America's Jewish Violin Sensation
The Life of Joyce Renée

ISBN 979-8-9850308-3-9

Published by Sola Hill Press

Contents

America's Jewish Violin Sensation

The Life of Joyce Renée

Steven Wasserman

"To live in the minds of the living and to be loved, is never to die."

(Inscribed on the gravestone of Joseph E. Maddy,
founder of Interlochen Center for the Arts.)

FOREWORD

This book is the story of my aunt, Esther Joyce Wasserman. Esther, who eventually went by the stage name Joyce Renée, was born to Max and Anna Wasserman on July 13, 1911. The Wasserman family lived in Cincinnati. Esther, later Joyce, grew up to become a world-renowned violinist who achieved great fame at a time when women virtuosos were few and far between, as well as during a time when being Jewish was not necessarily an asset. I decided to tell her life story to honor her memory and ensure that her extraordinary talent, incredible career, and tremendous generosity are not forgotten.

INTRODUCTION

From her name and from her voice, you would think that Joyce Renée is the most French Mademoiselle you could meet anywhere removed from the Champs Elysée or removed from Avenue D'Orleans or the Louvre.

It is true that she has a great deal of French background, but Mlle. Renee is truly American. She was the youngest honor graduate in the history of the Cincinnati Conservatory of Music. But, in Paris, she studied with Georges Enesco, one of the masters, and she also studied with such famous teachers as Kochanski, Arthur Hartmann, Rubin Goldmark and Dr. Eggar Stillman-Kelley.

Mlle. Renee has also been acclaimed for her violin solos in Carnegie Hall, Madison Square Garden, Radio City Music Hall and at West Point and Annapolis.

During the war, she did what many other musical artists did. She gave up her professional career while she performed for soldiers and hospitalized veterans. For her shows, she received citations from the Stage Door Canteen, the Merchant Marine, USO Camp Shows, the United States Theater Wing Hospital Committee and the Merchant Seaman's Club.

Mlle. Renee is an artist of the violin, but this Cincinnati girl uses her talent to benefit the underprivileged. In her native Cincinnati, for instance, the proceeds from her concerts are given to children who may not get all the nourishment they need.

Joyce Renée, the curly-haired girl from Cincinnati, was an international violin virtuoso. She was at the height of her powers. Nothing could stop her.

Max Wasserman: From Ukraine to Cincinnati

Komenitz Podolsk is a city in what is now western Ukraine, some 290 miles (450 kilometers) southwest of Kiev, not far north of the present-day borders where Moldova and Romania abut southwestern Ukraine. The city's name stems from the old Slavic word for stone ("kamy") and the word "podolia," the historic name of the area known for its rich, dark soil well-suited for growing wheat, potatoes, and corn.

Komenitz-Podolsk was established on an island in the Smotrych River, a tributary of the Dniester River that bisects modern day Ukraine. The Smotrych weaves its way through the town that, over time, expanded from the island on which it was founded to the banks on both sides of the river. On the eastern side of the town, the river cuts through the Smotrytsky Canyon, which has an escarpment on one bank that rises as high as one hundred feet above the riverbed.

Komenitz was the capital of Podolia Province for over one hundred years, from 1795 to 1917. Guards protected the town from the parapets of the Kamianets-Podolskyi castle perched on a hill above the town. The castle, a Ruthenian-Lithuanian structure (Ruthenia is an area in western Ukraine that extends into parts of present-day Poland and Slovakia), was built with high stone walls. The castle has more than a half dozen towers, some round while others are square, overlooking the town and the Smotrych River. The round towers are topped with conical roofs and weathervanes. The thick stone walls are punctuated with portals from which defenders could fire down on attackers seeking to storm the impressive redoubt.

Like most Jews in eastern Europe, Jews living in Komenitz-Podolsk endured a difficult history. Lithuania controlled the area from the fourteenth century until Poland and Lithuania were unified in 1569. For many years, the town barred Jews from settling in its thriving commercial center. In 1447, Komenitz did not allow Jews to visit the town for longer than three days. In 1598, Poland's King Sigismund III prohibited Jews from even visiting Komenitz, let alone permit them to trade there.[1] At various times during the 17th century, Crimean Tatars and Russian Cossacks attacked Jews living in the area.

When the Ottoman empire seized control of the area in 1672, it lifted the ban on Jews settling there, allowing the Jewish community to grow.[2] However, when Komenitz returned to Polish control in 1699, the Christian residents, comprised of Catholics, Lutherans, and Greek Orthodox, renewed their opposition to having a Jewish population in the town. In 1750, August III, King of Poland and Grand Duke of Lithuania, expelled Jews from Komenitz-Podolsk. The town's non-Jewish residents seized Jewish homes and destroyed the town's only synagogue.[3]

The area passed to Russian control in 1795.[4] In 1797, Czar Paul I permitted Jews to settle among the town's 2,617 residents.[5] Most Jews in the area spoke Yiddish; they also spoke and read Hebrew. It was not until Russia took control of the area that speaking Russian became common place. Most Jews made their living as traders, artisans, administrative personnel, or factory workers.[6]

Notwithstanding the Czar's edict allowing Jews to settle in Komenitz, the local Christian population was not to be denied. In 1832, they petitioned the government to once again expel Komenitz's Jewish residents. While the government rejected the petition, it restricted the right of Jews to build shops and homes and restricted them to living in two areas outside the town.[7]

Such was the history of Komenitz-Podolsk, the town where Aaron Leib Wasserman and Sarah Bayla ("Belle") Prosinate lived.[8] Sarah gave

---

1 *Id.*

2 *Id.*

3 *Id.*

4 WWW.JEWUA.ORG/KMANENETS_PODOLSKI.

5 Czar Paul succeeded to the throne when his mother, Catherine the Great, whom he apparently detested, died. Paul was emperor of Russia from 1790 until 1801, when he was deposed and assassinated in a palace coup.

6 *Id.*

7 WWW.JEWUA.ORG/KMANENETS_PODOLSKI.

8 Aaron Leib Wasserman was born on January 15, 1861; he died in Cincinnati at age fifty-six on January 18, 1917. Sarah Prosinate was born in Komenitz on February 1, 1858; she died in Cincinnati on April 19, 1930. Aaron and Sarah were married in Komenitz.

birth to their son Max Wasserman, one of Aaron and Sarah's nine children, on September 17, 1881.

Sarah likely prepared a variety of Ukrainian-Jewish dishes for her family. Dumplings filled with meat, potatoes, or sour cherries, the latter served with sour cream, were common at Jewish tables. Gefilte fish was also a staple. The name gefilte fish comes from the Yiddish word meaning stuffed fish. Mothers and grandmothers made the dish by grinding deboned fish such as whitefish, mullet, carp, and pike, adding breadcrumbs, eggs, and vegetable scraps, then stuffing the mixture into the skin of a whole fish. Preparing it took several days, and the home, or at least the kitchen, would be redolent (some might say reeked) with the smell of fish. At least in the United States, the ground mixture is typically served in the form of a croquette, without a fish skin casing.

Many Ukrainian-Jewish families enjoyed nalistniki, crepes filled with cottage cheese and raisins, or meat in a savory version, like blintzes. Another common dish was sheika ("neck"), the skin from a chicken neck stuffed with meat, vegetables, and a flour mix. The neck is stitched shut and boiled. Many families also enjoyed mimosa (American brunch devotees will be disappointed here), a salad composed of herring, boiled eggs, beets, and mayonnaise, set out in colorful layers. Tefteli—chicken and rice meatballs in a tomato sauce—were a favorite comfort food.

Notwithstanding Komenitz being home, the ever present antisemitism was likely the motivating factor behind Max and his family's decision to seek a new life elsewhere. Upon deciding to emigrate to the United States, Max may have headed southeast from Komenitz to Odessa on Ukraine's Black Sea coast, where he could have booked passage on a ship to the United States. The distance from Odessa to New York was roughly 4,858 miles (7818 kilometers) as the crow flies, but the route Max may have taken was hundreds of miles longer.

From Odessa, ships would have taken Max southwest across the Black Sea, through the Bosporus and Dardanelle Straits, southeast through the Aegean Sea, before turning west to cross the Mediterranean Sea and Atlantic Ocean to New York City. Any ship on which he booked passage likely made stops across the Mediterranean to refuel as well as to pick up passengers and freight.

An alternative route would have taken Max northeast from Komenitz to Kiev and then northwest to Gdansk on Poland's Baltic seacoast, or northwest from Kiev across Belarus to either Riga or Tallin on the Baltic Sea. From those ports Max and his family would have booked passage to the United States, traveling southwest across the Baltic and North Seas and then west across the Atlantic to New York.

Since the family likely had limited funds, they may have booked passage on a freighter to reach the United States. Given their lack of money, they probably fueled themselves on the weeks-long voyage with a sparse diet of tea, rough brown bread, along with perhaps pickled eggs, sausage, and cheese.

The history of Jews in Komenitz-Podolsk shows that Max and his family were fortunate to have emigrated to the United States. Despite the recurrent and sometimes violent antisemitism that plagued the area, much of the Jewish populace stayed, and the community grew. An 1893 census showed that Jews made up fifty percent of the town's 40,000 residents, while the balance was thirty-two percent Ukrainians and sixteen percent Poles. At the outset of WWI, Jews still made up more than half of the town's population of 60,000 residents.

Komenitz was in the region known as the "Pale of Settlement," an area in the western portion of the Russian Empire where Jews were allowed to live. Jews were not allowed to live outside the Pale or in many cities inside the Pale. The Pale included contemporary Belarus, Lithuania, Moldova, much of Ukraine, and portions of Poland. Most Jews in the Pale lived in small towns known as shtetls.

After the Russian Revolution, Zionist organizations became active in the area and developed into a formidable political force. The Zionists worked to advance local Jewish welfare and education as well as advocate and prepare residents for emigration to Palestine. After pogroms swept the area in 1903, Jews in the Pale formed branches of the Hagana—the Jewish self-defense force[9]—to defend the Jewish community against roving bands of hooligans who intermittently harassed and attacked Jews.

Once the Soviets took power in Russia in 1917, the revolutionary government severely suppressed Jewish cultural and communal life. Many Jews left the Pale for the United States, Canada, Brazil, and Palestine. Others fled to Kiev, Odessa, and Moscow, seeking better education, greater economic opportunities, and, hopefully, safety from the pogroms that plagued Jews in smaller towns and communities. Komenitz-Podolsk offered limited economic prospects since it lacked a railroad and significant raw materials. The few items produced locally—cigarettes, mineral

9 www.jewishgen.org/Yizkor/Kamyanets_Podilskyi.

water, cotton products, and flour from a few mills—were largely consumed by the town's residents.

When the Nazis came to power, anti-Semitism surged in Komenitz. "Fifteen synagogues and prayer houses were closed after 1936, though synagogue officials managed to conceal some thirty Torah scrolls which survived the Holocaust and were later used by clandestine religious communities."[10]

"Kamenitz-Podolski was occupied by German and Hungarian troops on July 11, 1941... Soon after the start of the occupation some 60 Jewish men were shot in the Old Town."[11] The Nazis appointed Ukrainian ultra-nationalists to administer the town. The appointees registered the entire Jewish population and demanded that Jews wear a yellow Star of David, which was followed by an order in August 1941 forcing the city's Jews to live in a small ghetto.[12]

The Hungarian Nazi regime deported 10,000 Jews, many of whom were originally from Poland and Russia, to Komenitz. The Nazis then murdered the deportees:

On August 26, 1941, between 12,000 and 14,000 Jews deported to Kamenitz-Podolski from Hungarian controlled Carpatho-Rus were murdered around the area of the munitions' depot in the eastern area of Kamenitz-Podolski. Jews of all ages and both sexes were told to assemble at the city's train station in order "to return home or be resettled in Palestine." Instead, they were taken to the site of mass execution. There they were forced to run a gauntlet of policemen and to surrender their valuables. Some of them were ordered to undress and then lay face down in a pit and were shot in the back of the head.[13]

Those Jews who were not shot were forced into a new ghetto. The killing of the town's Jews continued through 1942. In October and November 1942, 4,000 of the remaining Jews were shot. While some 500 Jews escaped, the Nazis ultimately captured and killed them. This was one of the Nazis' first mass murders of Jews.[14]

"A total of almost 30,000 Jews were victims of the Nazi genocide in Kamenetz-Podolski (12,000 of local Jews and 18,000 from Hungary,

---

10 *Id.*

11 *Id.*

12 *Id.*

13 www.jewua.org/kanenets_podolski.org)

14 *Id.*

Czechoslovakia, Poland and Romania)." A commission established after the Red Army liberated the area on March 27, 1944, found seven mass graves, including a grave containing the bodies of 500 children. Of those Jews who returned to the area after the war, most eventually left for Israel or the West in the 1990s.[15]

Whatever spurred Max Wasserman, his parents, and siblings to leave Komenitz, the town's subsequent history makes clear that their decision to emigrate saved their lives.

---

15 *Id.*

Anna Rabkin: From Belarus to Cincinnati

The city of Vitebsk, located in an area that today is part of Belarus, is situated along the Vicba River, which is the source of the city's name. The city began as a settlement in 974. By late in the 12th century, it had developed into a trade center. In 1320, it was incorporated into the Grand Duchy of Lithuania. In 1569, it became part of the Polish-Lithuanian Commonwealth. However, during the first partition of Poland in 1772, the Russian Empire annexed the city.

Anna Ida Rabkin was born in Vitebsk on August 10, 1892, when Vitebsk was part of Russia. Anna's parents were Nathan ("Nissan") Rabkin and Henia (sometimes spelled "Henya") Rabkin. Henia's parents were Saul Shaul Aronoff and Bessie Aronoff. A photograph of Henia, possibly from the 1920s, shows her with a kind smile and sparkling eyes. Her dark dress is set off by broad lace lapels; she wore dark, button-shaped, clasp earrings.

Nissan Rabkin was a bricklayer. He and Henia had six children: Arthur, Sam, Jack, Dave, Bess, and Anna. Henia would have been more than busy maintaining the home, doing the laundry, mending clothes, and feeding the family. Classic Belarusian foods include homemade sausages, draniki (thick potato pancakes), kletski (dumplings), and mushroom soup. In a Jewish home, the counterparts would have been a year-round equivalent of potato latkes, potato knishes, and kreplach (dumplings filled with ground meat and onions).

Borscht was likely a regular dish on the Rabkin family table, either plain or, if the budget allowed for it, a dollop of sour cream mixed in. Henia no doubt prepared cabbage rolls ("prakas"), in which boiled cabbage leaves were stuffed with a mixture of ground beef, rice, and onions, and then cooked in a sauce made with tomatoes, onions, and shredded cabbage.

Family lore has it that Sam Rabkin was a dissident and was jailed for "subversive activity." The family bribed the jailer to obtain Sam's release and decided it would be best if Sam left Vitebsk to get out of harm's way. As a result, Sam, Nissan, and Anna were the first members of the family to flee. Nissan took Anna with him, so he did not leave Henia to care for all six children.

Sam, Nissan, and Anna made their escape to Finland and then emigrated to the United States. While no records were located establishing when they emigrated, family members believe it was in the late 1890s. To reach Finland from Vitebsk's location in northeastern Belarus, Sam, Anna, and Nissan may have traveled overland through Russia to St. Petersburg and then taken a ferry to Helsinki. From there, they could have obtained passage on a passenger liner to the United States.

However, rather than put themselves in harm's way in Russia where Jews were always subject to violence, they more likely traveled northwest from Vitebsk to Riga or Tallinn to seek passage. Their voyage likely required a stop in Great Britain to board an ocean liner headed to the United States, as there probably were few ocean-going ships departing from the Baltic nations all the way to New York.

Many immigrants entered the United States at Ellis Island in New York. However, searches of Ellis Island databases have not uncovered entry records for Sam, Nissan, and Anna using the Rabkin surname, so they either entered the United States elsewhere or used pseudonyms.

As with Jewish history in Komenitz Podolsk, it is worth taking a brief look at the history of Vitebsk after Anna, Nissan, and Sam Rabkin left. Vitebsk became part of the Soviet Socialist Republic of Byelorussia in 1919. It was soon made part of the Russian Republic, but by 1924 was returned to Byelorussia.

Prior to WWII, Vitebsk was just over fifty percent Jewish. Marc Chagall is the most famous of Vitebsk's Jews. The city grew into a center of Jewish culture; it was one of the main cities in which Jews were allowed to live in the Pale of Settlement.

The Nazis occupied Vitebsk during WWII. The Russian and German armies fought fierce battles that ultimately destroyed much of the old city. The Nazis claimed that the ghetto in which they forced Vitebsk's Jews to live was a health hazard and the cause of an epidemic. These claims were pretexts the Nazis used to justify their massacre of Vitebsk's Jews. The Nazis killed most of the city's Jews in the Vitebsk ghetto massacre of October 1941. At the start of the war, roughly 16,000 Jews lived in Vitebsk. The Nazis marched the city's Jews to the Daugava River that bisected Vitebsk, where they shot the Jews and threw their bodies into the water. Investigations have not determined a definitive number of victims, but the result was the Nazis made Vitebsk "Judenrein," that is, "free of Jews."

Like Max Wasserman and his family, Nissan Rabkin's decision to leave Vitebsk and take Anna and Sam with him unquestionably saved their lives.[16]

16 Research has not revealed how and when Henia and the rest of her and Nissan's children emigrated to the United States.

Cincinnati's Jewish Community

Cincinnati was founded in 1788 on the banks of the Ohio River. The site was surrounded by hills, the most prominent of which was eventually christened Mt. Adams, so named because John Quincy Adams visited the area to dedicate an observatory built there. From the crest of Mt. Adams, Cincinnatians could look across the Ohio River's swift, muddy waters to Kentucky on the southern bank. The settlement grew rapidly during the early nineteenth century and soon became the largest city west of the Allegheny Mountains.[17]

By the middle of the nineteenth century, the city had become a major manufacturing and commercial center. It came known as the "Queen City of the West."[18] In 1866, at the time the John A. Roebling Suspension Bridge opened, spanning the Ohio River and connecting Cincinnati with Covington, Kentucky, it was the longest suspension bridge in the world, with its main span stretching just over one thousand feet. Its fieldstone towers and sky-blue railings and suspension cables made it a major landmark.[19]

Joseph Jonas, who claimed to be the first Jew to settle in Cincinnati, settled there in 1817 and set up shop as a watchmaker and silversmith. By 1824, enough Jews had joined Jonas to allow them to establish Congregation Bene Israel, the oldest synagogue west of the Alleghenies.[20] The congregation came to be known as Rockdale Temple when it moved

17 *Images of America: Jews of Cincinnati*, 2007, John S. Fine and Fredric J. Krome, Arcadia Publishing, p. 7.

18 *Id.*

19 Cincinnati's Roebling Bridge was eventually surpassed by Roebling's most famous structure, New York's Brooklyn Bridge, which opened in 1883.

20 *Id.*

to a building in the Avondale neighborhood at the corner of Harvey and Rockdale Avenues.[21]

Cincinnati also became known as "Porkopolis" due to it being a center of pork production and distribution.[22] As evidence of how involved Jews were in the local community and how they were willing to "cross religious lines" when it came to business, one of the city's major pork production companies—E. Kahn and Sons—was owned by Jewish immigrants from Bavaria.[23]

Polish Jews founded Cincinnati's Adath Israel congregation in 1847. Initially located in downtown Cincinnati, the Conservative congregation later built a synagogue in Avondale and eventually constructed a much larger synagogue complex in Cincinnati's Amberley neighborhood in 1967.

By 1850, "Cincinnati's Jewish community was one of the largest in the country," although it only had between 2,500 and 3,300 Jews.[24] However, during the 19th century, Jews continued to arrive from central Europe, primarily Germany, and the Jewish community steadily grew. Samuel Pike, an early Jewish immigrant, built the city's first opera house.[25]

Cincinnati's Jewish community played a significant role in how Judaism was practiced in the United States. In 1853, a local congregation hired a young rabbi by the name of Isaac Wise to serve on its pulpit.[26] Wise not only served as a rabbi, but he also founded a Jewish newspaper named The *Israelite*, which ultimately became known as the *American Israelite*. The *Israelite* included a supplement in German titled "*Die Deborah*" formulated for Jewish women.[27]

Rabbi Wise is perhaps best known for developing and advocating on behalf of what he believed was a distinctly American form of Judaism suited to the conditions Jews faced in the United States. His ideas and

---

21 The building was destroyed in the race riots in Cincinnati in the late 1960s. The lot is still vacant.

22 In a nod to its history as a center of pork production, Cincinnati holds a "Flying Pig" marathon every year.

23 *Images of America* at p. 7.

24 *Id.*

25 *Id.*

26 *Id.* at 8.

27 *Id.* the *American Israelite*, still in publication, is the oldest continuously published Jewish newspaper in the United States. *Id.* at 56.

changes to Jewish liturgy and rituals ultimately became the Reform Judaism movement in the United States.[28]

Wise also was responsible for construction of the magnificent Plum Street Temple completed in 1868 in downtown Cincinnati. To this day, the Plum Street Temple, with its elegant and intricate Moorish features and decoration, is one of Cincinnati's most recognizable structures. The congregation built the temple opposite the city's leading Catholic and Unitarian churches, perhaps signifying that the Jewish community was staking a claim to equal status with the city's other major faiths.[29]

In 1875, Rabbi Wise founded the Hebrew Union College to train a rabbinate that reflected American and specifically Reform practices.[30] At the time, it was "the only rabbinical seminary in America, [and] became particularly important in the life of the city. It served as a magnet for attracting important Jewish scholars," as well as talented students, and spread Cincinnati's name across the country as the leading community of the Reform movement.[31]

Hebrew Union College sponsored a banquet in 1883 to celebrate the ordination of its first four graduates. The banquet became known as the "Trefa Banquet" because the menu for the event included clams, shrimp, and crab, as well as ice cream for dessert following entrees that included meat.[32] (Trefah means non-Kosher food.) The caterer apparently had only limited knowledge of Kashrut and, therefore, did not include pork in the meal, believing that made the meal Kosher.[33] While the Reform Jewish movement believed in less rigorous adherence to many Jewish traditions and laws, the infamous "Trefa banquet" may have been more a misunderstanding than indulgence in an intentional breaching of the laws of Kashrut.

---

28 The Reform movement began in Germany's Jewish community in the early twentieth century. The reformers wanted to "modernize" Jewish worship and make it less different from how other faiths in Germany practiced their religions. The reformers added organ music to the services, placed far less stress on adhering to the rules of keeping Kosher ("Kashrut"), and conducted portions of the services in German. These same elements became part of Reform Judaism in the United States, with clergy conducting much of the synagogue services in English.

29 *Jews of Cincinnati* at 15.

30 *Id.* at 20-21.

31 *Id.* at. 15.

32 *Id.* at 30.

33 *Id.* at 87.

The Manischewitz family were early Jewish pioneers in Cincinnati.[34] They opened a small bakery in 1888 and eventually figured out how to make matzos using modern mass production techniques. This allowed them to produce greater quantities of matzo and do so quickly and inexpensively. Manischewitz soon was distributing matzos to appreciative Jewish families around the world.[35]

Cincinnati's Jewish population was soon large enough that companies began developing and advertising products to suit the community's needs. For example, Proctor and Gamble offered Kosher Crisco, "an economical solid Kosher fat, made entirely of pure vegetable oil," for Jewish bakers.[36]

Julius Fleischmann, who emigrated to the United States from Hungary in 1868, was another Cincinnati Jewish pioneer. He brought with him a tube containing yeast cells, which he used to establish the Fleishmann Yeast Company. Not content with being a successful businessman, Fleishmann was elected mayor in 1900. His family also operated a whiskey distillery until the advent of Prohibition in 1920.[37] Fleischmann's heirs donated land to the city to create a park in the Avondale neighborhood. The four-acre park features gardens, an evergreen maze, playground, and ornamental iron gates topped with an old-fashioned gaslight fixture.

As the nineteenth century ended, Cincinnati's Jewish community was respected throughout the United States. While it was smaller than Jewish communities in large east coast cities such as New York, Boston, and Philadelphia, and the community was not particularly observant when it came to Jewish traditions and liturgy, it was dynamic, successful, and the oldest and most cultured Jewish community west of the Alleghenies.[38]

While Cincinnati's first Jews were from England, from 1820 to 1870 more and more Jews came to the city from Germany.[39] Until late in the nineteenth century, most of Cincinnati's Jews were of German descent. They saw America (and Cincinnati) as "a promised land where economic

34 *Id.* at 8.

35 *Id.* at 8. Manischewitz later moved to New Jersey to better serve the larger Jewish community in the greater New York area.

36 *Id.* at 61,

37 *Id.* at 65.

38 *The Jews of Cincinnati*, by Jonathan D. Sarna and Nancy H. Klein, (1989), Center for the Study of the American Jewish Experience, p. 1.

39 *Id.* at 3.

opportunities abounded and Jews faced none of the restrictions that had so embittered their lives in the German states."[40] They came "seeking a place where Jews could settle as citizens, succeed economically, practice their religion freely, and coexist happily and on equal terms with their Christian neighbors."[41] Many Jews in Cincinnati felt they had excellent relations with their Christian neighbors and believed they could live there safely. Nevertheless, there remained a layer of prejudice that at times reared its ugly head in the city.[42]

Many of the early Jewish immigrants started out as peddlers. After amassing a small bit of capital, they opened stores.[43] A large percentage of Cincinnati's Jews went into the garment industry. By 1860, "'the manufacture, distribution, and sales of men's ready-made clothing and other apparel supplied at least a portion of the livelihood for well over one-half of Cincinnati's Jews.'"[44] The ready-made clothing trade was largely a Jewish industry.

Cincinnati's Jews also proved to be extraordinarily civic-minded. Cincinnati's Jews "played a central role in creating and maintaining their city's cultural institutions."[45] They played leading roles in the symphony and art museums, established the first Jewish hospital in the United States, and the stunning Art Deco botanical conservatory in Cincinnati's Eden Park neighborhood. The latter was named the Krohn Conservatory in honor of Jewish Cincinnatian Julius Krohn, who served on the city's Board of Parks Commission from 1912 to 1948.

The 1880s saw the advent of mass immigration to the United States from Poland, Russia, and other eastern European countries. A series of pogroms against Russia's Jews after the assassination of Tsar Alexander II in 1881 sparked a wave of emigration to the United States.[46]

Those Jews already in Cincinnati were anxious to have their newly arrived co-religionists fit in as quickly as possible.[47] To that end, the *American Israelite* advocated that immigrants' children be sent to public

---

40 *Id.*

41 *Id.*

42 *Id.* at 9.

43 Fred Lazarus Jr., a Jewish immigrant, was the founder of Federated Stores. *Jews of Cincinnati* at p.5.

44 *Jews of Cincinnati* at 6.

45 *Id.* at 12.

46 *Id.* at 62.

47 *Id.* at 63.

schools to learn English, as well as to learn "how to fit in." Young working people were to be sent to night school to study English. Immigrants were advised to become citizens as quickly as possible.[48] However, there was no denying that Cincinnati's German Jewish community, having established itself in the city, looked somewhat askance at the poor Russian immigrants.[49] The German Jews were at times skeptical of the new arrivals, with their different language, customs, and Yiddishkyte culture.[50]

The Jewish community grew to such an extent that in 1917 a group decided to establish a summer camp where Jewish children could enjoy outdoor activities.[51] With a generous contribution from Mrs. H.S. Livingston, who offered to pay for the land and improvements if the camp was named for her son who had died in World War I, the community purchased sixteen acres of undeveloped land alongside the Little Miami River roughly sixteen miles from Cincinnati.[52] Over the years, thousands of Jewish children spent their summers at Camp Livingston enjoying outdoor sports, arts and crafts, and Shabbat services at which they demonstrated their ruach (spirit) by singing Jewish songs.

Cincinnati's Jews initially lived downtown, where they built their earliest synagogues. Over time, however, they moved northwest of the city center to the Avondale neighborhood, and later, beginning in the 1950s, to Bond Hill, Golf Manor, Roselawn, and then (if they were affluent) to Amberley Village.[53] Beginning in the 1970s and continuing today, the Jewish community resides largely in the northeastern suburbs of Blue Ash, Montgomery, and beyond, with a small contingent in Wyoming (a northern Cincinnati suburb).

In the 1950s, another member of the Jewish community, David Frisch, established Frisch's Big Boy restaurants, a popular local chain.[54] One of the earliest Big Boy restaurants was on Reading Road, north of downtown. Frisch's restaurants became famous for their sandwiches such

---

48 *Id.* at 63.

49 *Id.* at 81.

50 *Id.* at 51. Also spelled Yiddishkeit, the word refers to the customs and practices of Jewish life, particularly eastern European Jews who spoke Yiddish.

51 Id at. 77.

52 *Id.*

53 *Id.* at 8. There was a period when Jewish migration from downtown Cincinnati took them up Queen City Avenue to Price Hill, where Cincinnati's Conservative and Orthodox Jewish cemeteries are located.

54 *Id.* at 117.

as the Big Boy (two burgers with cheese on a double-deck bun), the Swiss Miss (a single burger with cheese), the Buddie Boy (ham and Swiss cheese) and Brawny Lads (a burger on a rye bun presumably intended for eastern European tastes familiar with rye and pumpernickel breads), along with French fries, shakes, and pies.[55] The decidedly non-Kosher menu demonstrates how assimilated the Jewish community was in some respects, or at least how willing it was to adapt its commercial undertakings to suit the tastes of the community at large.

One neighborhood near downtown became known as "Over the Rhine" because of the presence of so many German immigrants. However, in the second half of the nineteenth century, particularly after 1881 when more immigrants arrived from eastern Europe, the Jewish community's demographics changed considerably and became less "German-centric." It was in this successful, growing, and dynamic Jewish community that Max Wasserman and Anna Rabkin began their lives in the United States.

---

55 The author has fond memories of eating at Frisch's in Dayton, where he grew up, and in Cincinnati where his grandmothers lived and where his mother and sister eventually came to live. Whenever the author returns to Cincinnati, he stops at the Frisch's on Vine Street to enjoy a Big Boy platter and purchase a jar of Frisch's famous tartar sauce. Frisch's strawberry pie also deserves mention.

Max and Anna in Cincinnati

Cincinnati's prominent, growing Jewish community made it an attractive destination for Jewish immigrants. Since Max was a tailor, the emergence of Cincinnati's ready to wear industry and the predominance of Jews in that business no doubt made the city a place where he felt he could secure work. A 1908 business directory identified Max as a tailor and later a foreman at a business located at 1521 Central Avenue in Cincinnati (the directory does not provide the name or nature of the business).

The Rabkin family probably settled in Cincinnati due to the city's burgeoning and prominent Jewish community. A Cincinnati business directory from 1908 identified Nissan Rabkin as a tilemaker with a home address of 413 Armory Avenue. A subsequent directory identified him as a bricklayer. Nissan eventually became involved and did quite well in real estate and construction. However, the Great Depression devastated his business and he lost almost everything.

The same 1908 business directory lists Anna Rabkin as a saleslady at 1531 Central Avenue and later as a saleslady and clerk at 1523 Central Avenue. The directory does not identify the businesses that employed Anna, who spoke Yiddish and eventually English, but never Russian.

Max and Anna met when Anna was working as a cashier at a Kroger's grocery store and Max struck up a conversation with her as she rang up his purchases. While they came from different countries and backgrounds, they shared the experiences of Jewish persecution and immigration to a new country. They were married on August 7, 1909, when Max was twenty-seven and Anna was seventeen. Their ketubah (Jewish marriage contract) states that Max (Hebrew name Mordechai) was the son of Aharon Aryeh. The ketubah identifies Anna as Chana Zlita, daughter of Nison. Anna was a common diminutive name for Chana. The ketubah identifies Moshe, son of Dovid the Levite, as one of the witnesses to the signing of the marriage contract; the name of the other witness is illegible.

Max and Anna's application for a marriage license states that Max lived at 1307 Sutton St., was a tailor, and his parents were Aaron Wasserman and Sarah Bussman (this is incorrect; Max's mother was Sarah Prosinate). The application states that Anna was eighteen, lived at 413 Armory Avenue, and worked as a saleslady. The "Marriage Return" portion of the application erroneously states they were married on August 4, with Rabbi S. Lipsitz presiding.

A wedding photograph shows Anna and Max as a handsome couple. Max sat in a chair with a high, carved back, while Anna stood next to him with her right arm on the chair back. Her left arm cradled a bouquet that trailed a four-foot braid of roses, baby's breath, and fern fronds. Anna wore a beautiful white hat with a six-foot veil cascading down from her dark curls. Her ankle-length wedding gown featured lace trim on the bodice and sleeves. Max wore a dark suit with a white shirt and white tie, along with a boutonniere on his left lapel comprised of a rose and a small fern frond. His expression was calm and thoughtful.

A 1909 city directory states that Anna worked at W. & Krauss at 933 Central Avenue in downtown Cincinnati. Max worked as a foreman/tailor at 615 West Court Street just west of downtown, close to Cincinnati's renowned Fountain Square, at the corner of Vine Street and West 5th Street, named for the Tyler Davidson Fountain in the center of the Square. The Davidson fountain, intended to rival famous fountains in Europe, was designed to glorify the "blessings of water." Water flowed from the hands of the nine-foot main statue named the "Genius of Water" which locals referred to as "The Lady." Beneath The Lady were four adult figures representing practical uses of water, while figures of four children represent the pleasures of water.

The 1909 directory lists Max and Anna's home address as 1307 Cutter Street, northwest of downtown. Photographs reveal 1307 Cutter as part of a set of red brick row houses. The front door of 1307 was framed by round columns, with a bay window on the ground floor and four standard windows across the second floor.

The 1910 Census Record for Hamilton County, where Cincinnati was located, identified Max as the head of household and Anna as his wife. The record provides that he was twenty-eight and she was nineteen. The census listed their place of birth, and that of their parents, as "Rus Russian" but states they could speak English. Rus Russian was a phrase used to describe people from Belarus, Ukraine, and western Russia. The form identified Max's occupation as pants maker and custom tailor but does not include an occupation for Anna. The record says they emigrated to the United States in 1897, although it is unlikely that they emigrated the same year.

In 1911, after two years of marriage, Max and Anna began their family, having four children in quick succession:

- Esther Joyce Wasserman, born July 13, 1911.
- Hilda Ruth Wasserman, born Nov. 11, 1913.
- Jules ("Jay") Robert Wasserman born May 12, 1915.
- Rose Wasserman born Dec. 21, 1917.

Esther was born in the family home at 817 Laurel Street at 8:00 a.m. on July 13, 1911. The birth certificate identifies her parents as Anna Ida Rabkin (age nineteen) and Max Wasserman (age twenty-seven), states that her parents were born in Russia, and lists Max's occupation as tailor and Anna's as housewife. The printed State of Ohio Certification of Birth from the Department of Vital Statistics contains an error; apparently someone misread Max's name as Mark and entered the name of Esther's father as Mark Wasserman.

By the time Rose Wasserman was born six years later, the family had moved to 423 Betts Street, part of a neighborhood known as Betts Longworth just northwest of downtown. The area (now a historic district) was populated with houses built in the Federal, Italianate, and Queen Anne styles. The oldest Jewish cemetery in Cincinnati is located there. By then, Max was thirty-seven and Anna was twenty-six.

On Sept. 12, 1918, nine months after Rose was born, Max registered with the Selective Service Board, Local Number 6 for Hamilton County, just two months before WWI ended on Nov. 11, 1918.[56] The registration card stated he was a "taylor" with his place of employment at 615 West Court Street in downtown Cincinnati. His height and build were listed as medium; the form noted he had grey eyes and black hair.

Max and Anna eventually moved to 765 Greenwood Avenue, one block off Reading Road, in Cincinnati's Avondale neighborhood. The

56 Aliens and holders of first nationalization papers were not eligible for the draft. (*Jews of Cincinnati* at 106.) Since Max registered with the Selective Service, that suggests he was, by 1918, a United States citizen. Those Jews who wanted to serve, but were ineligible for the draft, joined the "Jewish Legion," a group of Jewish volunteers who fought in the British army during WWI to help end Turkish rule in Palestine. (*Id.*)

two-story home's main floor had brick siding, while the second-floor exterior was shingled. The peaked roof covered a small attic. The home featured a wide porch across the front that continued down the left side as you faced the house from the street. Chairs and planters were placed on each side of the front door. Flowers and vines cascaded from baskets hung along the front edge of the porch, while a mezuzah on the right side of the front door frame marked the house as a Jewish home.[57]

The 1920 census records for Hamilton County include Max (age thirty-seven) and Anna (age twenty-six), as well as well as their children Esther (age nine), Hilda (age seven), Julius (age four), and Rose (age two). The form states that Max and Anna could read and write (presumably English), but their "mother tongue" was Yiddish. The form included a few details regarding Anna's parents, stating they were born in Petrograd[58] and their mother tongue was Yiddish. The spreadsheet states that Max was a tailor who owned his own shop.

Anna prepared many of the dishes Max knew from his childhood. One such dish was lenivuye ("lazy") vareniki, which are small cheese dumplings served with honey and sour cream. They are called lazy because they were less difficult to make than other, more elaborate dumplings. Zharkoe was a hearty beef and potato stew that could fuel a person for the better part of a day. Sate (pronounce like pâté) was a Ukrainian dish reminiscent of ratatouille in which vegetables are cut, seared, and arranged in layers. It was labor intensive but delicious.

As to borscht, the classic eastern European beet soup, some people enjoyed it with a slice of dark, rye bread smeared with a bit of shaved, raw garlic. Other people added sour cream to the soup. Apple/zucchini blinchiki were like latkes prepared with a combination of apples and zucchini instead of potatoes. More apples made for a sweeter version; fewer apples made the dish savory. Dessert might be vertuta, an apple dish akin to apple turnovers or strudel.

---

57 The Hamilton County Real Estate Tax List provides a confusing and seemingly incomplete record for the property. It shows Hilda Cohen as the owner in 1938, then Jules Wasserman in 1939, then Anna Wasserman in 1953, and back to Jules in 1962. The first assessed value on the record for 765 Greenwood values the house at $6,270 and the lot at $2,490 but does not list a date for the valuation.

58 The Soviets changed the city's name from St. Petersburg to Petrograd in 1914 at the start of WWI because the previous name, with the inclusion of "burg," sounded too German. In 1924, five days after Lenin died, the Soviets changed the name again, this time to Leningrad. In 1991, after the collapse of the Soviet Union, Russia changed the city's name once more, this time back to St. Petersburg.

While Anna likely prepared dishes she knew from Belarus, she may also have learned to make dishes that Max knew from Ukraine. Those likely included potato pancakes (known as deruny in Ukraine) and vareniki, which were dumplings stuffed with a variety of fillings, including cabbage, beef, mushrooms, cottage cheese, cherries, currants, or potatoes. The dumplings often were topped with sour cream.

Another classic Ukrainian dish was stuffed cabbage rolls (goluybtsi) made by filling boiled cabbage leaves with ground beef and onions. The leaves were then rolled into a shape much like egg rolls and slowly cooked in a pot filled with tomatoes, sliced cabbage, and onions. Whatever dishes Anna prepared for the family, she kept a strictly kosher home, with two sets of dishes (milk and meat—*milchig* and *fleishig* in Yiddish) and another set for Passover.

At some point, Max and Anna began attending services with the Adath Israel congregation in Cincinnati. Adath Israel was founded in 1847, with its original name being the "Polish Synagogue." It was the oldest traditional synagogue in Cincinnati and one of the oldest Conservative congregations in the United States.[59] Adath Israel initially was located downtown, where much of Cincinnati's Jewish population lived. The first site for the congregation was on Lodge Alley between Fifth and Sixth Streets.

In 1860, the congregation moved to the corner of Seventh and Walnut streets downtown. During the 1880s, which saw the onset of mass migration of east European Jews to the United States, the congregation grew. As the Jewish population began to move from downtown to Cincinnati's suburbs, Adath Israel followed, moving to Rockdale Avenue and eventually to a synagogue complex at Lexington and Reading Roads in the Avondale neighborhood.

Max and Anna's fifth and last child, Allan Lee Wasserman, was born at Cincinnati's Jewish Hospital on February 25, 1924. It seems likely that Allan was a "surprise" baby, since he arrived seven years after Rose, Max and Anna's fourth child, was born.[60] Allan was named after Max's father Aaron Leib Wasserman. The birth certificate lists his name as Aron Lee Wasserman. The original birth certificate did not state a name for the baby, and his name was added a few days later by affidavit. Research has

59 Adath Israel website.

60 Allan Wasserman was the author's father.

not revealed how, when, or why Aron's name was changed from Aron Lee to Allan Lee Wasserman.

Allan's birth certificate states that Max was a "manufacturer" and Anna was a housewife residing at 3413 Hartford Street, which was northeast of downtown Cincinnati, between Avondale on the west and the Walnut Hills neighborhood to the east. Anna and Max's family was now "complete" with the birth of their fifth child.

The Wasserman family, mother, father, and five children, was well-settled. They were safe from the progroms of eastern Europe, Max was employed, and their American-born children hopefully had bright futures.

Esther Joyce Wasserman

The earliest known photograph of Esther Joyce Wasserman was taken around 1920 when Esther was nine years old. It shows her perched on a fence next to her youngest sister Rose, in what looks like a photographer's studio. Esther wore a simple dress with decorative stitching around the collar, sleeves, and at the knees. She smiled broadly; her head was covered with a mass of auburn curls.

Esther began taking violin lessons as a child, although research has not revealed when or whether she did so due to her own interest or at the behest of her parents. Whatever may have instigated her taking up the instrument, Esther practiced diligently, sometimes using a metronome to help develop her sense of pace and timing.

Esther made her debut as a performer in 1920 when she was a bright-eyed, curly-haired nine-year-old, playing on WLW radio in Cincinnati. She got her big break courtesy of Dr. Frank Simon, who invited her to join his orchestra for New Year's Eve. Frank Simon, born in Cincinnati and raised in nearby Middletown, Ohio, was cornet player. He played with John Phillip Sousa's band as a principal cornet player and assistant conductor. Simon later started the Armco Band, sponsored by Armco Steel Company, which became the finest industrial band in the country. Simon was also on the faculty at the Cincinnati Conservatory of Music.[61]

---

61 For many years, the American Rolling Mill Corporation ("Armco") sponsored a concert band, "The Armco Band," led by Middletown, Ohio, native Frank Simon. The Armco Band achieved success as a regional and national entertainment act during its twenty years of operation from 1920-1940. (Thesis by Christopher Chafee, Nov 20, 2003, University of Cincinnati.) The "Blue Network" was the name of an American radio network that operated from 1927 through 1945. It was initially owned by NBC but was later divested due to antitrust litigation, and later became the American Broadcasting Company. The Blue Network was the original home of broadcasts by the NBC Symphony Orchestra led by conductor Arturo Toscanini. The network also aired programs by Lowell Thomas and Walter Winchell. Joyce played many times on three major radio networks as a soloist, being featured on programs such as "Music at Twilight," "Works of the Masters," the "American Festival Series," and several television shows.

For her debut with Simon's Armco Band, Esther performed the "Faust Fantasie" by Pablo de Sarasate, along with "En Bateau" by Claude Debussy. Pablo de Sarasate was a Spanish violin virtuoso, composer, and conductor of the Romantic period. Debussy, a French composer, is sometimes regarded as the first Impressionist composer, although Debussy did not like that term. His composition "In the Boat" was part of the "Petite Suite" Debussy composed as a four-hand piano piece.

Since this performance was Esther's grand debut, her family was rapt as they listened to the radio broadcast in their living room. Esther's performance was so successful that it initiated a life-long friendship with Dr. Simon and led to her appearing many times with him.

Esther went on to make her orchestral debut with the Cincinnati Symphony in 1924 at the age of thirteen. The Symphony's archivists suspect Esther won a talent competition and appeared in a concert for which the symphony did not print, or at least did not retain, programs. In any event, it was obvious by this time that Esther was a rare talent with a bright musical future.

Esther Devotes Herself to Music

Esther attended Hughes High School in Cincinnati from 1925 to 1928, where she majored in music and art. Located at 2515 Clifton Avenue, Hughes was just a few blocks from the main campus of the University of Cincinnati. Designed in a Tudor Gothic style, Hughes was built in 1910. It had four floors and a seven-story central tower bordered by round columns from street level to the top of the tower. The building's exterior featured stone gargoyles grimacing down from the roof lines. The interior had a dozen fountains made by the Rookwood Pottery Company, along with lovely Rookwood panels on the walls.[62] Esther completed high school in three years, graduating from Hughes in 1928 when she was sixteen.

Esther also attended the Cincinnati Conservatory of Music, starting in 1923 when she was only twelve years old. She majored in violin, with minors in composition and English.

Esther's professors at the Conservatory were pleased with their young student. During her first year, her violin instructor Mr. Perutz considered her to be a good pupil who was both ambitious and talented. As time went by, Professor Perutz noted she was diligent and had become "an excellent pupil in every way." He commented further that Esther was conscientious and improving remarkably.

Esther received her diploma in violin from the Conservatory on June 17, 1929, when she was only seventeen, the youngest honors graduate in the Conservatory's history. The Conservatory awarded her a Bachelor of Music degree on June 11, 1930, when she was only eighteen.

---

62 Maria Longworth Storer founded Rookwood Pottery in 1880. Rookwood was the first large manufacturing business founded and owned by a woman in the United States. It was also the birthplace of the art pottery movement in the U.S. Rookwood quickly became a huge success. It won the Gold Medal at the 1889 Exposition Universelle in Paris, which established the U.S. art pottery movement on the world stage. Rookwood artware is held in museum collections around the world, including San Francisco's DeYoung Museum. In 1902, Rookwood added architectural tiles to its product line; Rookwood tiles were used to decorate buildings around the country as well as many stations in the New York City subway system.

Music Between the Lakes

Esther was awarded a scholarship to attend the Interlochen Center for the Arts during the summer of 1930. Interlochen was situated in the northwestern portion of Michigan's lower peninsula. Founded in 1928, it was, and still is, one of the nation's foremost institutions for arts training, including music, visual arts, and theater. One of the music camp's main reasons for being was its renowned National High School Orchestra. While research has not disclosed if Esther performed in the orchestra, given her success to that point, it is almost certain she did. Esther's summer at Interlochen not only gave her a chance to enjoy outdoor activities, but also opportunities to study with new instructors and compare notes with other aspiring young performers.

Interlochen was divided into boys' and girls' camps, each of which had assembly and mess halls, athletic fields, and performance and practice space for musicians. Esther continued to concentrate on violin, while also studying composition.

A typical day at camp involved getting up at 6:30 (perhaps one of the trumpet students played reveille to awaken the campers) and taking a quick dip in the lake before breakfast at 7:00. Then came clean up and inspection (campers needed to have tight hospital corners on their bunks), orchestra rehearsal, music classes or recreation, dinner (lunch in modern parlance) and a rest period from noon to one. The afternoon schedule called for music, dramatics, or recreation, followed by band rehearsal, and then baseball and sports.[63] Campers could also go swimming. Supper and a rest period went from six to seven o'clock, followed by ensembles, chorus, cottage orchestra, and dramatics. Campers were to report to their cabins by nine o'clock; taps and lights out were at ten. The campers' days were a rich mix of arts and typical summer camp activities.

63 The camp history mentions baseball separately, which makes one wonder if the camp did not consider baseball to be a sport.

Interlochen was named for its location: "Tween lakes so far God placed thee there and called thee Interlochen."[64] The lakes between which the camp was located were Lake Wah-Be-Ka-Ness and Lake Wah-Be-Ka-Netta. Today they are known by the more prosaic names of Duck Lake and Green Lake.

The town closest to camp was Traverse City, Michigan. One of the better places to stay in town was the Park Place Hotel, which offered "all foods in season." Guests could enjoy snacks and light food at a soda fountain or indulge in more elaborate meals, prepared by a French chef de cuisine, in the dining room. The hotel offered music for its guests, including "the sounds of the Cherry Land Trio," no doubt so named because Michigan was famous for its cherries. The Whiting Hotel challenged the Park Place for hotel supremacy in Traverse City, billing itself as "the coolest place in town."

For clothing, visitors could look to "The Irishman and the Jew Clothiers" who provided "Haberdashery for Any Occasion." If a snack was in order after shopping, Max Bauer's Creamery was ready to quell hunger pangs with ice cream and butter "noted for their Nutritious Flavor—That's Why They're used by Leading Hotels in the North."

If guests visited Interlochen in midsummer, they could enjoy the Michigan Cherry Festival during the second week of July. Promoters billed the festival, held in Traverse City, as "The Midwest's Mardi Gras." The festival featured "three spectacular days of parade, pageantry, and revelry celebrating the picturesque cherry harvest in the nation's cherry capital." According to an advertisement in the "Interlochen Bowl" program for 1930, the festival included boat races, concerts, orchard tours, airplane races, street dancing, athletic events, glider stunting, "juvenile activities," the "Governor's Ball," a "Grand Fireworks display," coronation of the Cherry Queen, and a full "Three Days of Merrymaking." The festival was so popular and accommodations so tight that the sponsors suggested attendees make reservations on "any lake in a fifty-mile radius." Today it is called the National Cherry Festival and runs for a week during the first week of July. One might consider it a cherries jubilee.

64 Interlochen newsletter 1930.

The Juilliard School

After graduating from the University of Cincinnati's Conservatory and Hughes High School, Esther attended the Juilliard Graduate School of Music in New York City from 1930 to 1931. She matriculated in October 1930 at the age of eighteen.[65] The Juilliard School was a world leader in performing arts education. Its mission was to provide the highest quality education possible to gifted musicians from around the world.

Dr. Frank Damrosch founded the "Institute of Musical Art" in 1905.[66] Damrosch, a German American music conductor and educator, was born on June 22, 1859, in Breslau, Germany. His mother, Helene von Heimburg, was an opera singer, and his father Leopold was a conductor. Frank, along with his father and his brother Walter, emigrated to the United States in 1871. Frank was the godson of Franz Liszt.

In 1897 Damrosch became the head of music education for the New York City public schools. Damrosch believed the United States needed a music academy that could provide an education like that offered at established European conservatories. His Institute of Musical Art was first housed in a building on Fifth Avenue at 12th Street in Manhattan but grew quickly and, in 1910, moved uptown to a location near Columbia University.

In 1919, a wealthy textile merchant by the name of Augustus Juilliard died. In his will, he provided what was then the country's largest bequest for music education. The trustees for the bequest honored Juilliard's

65 The 1930 Census records include entries for Esther's family: Max, Anna, Esther, Joyce, Julius (who went by Jay), Rose, and Allan, who by then was six years old. The records do not list an occupation for Max, so he may have stopped working by then. The form states that Max emigrated to the United States in 1898 and Anna in 1907. Anna's date of emigration seems wrong since she and Max married in 1907 and family lore has it that she emigrated in the 1887-98 timeframe. The form states that Max and Anna were not naturalized, although as to Max that seems odd since he registered for the draft in 1918, which he could not have done unless he was naturalized or a citizen.

66 Julliard School Website.

desire by founding the Juilliard Graduate School in 1924, which merged a few years later with Damrosch's Institute of Musical Art. The combined entity became the Juilliard School of Music.[67]

Esther took classes in violin, orchestra, piano, and counterpoint. She studied violin with Paul Kochański, a Polish violinist. Kochański, born in Odessa to Polish-Jewish parents, studied violin as a child. He was asked to become the concertmaster of the Warsaw Philharmonic Orchestra when he was only fourteen. He became close friends with Arthur Rubinstein, a Polish musician widely regarded as one of the greatest pianists of all time. Kochanski and Rubenstein traveled together to New York in 1921. Kochański took a position at Juilliard, leading the violin faculty from 1924 until his untimely death in 1934 at age forty-six. As evidence of his extraordinary talent and the esteem in which he was held by his fellow musicians, Kochanski's pallbearers included Arturo Toscanini, Jascha Heifetz, Vladimir Horowitz, and Leopold Stokowski.

While at Juilliard, Esther also studied music theory and composition with Bernard Wagner and Professor Rubin Goldmark, as well as studying ensemble with Hans Letz and English literature with Professor John Erskine.

Esther was anxious to pursue her performing career, so she filled out a form for the Juilliard Placement Bureau. She wrote that her present position was "concertizing." She was looking for opportunities to perform at concerts and recitals, to solo with symphony orchestras, as well as teach violin. Esther was ready to study, but she was also eager to perform.

At age nineteen, Esther was living at the Hotel Lincoln on Eighth Avenue between 44th and 45th Streets in Manhattan's theater district. Opened in 1928, the Lincoln was a massive hotel, with 1,300 rooms spread over twenty-seven floors. Its clientele included people associated with the theater district, businessmen, and tourists. This was back in the day when telephone numbers started with prefixes, so Esther noted on the Juilliard Placement form that she could be reached at "Avon 2470 or Circle 6-4500."

After graduating from Juilliard, but while still in New York, Esther studied violin with Remo Bolognini from 1931-1934. Bolognini was the assistant concertmaster of the New York Philharmonic under Arturo

67 In 1945, the school added a dance program. In 1968, it added a division to teach drama; John Houseman was its first director. To reflect the added disciplines, the school changed its name to The Juilliard School. In 1969 the school moved to its present location in Lincoln Center at Broadway and 66th Street.

Toscanini, the orchestra's music director. She also studied ensemble and repertoire with Arthur Hartmann from 1933-1934, while Erno Balögh coached her in repertoire from 1934 to 1936.

Esther's reputation grew to such an extent that she was awarded several National and International Fellowships, including scholarships from the Schmidlapp Foundation (1931-1933) and Fleischmann Foundation (1934-1936). These years in New York were exhilarating. Esther was studying with some of the most famous violinists and conductors in the United States. She was recognized throughout the music world as a talented, up and coming artist, while she sought as many opportunities to perform as she could find.

Esther's Post-College Career Begins

The earliest available publicity photograph of Esther is from 1932, when she would have been twenty-one. The portrait shows her looking like a classic movie star of that era. Her hair was styled in waves, with a clip holding it in place on one side. She looked glamourous in a white fur coat. In another photograph, Esther looked off to the side with her lips parted in a slight smile. She was seated, wearing a silk scarf embroidered with flowers and long tassels that dangled over Esther's legs.

Esther's reputation as an outstanding violinist grew. In 1937, Dr. Stephen Wise engaged her to be the only guest soloist at the thirtieth anniversary event celebrating the founding of the Free Synagogue in New York and honoring Dr. Wise. The Free Synagogue, a Reform congregation, was located at 30 West 68th Street on Manhattan's upper West Side, just west of Sheep Meadow in Central Park. The gala event, featuring New York's Mayor Fiorella LaGuardia and Albert Einstein as speakers, was held in the main ballroom of Manhattan's Hotel Commodore. Esther was clearly becoming a top-of-the-line performer.

The Commodore, named after "Commodore" Cornelius Vanderbilt who founded the New York Central Railroad System, was located at 109 East 42nd Street next to Grand Central Station. It opened in 1919 to provide rooms for rail travelers passing through Grand Central. The Commodore's nearly 2000 rooms, spread over twenty-eight floors, made it one of the largest hotels in New York City. Its ballroom could seat 3500 guests and hosted many of the nation's most important functions. Scott and Zelda Fitzgerald spent their honeymoon at the Commodore. President Franklin Roosevelt watched election returns there and John Kennedy began his 1960 Presidential campaign at the Commodore. It was renovated in 1980 and today, it is the Hyatt Grand Central New York, but is expected to close this year.

Unfortunately, Esther's rapid ascent as a violin virtuoso was interrupted by sad news from Cincinnati. After suffering a lengthy illness,

Esther's father Max died on March 15, 1937, at age fifty-five. The Hamilton County Death Certificate states the cause of death was acute coronary occlusion, that is, Max had a massive heart attack. The death certificate said Max had retired from manufacturing pants. The obituary in the *American Israelite* stated Max had retired in 1924, when he was only forty-two years old, from manufacturing clothing at Parkway and Elm Streets in downtown Cincinnati (Parkway is now known as Central Parkway). Max's gravestone at the Love Brothers' Cemetery in Cincinnati reads: "Mordechai son of Aharon Aryeh passed on March 15, 1937."

Esther, as Max and Anna's eldest child, felt terrible that she was in New York and could not be with her mother for an extended period during this difficult time. Fortunately, Esther's siblings Hilda, Rose, Jules, and Allan lived in or near Cincinnati, so they were able to comfort Anna and help her adjust to life without Max while Esther pursued her career in New York.

The View from Cincinnati

Cincinnati's newspapers provided frequent coverage of Esther's career. The *Cincinnati Times Star* reported on February 22, 1938, that Esther, by then age twenty-six, had recently appeared on the National Broadcasting (NBC) and Columbia Broadcasting (CBS) networks. The *Times Star* noted Esther had been featured on television programs such as the Golden Rule Mothers' Foundation Hour, Music at Twilight Hour, Federation of Music Clubs Hour, the Cincinnati Conservatory Hour, the Music Masters' Symphonic Hour presented by the New York Civic Orchestra, and the Federation of Churches broadcast.

Esther occasionally returned to Ohio to perform in local venues. The *Times Star* reported on February 19, 1938, that Esther would be playing a program for Cincinnati's Mt. Auburn Music Club. Her repertoire was to feature works by Arcangelo Corelli (an Italian violinist and composer of the Baroque era), Johann Sebastian Bach, Samuel Richards Gaines (an American composer, conductor, and pianist), Igor Stravinsky, Granville English (an American composer), Ernest Bloch (one of the early presidents of the San Francisco Conservatory of Music), and Manuel de Falla.

In 1939, when Esther was twenty-eight, she began performing as Joyce Wasserman. The *Cincinnati Enquirer* published a review of one of her hometown concerts:

A large audience received the entire program with the utmost enthusiasm. The breadth and sweep of the first movement, the melodious quality of the second, and the brilliance of the Finale of the Mendelssohn Concerto demonstrated the singing tone of the wide variety of violin technique of the performer. She displayed a wide range of moods in the short numbers. Gifted, well trained, and versatile, Miss Wasserman should, and no doubt will, go far—and probably famously—in her chosen career. She swung into her program with verve, ease, and rhythmic aplomb, that seemed to mark her as one of those rare souls to whom Music becomes a passion, and which offers those who listen an intense sensation of a vivid personality at the helm, and which makes for musical, artistic and personal success upon the artist's rostrum!

The *Times Star* reported Joyce "handled a difficult program with astonishing ease, poise and flexibility." The *Norfolk Ledger Dispatch* commented that Joyce "played with facile technique, vigor, velvety texture of tone, and sound interpretation. Miss Wasserman was given an ovation following the final rondo movement of Lalo's "Symphonie espagnole." (*Norfolk Ledger Dispatch.*) "We were impressed with her playing—she has that certain something—a very fine artist who should go a long way in her chosen profession." (Reginald Billen, Louisville, Kentucky.)

On January 9, 1939, the *Cincinnati Times Star* reported further regarding Esther's career:

> Miss Joyce Wasserman, who will be presented by the Music Department of the Cincinnati's Women's Club at a recital at 8:30 o'clock Thursday evening, represents one of the sensational violinists among the younger American artists. She is a holder of many fellowships, including the Juilliard Graduate School and the Fleishmann scholarship. She is a graduate of the Cincinnati Conservatory of Music, where she has the distinction of being the youngest artist ever to have achieved the highest honor diploma in violin and a Bachelor of Music Degree conferred upon her at the age of seventeen.
>
> Joyce Wasserman has appeared extensively in concerts and as a soloist with symphony orchestras, here and in Europe, as well as in numerous broadcasts over the National Broadcasting, Columbia, and Mutual Networks. Recently she was presented with the coveted medal of the Ohio Society of New York, and last year at the music convention was chosen to demonstrate the valuable collection of violins for the Wurlitzer company.
>
> Miss Wasserman's musicianship is of a very high order—her playing is filled with the glow of youth, with a firm, sure tone and a variety of warmth and color. She encompasses the delicacy of a woman with the strength of a man, and in all her work she evidences good taste reflecting the absorption in her work and her serious innate love of the music.
>
> Last spring in an audition with George Enesco, the very outstanding and well-known violinist, orchestra director and composer, he was so impressed with Miss Wasserman's playing that he gave her a scholarship in his summer course in Paris...At the

close of this term Mr. Enesco wrote a fine letter in praise of her musicianship, talent, and splendid execution. She is (presently) in New York, coaching with Ernö Balogh, well-known pianist, accompanist, and coach.[68]

One of Joyce's first radio performances was on the "Golden Rule Mother's Hour," when she played as a soloist along with Dr. Emerson Fosdick and the Studio Orchestra. Afterwards, the president of the Golden Rule program wrote to Joyce: "I wish you could see the fan mail across my desk. There are 1018 letters commenting on about how much they particularly enjoyed the violin solos." Joyce's career was taking off to such an extent that, in 1939, the Cincinnati Conservatory honored her with its Institute Instrumental Award.

The *Miami Herald* commented in a March 24, 1940, article that "Miss Wasserman is considered one of the sensational younger violinists who has achieved great praise from press and public for her outstanding musical and artistic ability." The *Miami News* similarly reported that Joyce was a distinguished young violinist who had won laurels at home and abroad. Joyce's reputation by now was not only national, but international as well. This was heady stuff for a young woman from the Midwest, a first-generation United States citizen whose parents came from the humblest origins in Eastern Europe. For Joyce and her parents, the United States was indeed the land of opportunity.

68 The *Cincinnati Times Star*, Jan. 9, 1939. Enescu performed at a concert at the McMillin Theatre in Manhattan in the late 1930's or early 1940's; research has not determined the year, although a program for the concert gives the date of February 15. The Theatre was located on Columbia University's Morningside Heights campus at Broadway and 116th Street. Though Enescu was an internationally acclaimed conductor, composer, and violinist, tickets for the event were offered from $1.20 up to $2.40. How prices how have changed.

Joyce in Paris

In 1939, Joyce was awarded a Woolley International Fellowship to study abroad. Established in the early 1930s, the Harriet Hale Woolley Scholarship was awarded annually to a small group of exceptional artists and musicians from the United States who planned to pursue their studies in Paris. The Fondation des États Unis, which administered the grants, maintained a private student residence in the Cité Internationale Universaire de Paris in Paris' 14th arrondissement. The Cité Internationale Universaire de Paris ("CIUP") was established after World War I to create a place for students, researchers and intellectuals from around the world to meet and study in a spirit of peace and cooperation.

The Parisian press lauded Joyce as "America's violin sensation."[69] The fact that Joyce was able to speak and read French came in more than a little handy and likely went a long way towards endearing her to the French press. The "Institute Instrumental" in Paris conferred an award on Joyce in 1939 in recognition of her talent.

While in Paris, Joyce studied with George Enescu. Enescu is spelled "Enesco" in French; some of the quotations that follow used the French spelling of "Georges Enesco" rather than the Romanian spelling of George Enescu. Enescu was a world-famous conductor, composer, and violinist. Enescu, who was from Romania, performed and led concerts with orchestras across the United States. He is widely regarded as one of the greatest musicians in Romanian history. His "Romanian Rhapsody in A Major" was a staple of orchestral performances.

Enescu was born in Romania's Moldavian hill country in 1881 (making him the same age as Joyce's father Max). At age seven he enrolled in the Vienna Conservatory. By the time he was seventeen, he began a brilliant career as a violin virtuoso. Enescu made his debut as a composer in 1898 when his "Poème roumain" premiered. His "Symphonie

69 the *American Israelite's* 'Let There Be Light' podcast.

concertante" premiered in 1908. Enescu also composed a four-act lyric tragedy entitled "Oedipus Rex," which premiered in March 1938 at the Paris Opera.

Joyce studied violin repertoire with Enescu in 1939 at his master violin classes in Paris. She studied with him again after World War II, from 1946 to 1948. Enescu was enthused with Joyce's talent: "Her art is of the highest order and her knowledge of the instrument perfect. She has personality and great fire." (Note from George Enescu, April 24, 1939, Rue de Clichy, Paris.) Enescu went on to comment that her success was well-deserved. Joyce's time in Paris was magical, as she spread her musical wings beyond the United States and her reputation spread accordingly.

Photos

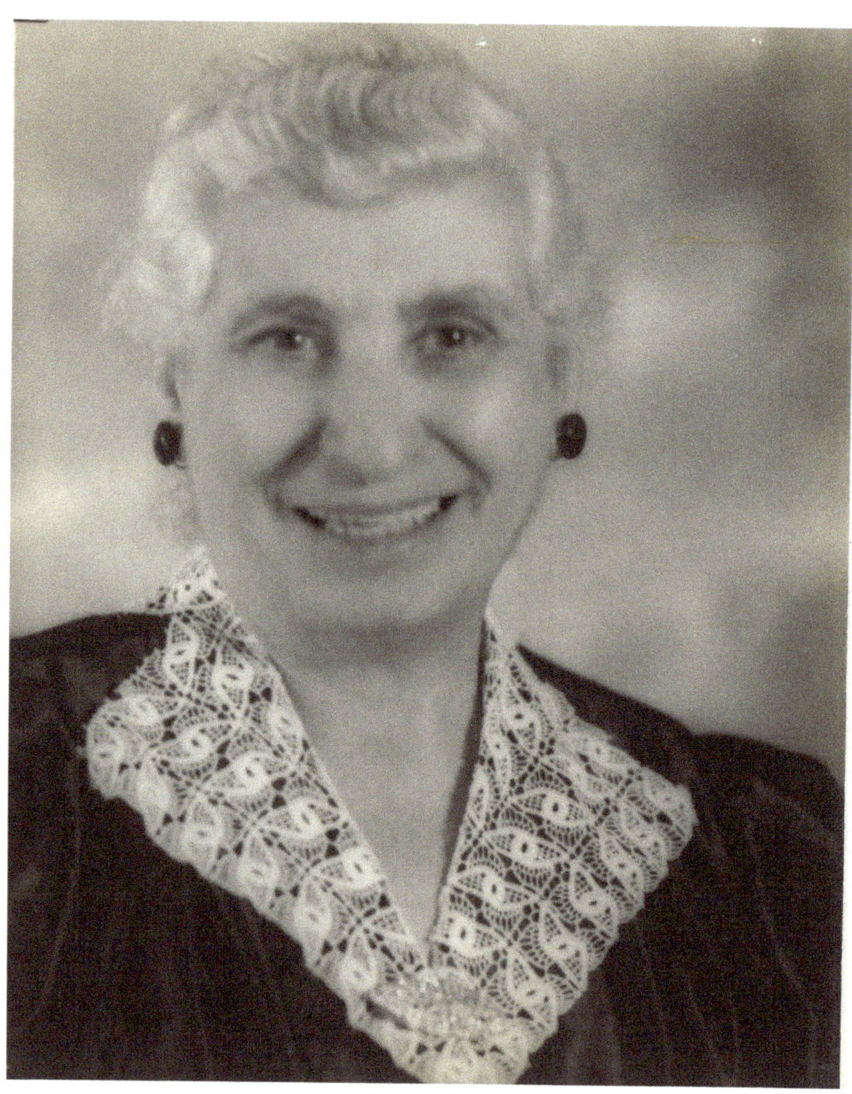

Henia Rabkin

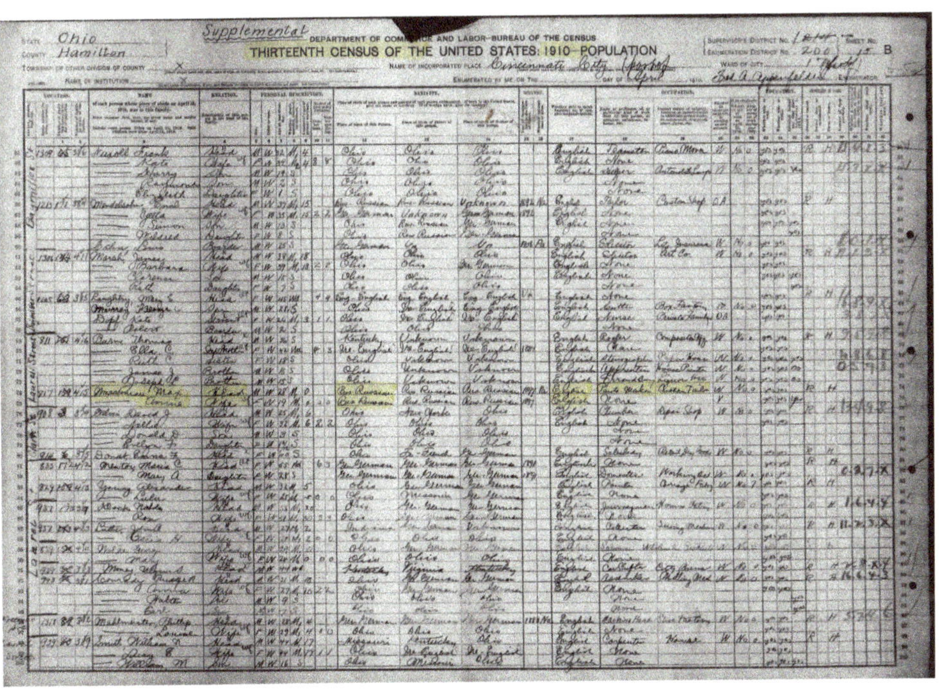

Supplemental
DEPARTMENT OF COMMERCE AND LABOR—BUREAU OF THE CENSUS
THIRTEENTH CENSUS OF THE UNITED STATES: 1910—POPULATION

State: Ohio
County: Hamilton
Township or other division of county: X
Name of institution: X
Name of incorporated place: Cincinnati City
Supervisor's District No.
Enumeration District No. 200
Sheet No. 15 B
Ward of city: 1
Enumerated by me on the ___ day of April, 1910.

Page from 1910 U.S. Population Census

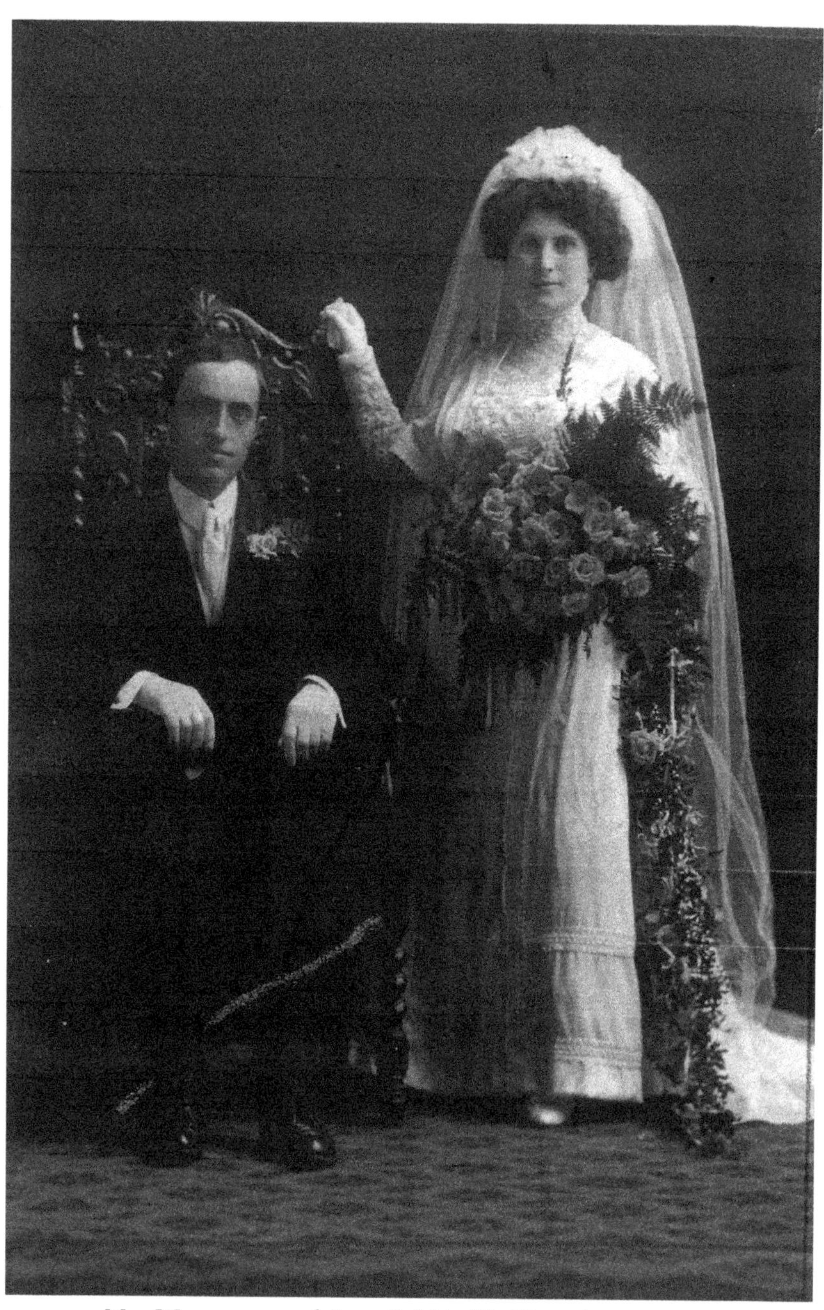

Max Wasserman and Anna Rabkin Wedding, Aug. 4, 1909.

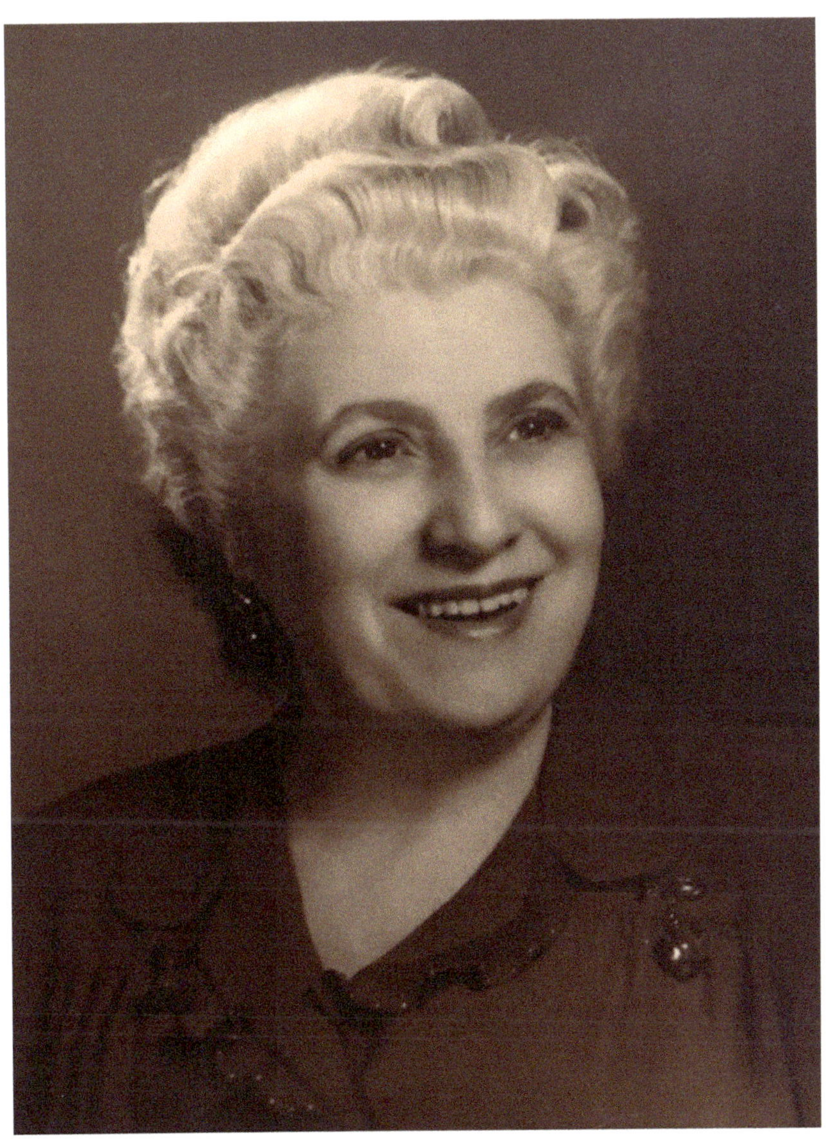
Anna Wasserman

PLACE OF BIRTH
County of Hamilton
Township of
Village of or City of Cincinnati
No. 817 Laurel St. 17 Ward.

STATE OF OHIO
Bureau of Vital Statistics
CERTIFICATE OF BIRTH

Registration District No. 494 File No. 98832
Primary Registration District No. 8227 Registered No. 7517
MAR 1912

FULL NAME OF CHILD Esther Wasserman

Sex of Child Female | Legitimate? Yes | Date of birth July 13 1911

FATHER		MOTHER	
FULL NAME	Max Wasserman	FULL MAIDEN NAME	Anna Ida Rabkin
RESIDENCE	817 Laurel St	RESIDENCE	817 Laurel St
COLOR OR RACE	White, AGE AT LAST BIRTHDAY 28 (Years)	COLOR OR RACE	White, AGE AT LAST BIRTHDAY 19 (Years)
BIRTHPLACE	Russia	BIRTHPLACE	Russia
OCCUPATION	Tailor	OCCUPATION	Housewife

Number of child of this mother 1st — Number of children, of this mother, now living One

CERTIFICATE OF ATTENDING PHYSICIAN OR MIDWIFE*

I hereby certify that I attended the birth of this child, and that it occurred on July 13, 1911 at 8 A.M.

(Signature) [illegible] M.D.

(Physician or Midwife.)

Given name added from a supplemental report.

Address 19 [illegible]

Filed MAR 22 1912

Registrar

JUL 18 2022

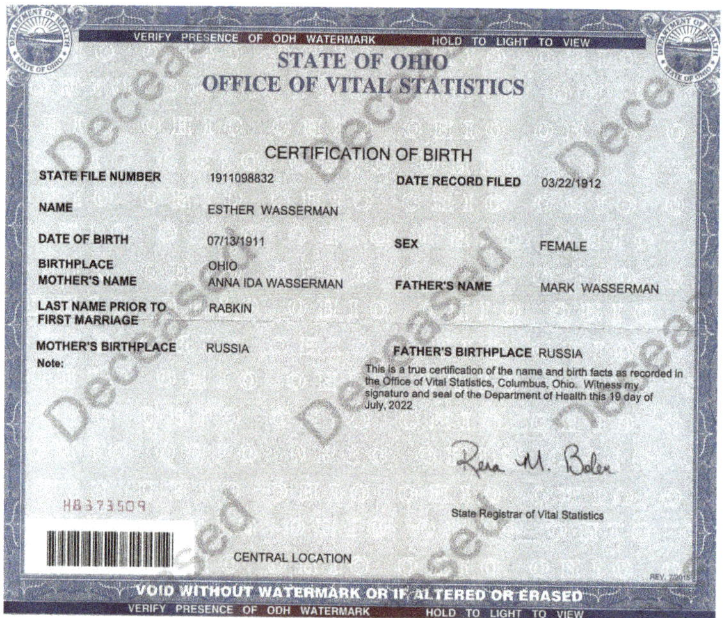
VERIFY PRESENCE OF ODH WATERMARK HOLD TO LIGHT TO VIEW

STATE OF OHIO
OFFICE OF VITAL STATISTICS

CERTIFICATION OF BIRTH

STATE FILE NUMBER	1911098832	DATE RECORD FILED	03/22/1912
NAME	ESTHER WASSERMAN		
DATE OF BIRTH	07/13/1911	SEX	FEMALE
BIRTHPLACE	OHIO		
MOTHER'S NAME	ANNA IDA WASSERMAN	FATHER'S NAME	MARK WASSERMAN
LAST NAME PRIOR TO FIRST MARRIAGE	RABKIN		
MOTHER'S BIRTHPLACE	RUSSIA	FATHER'S BIRTHPLACE	RUSSIA

Note:

This is a true certification of the name and birth facts as recorded in the Office of Vital Statistics, Columbus, Ohio. Witness my signature and seal of the Department of Health this 19 day of July, 2022

State Registrar of Vital Statistics

H8373509

CENTRAL LOCATION

VOID WITHOUT WATERMARK OR IF ALTERED OR ERASED
VERIFY PRESENCE OF ODH WATERMARK HOLD TO LIGHT TO VIEW

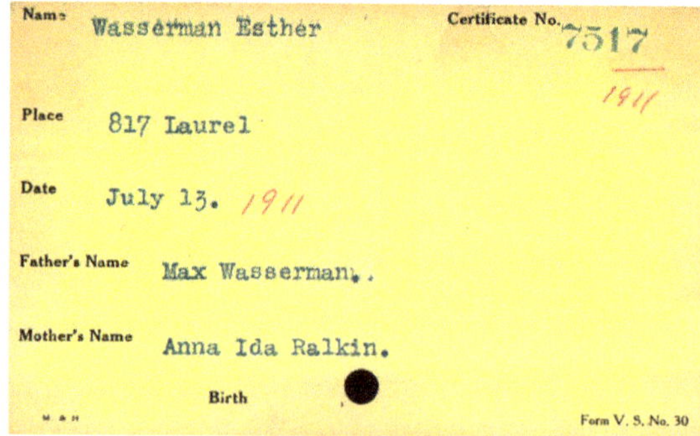
Name Wasserman Esther — Certificate No. 7517 1911

Place 817 Laurel

Date July 13. 1911

Father's Name Max Wasserman.

Mother's Name Anna Ida Ralkin.

Birth

Form V. S. No. 30

Top image: Esther Wasserman's Birth Certificate. Middle image: Esther Wasserman birth certificate retrieved from Hamilton County. Bottom image: Contemporaneous note of Birth of Esther Wasserman. Anna Rabkin's last name is misspelled on the note.

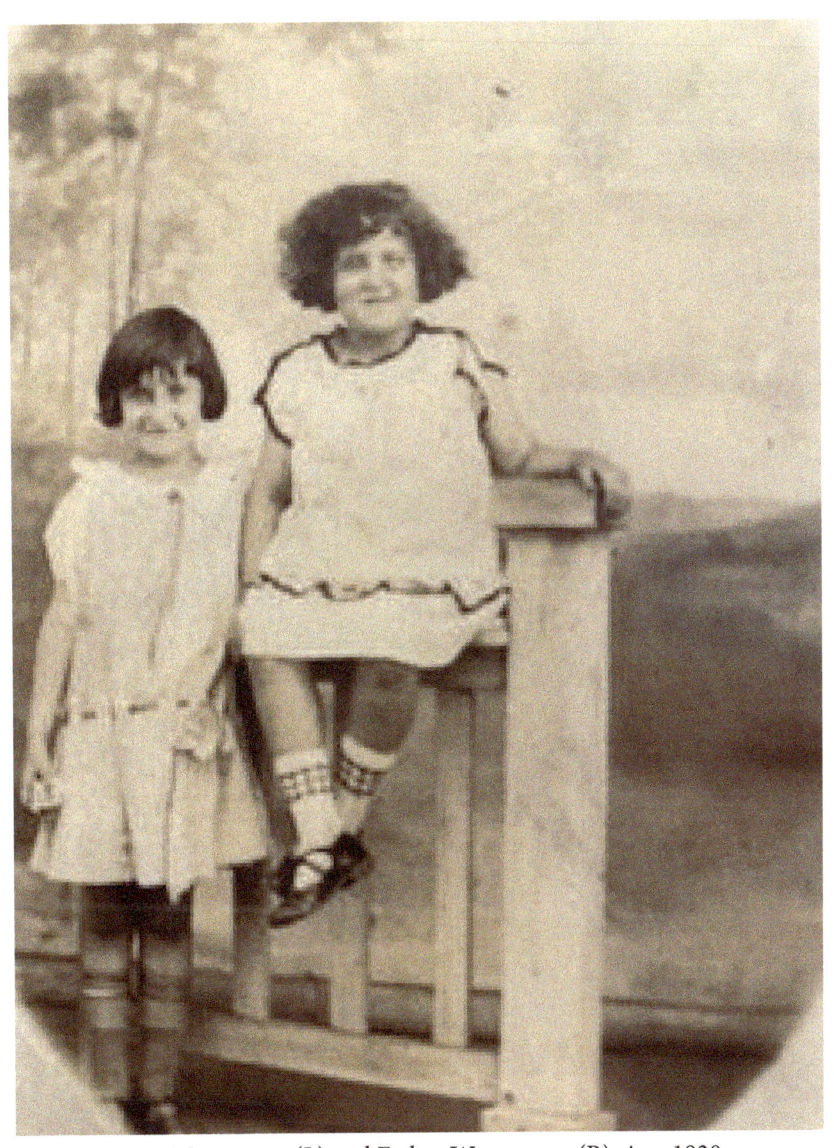

Rose Wasserman (L) and Esther Wasserman (R) circa 1920.

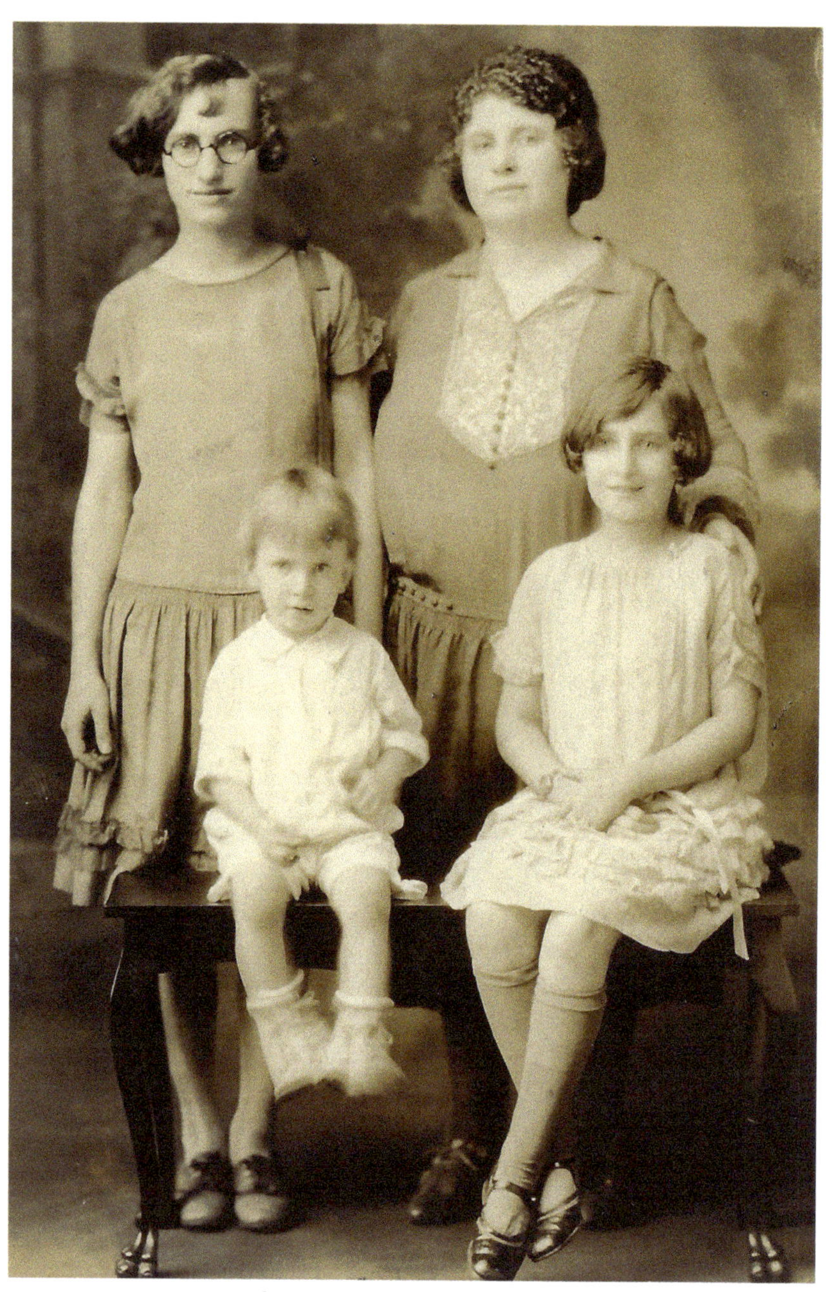

Standing: Hilda and Anna Wasserman;
Seated: Jay and Rose Wasserman. Circa 1920.

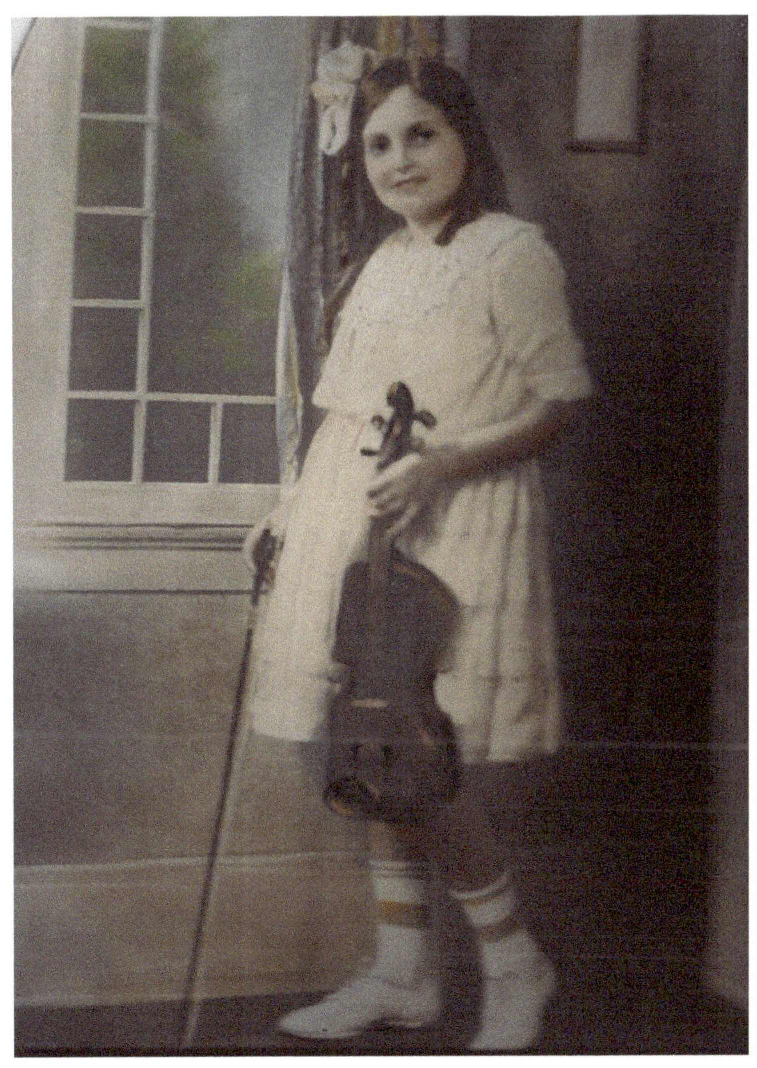

Esther Joyce Wasserman, age 11, circa 1922.

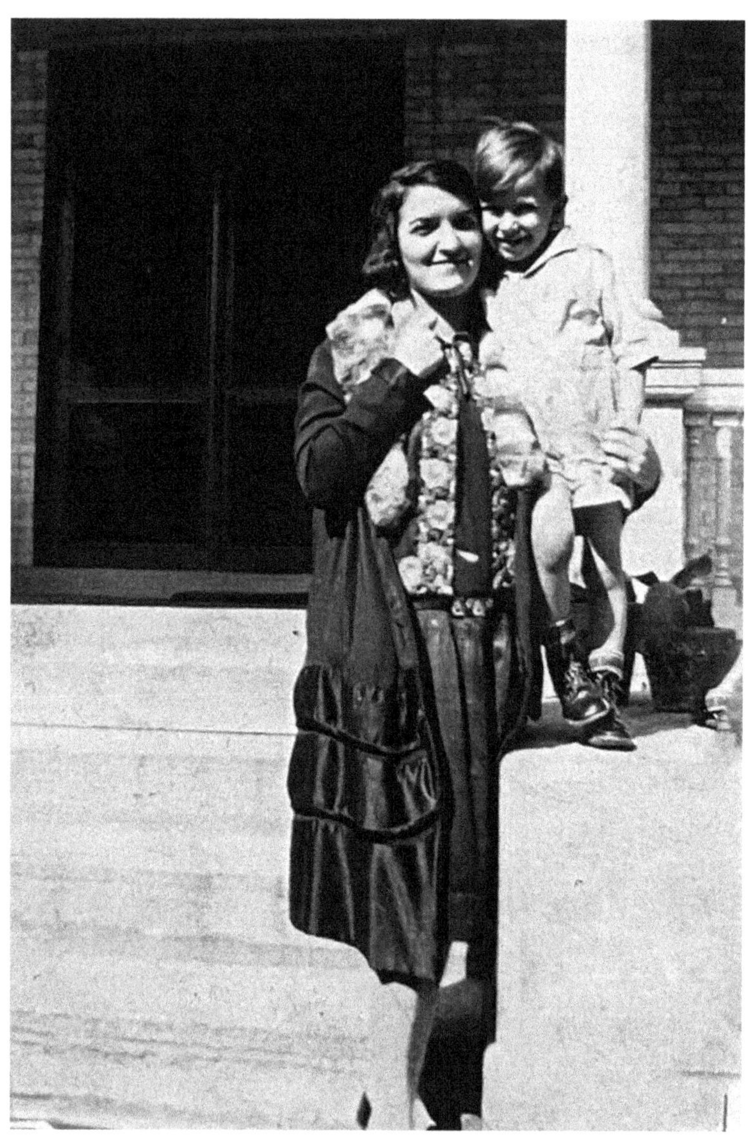

Esther with her younger brother Allan in 1928,
on the porch of the family home in Cincinnati.

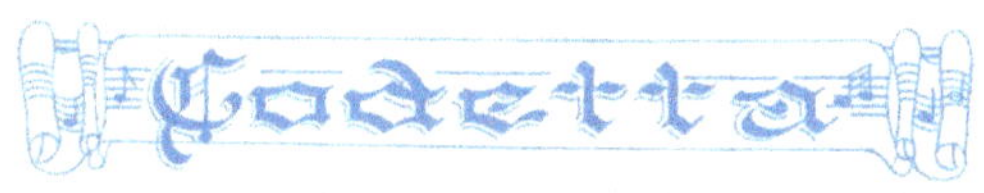

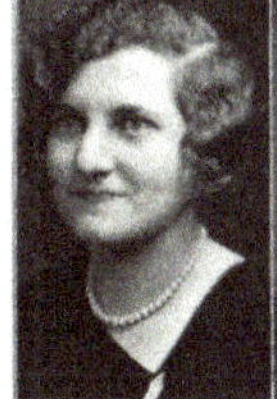
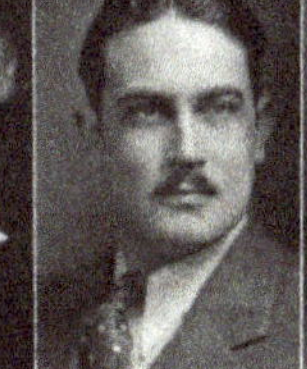
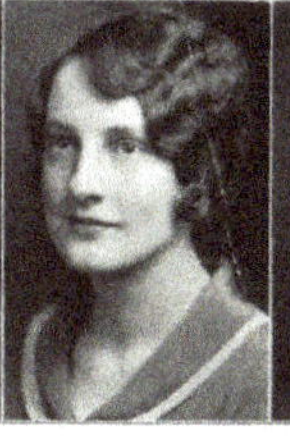
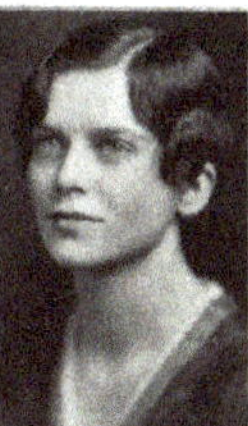

Wasserman *Watson* *E. Welker* *H. Welker*

ESTHER WASSERMAN
Cincinnati, Ohio
Violin—Diploma, '30.

JACK WATSON
Dillon, South Carolina
Voice—Diploma, '30.
Phi Mu Alpha; Opera Chorus; Opera; Beddoe Four.

EVELYN WELKER
Connellsville, Pennsylvania
Piano and Organ—Certificate in Piano.

HELEN WELKER
Connellsville, Pennsylvania
Voice.

ALICE WHARTON
Leesburg, Florida
Piano—Post-Graduate. Accompanist.
Delta Omicron.

FRANCES WHITTAKER
Bridgeport, Illinois
Violin—Certificate in Violin, '30. Diploma, Public School Music, '30.
Phi Sigma Mu.

DORIS WIGHTMAN
Gales Ferry, Connecticut
Voice and Piano.

LEONARD WITHERS
Parkersburg, West Virginia
Piano.
Opera Chorus.

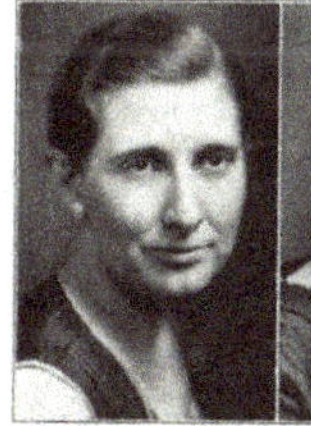
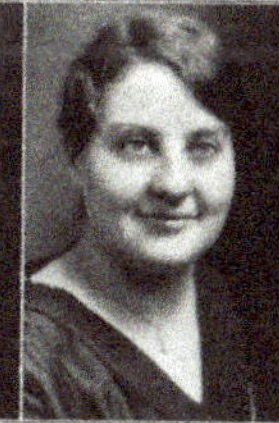
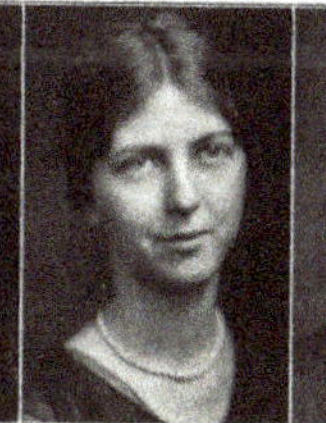
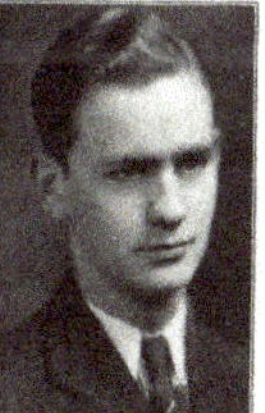

Wharton *Whittaker* *Wightman* *Withers*

[61]

Page from Esther's yearbook from the Cincinnati Conservatory of Music, circa 1928.

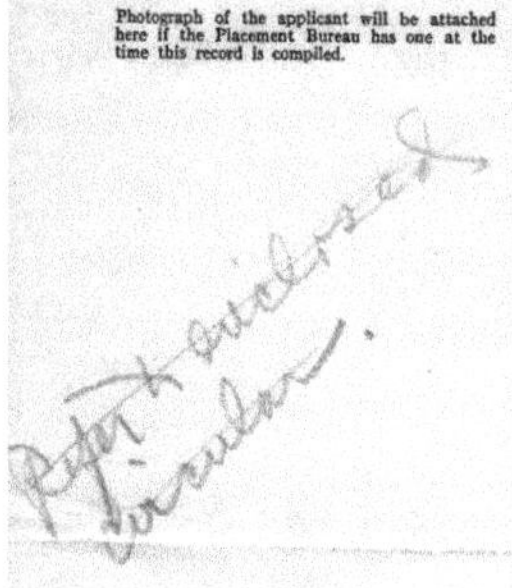

Photograph of the applicant will be attached here if the Placement Bureau has one at the time this record is compiled.

PLACEMENT BUREAU
JUILLIARD SCHOOL OF MUSIC
120 CLAREMONT AVENUE
NEW YORK CITY

1

CONFIDENTIAL INFORMATION

concerning

Name JOYCE RENEE

Address 765 GREENWOOD AVENUE
CINCINNATI 29, OHIO, 11

Telephone HOTEL LINCOLN, N.Y.C.
AVON 4470 or CIRCLE 6-4500

Date of birth JULY 13, 1911 Place of birth CIN. OHIO

If foreign born:

Date of arrival in U.S.A.

Citizenship status

Height 5' 6½" Weight 149

Physical handicaps NONE

Marital status SINGLE Children

Present position CONCERTIZING

Prepared to accept the following types of positions
CONCERTS, RECITALS, SOLOS WITH SYMPHONY ORCHESTRAS, AND TEACHING

This folder contains confidential information which may assist you in estimating the qualifications of the applicant. It is for the use of employing officers only. Under no circumstances is it to be given to the applicant. When it has served its purpose, it should be returned directly to the Placement Bureau, 120 Claremont Ave., New York City.

F-143A 10M 7-47

Esther's Juilliard Placement Information Form, p. 1.

JUILLIARD SCHOOL OF MUSIC, PLACEMENT BUREAU Registrant's Name ....

ACADEMIC AND PROFESSIONAL TRAINING 2

List in chronological order; start with high school or preparatory school and include undergraduate and graduate work both at Juilliard and in other institutions.

DATES From To	NAME OF SCHOOL	LOCATION	MAJOR	MINOR	DEGREES, DIPLOMAS, ETC.
1925–'28	HUGHES HIGH SCHOOL	CIN., OHIO	MUSIC AND ART	ENGLISH	DIPLOMA
1923–'29	CIN. CONS. OF MUSIC	CIN., OHIO	VIOLIN	COMPOSITION AND ENGLISH	HIGHEST HONOR DIPLOMA,
1929–'30	CIN. CONS. OF MUSIC AND UNIV. OF CIN.	CIN., OHIO	VIOLIN	ENGLISH	B.M. DEGREE
SUMMER 1930	INTERLOCHEN		VIOLIN	COMPOSITION	
1930–31	JUILLIARD GRADUATE SCHOOL	N.Y.C.	VIOLIN	COMPOSITION	

Major teachers at Juilliard

DATES From To	NAME OF TEACHER	SUBJECT OR INSTRUMENT
1930–'31	PAUL KOCHANSKI	VIOLIN
	BERNARD WAGNER + GOLDMARK	THEORY — COMPOSITION
	LETZ + SALMOND	ENSEMBLE
	JOHN ERSKINE	ENGLISH LITERATURE

Special training with distinguished private teachers (other than Juilliard)

DATES From To	NAME OF TEACHER	LOCATION	SUBJECT OR INSTRUMENT
1931–'33	REMO BOLOGNINI	N.Y.C.	VIOLIN
1933–'34	ARTHUR HARTMANN	N.Y.C.	VIOLIN
1934–'36	ERNO BALOGH	N.Y.C.	REPERTOIRE
1939	GEORGES ENESCO	PARIS	VIOLIN REPERTOIRE
–'48	GEORGES ENESCO	N.Y.C.	VIOLIN REPERTOIRE

F-143B 10M 7-47

Esther's Juilliard Placement Information Form p. 2.

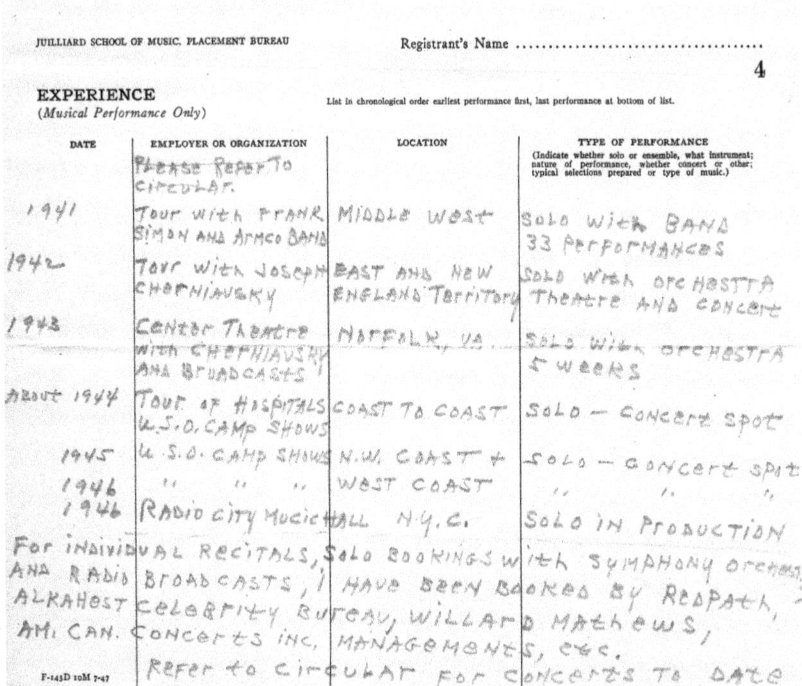

JUILLIARD SCHOOL OF MUSIC, PLACEMENT BUREAU

Registrant's Name ....

4

EXPERIENCE
(Musical Performance Only)

List in chronological order earliest performance first, last performance at bottom of list.

DATE	EMPLOYER OR ORGANIZATION	LOCATION	TYPE OF PERFORMANCE (Indicate whether solo or ensemble, what instrument; nature of performance, whether concert or other; typical selections prepared or type of music.)
	~~Please Refer To~~ Circular.		
1941	Tour with Frank Simon and Armco Band	Middle West	Solo with Band 33 Performances
1942	Tour with Joseph Cherniavsky	East and New England Territory	Solo with Orchestra Theatre and Concert
1943	Center Theatre with Cherniavsky and Broadcasts	Norfolk, Va.	Solo with Orchestra 5 weeks
About 1944	Tour of Hospitals U.S.O. Camp Shows	Coast to Coast	Solo — Concert Spot
1945	U.S.O. Camp Shows	N.W. Coast +	Solo — Concert Spot
1946	" " "	West Coast	" " "
1946	Radio City Music Hall	N.Y.C.	Solo in Production

For individual recitals, solo bookings with symphony orchestra and radio broadcasts, I have been booked by Redpath, Alkahost Celebrity Bureau, Willard Mathews, Am. Can. Concerts Inc. Managements, etc.

Refer to circular for concerts to date

F-143D 10M 7-47

Esther's Juilliard Placement Information Form p. 4

JUILLIARD SCHOOL OF MUSIC, PLACEMENT BUREAU

Registrant's Name ....

5

Honors and Distinctions (scholarships, fellowships, prizes, etc.)

DATE	CONFERRED BY	LOCATION	TYPE OF AWARD	SKILL, SERVICE OR PERFORMANCE MERITING AWARD
1928	Ohio Fed of Music Clubs Prize	Dayton, O.	First Prize	Performance
'29	Cin. Cons. of Music	Cin., O.	Highest Honor	Skill + Performance
'30	Juilliard School	N.Y.C.	Violin Diploma	
'31–'33	Schmidlapp Foundation	Cin. & NYC	Fellowship	
'34–'36	Fleischmann "	" " "	Scholarship	
'39	Institute Instrumental, Paris	France	"	
'39	Woolley Foundation	"	"	
'44, '45, '46	Ohio Society of N.Y.	N.Y.C.	Medals	

Publications (music, books, articles, etc.)

DATE	TITLE AND DESCRIPTION OF THE WORK	NAME OF PUBLISHER

Recordings (commercial)

DATE	NAME OF COMPANY	DESCRIPTION OF WORK Include all significant information, title, part in the performance, conductor, etc.

Languages (list and use code to indicate proficiency: S-speak, R-read, T-prepared to teach)

S.R. French

Memberships in professional and civic organizations

One of founder members of Musicians Club of Am., A.G.M.A., Local 802, Studio Club

F-143E 10M 7-47

Esther's Juilliard Placement Information Form p. 5

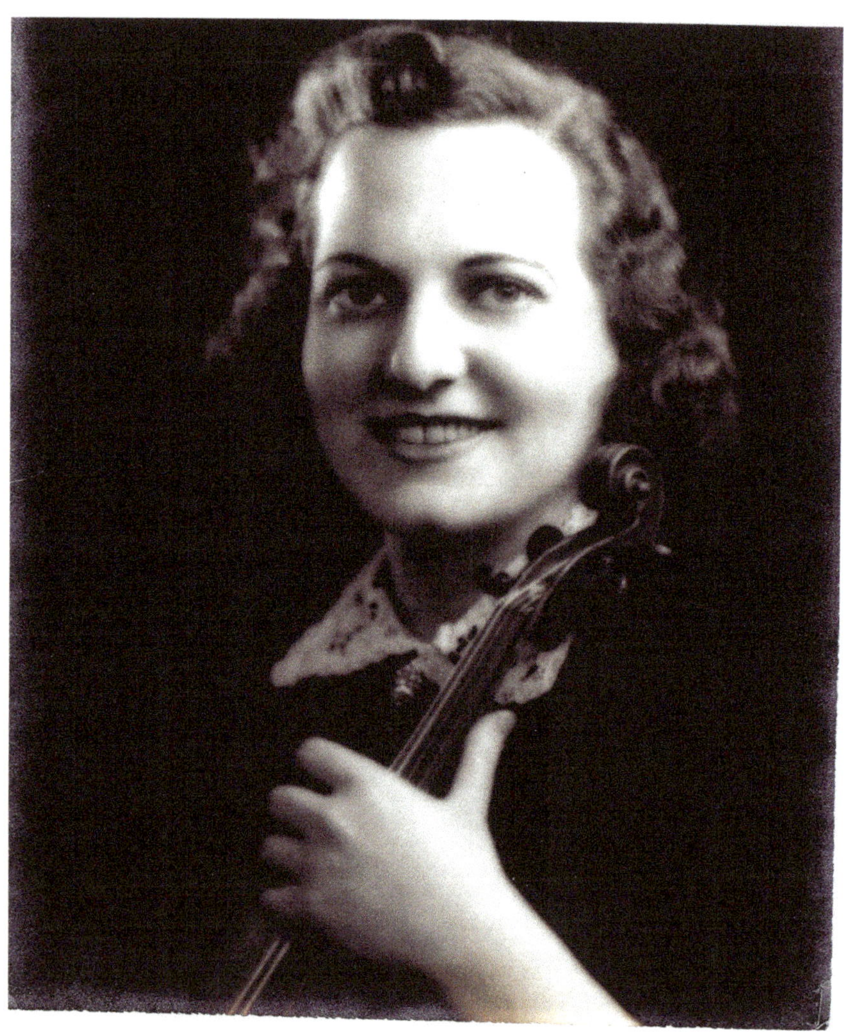

Esther promotional portrait photograph.

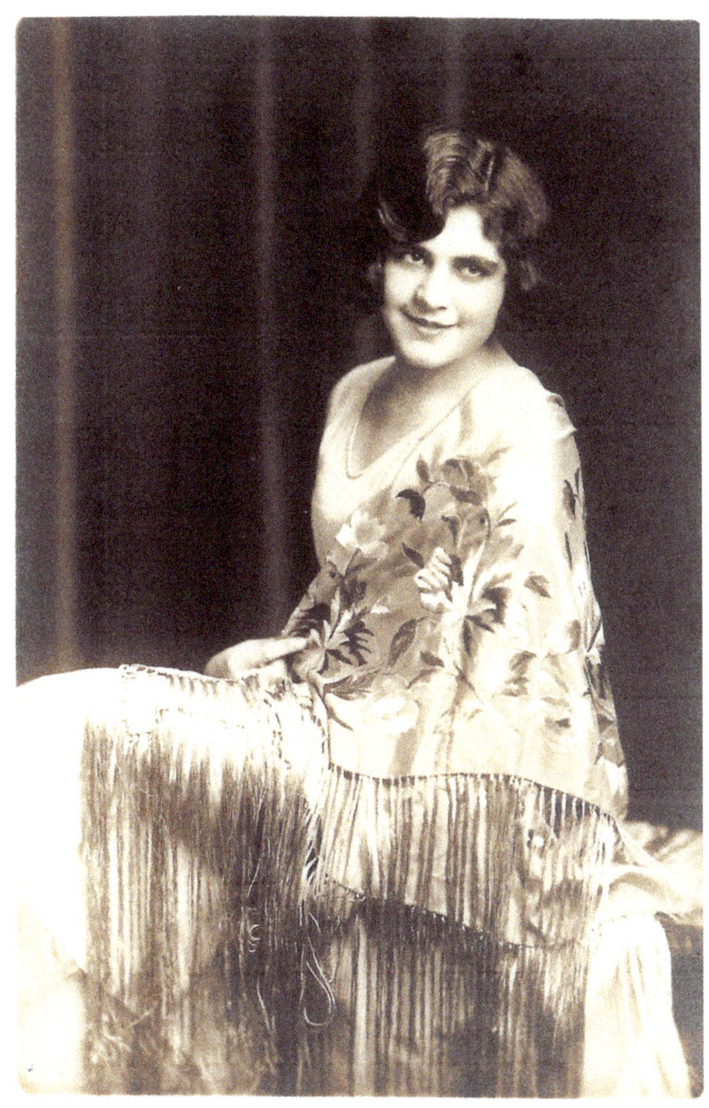

Esther promotional photograph, circa 1928.

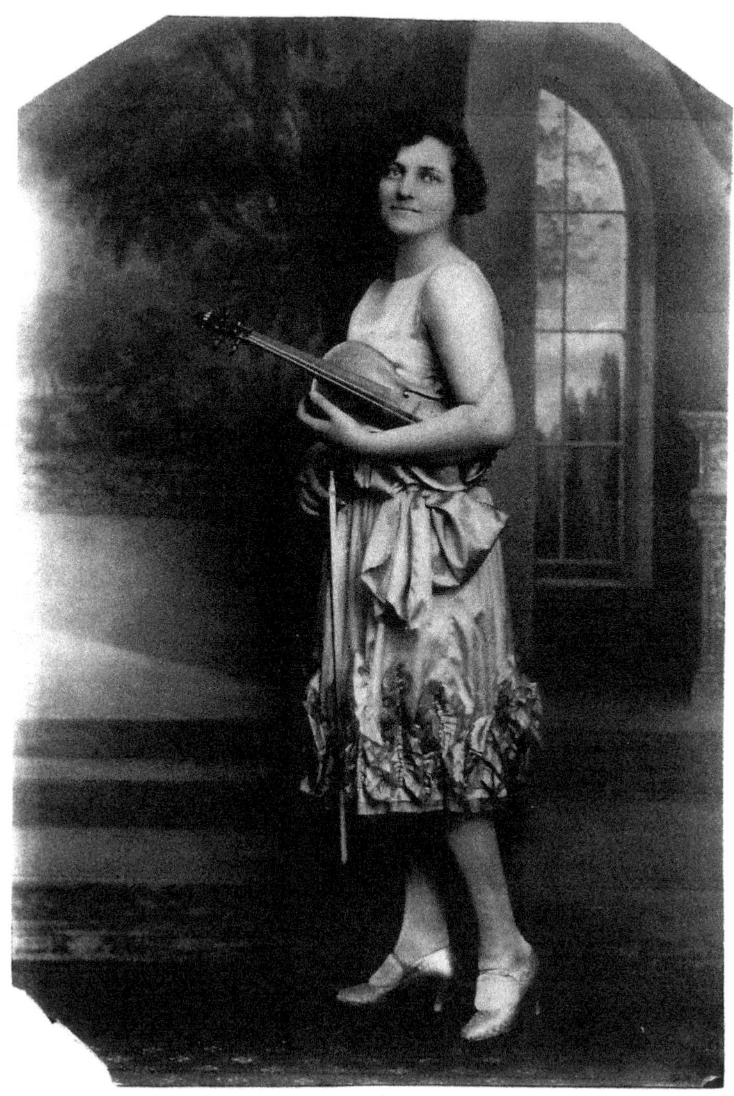

Esther promotional photograph, circa 1928.

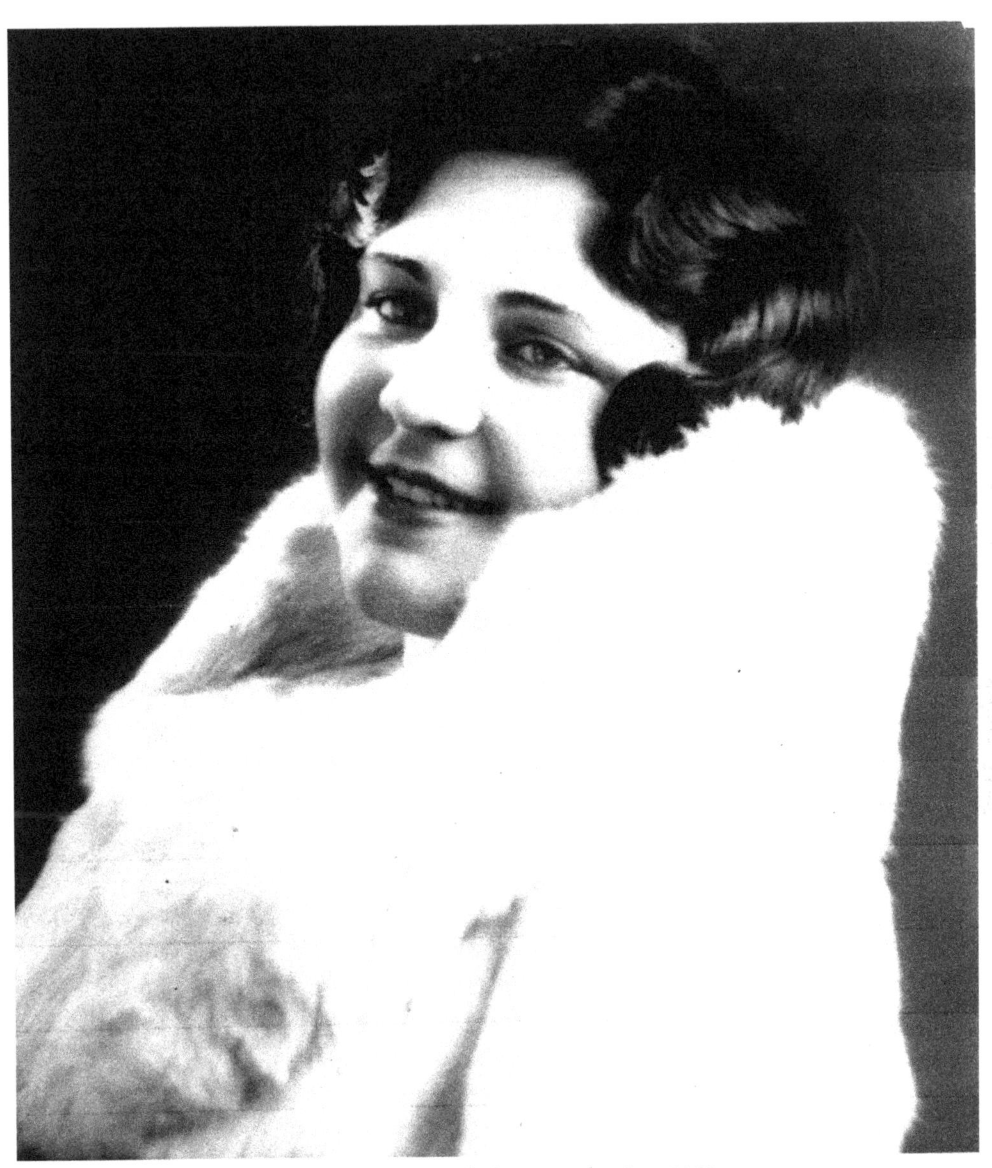

Esther promotional photograph, circa 1932.

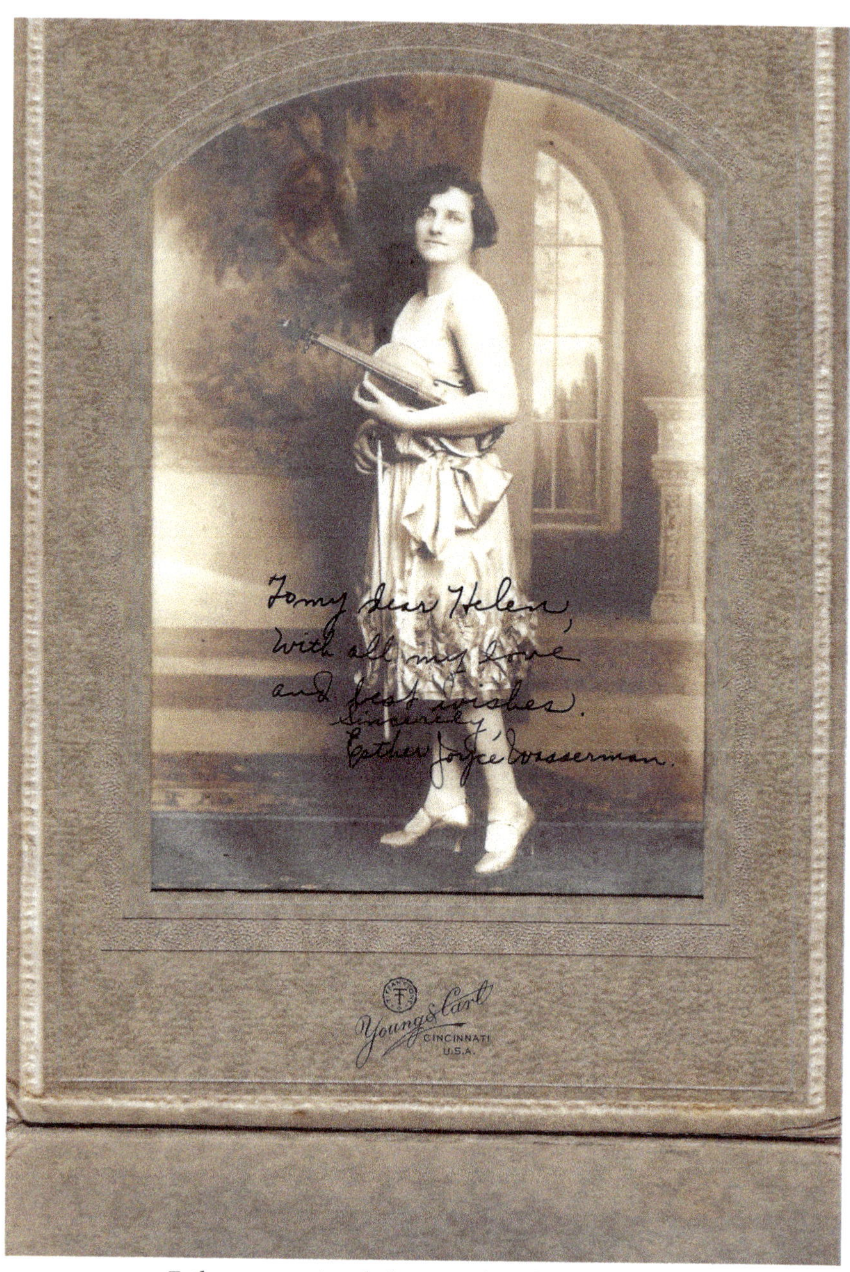

Esther promotional photograph with inscription.

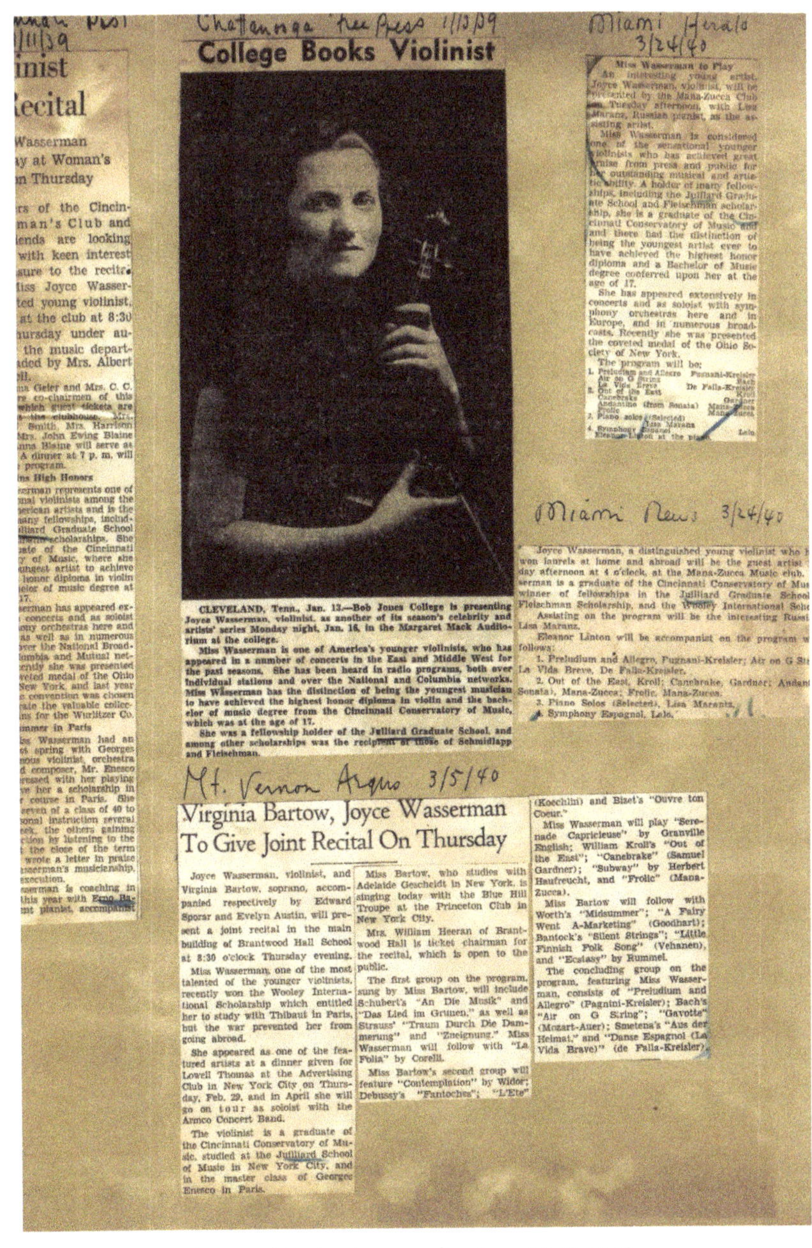

...man Post 1/11/39

...inist
...ecital

...Wasserman
...ay at Woman's
...n Thursday

...rs of the Cincin-
...man's Club and
...iends are looking
... with keen interest
...sure to the recital
...Miss Joyce Wasser-
...ted young violinist,
... at the club at 8:30
...hursday under au-
... the music depart-
...aded by Mrs. Albert
...ell.
...na Geier and Mrs. C. C.
...re co-chairmen of this
... which guest tickets are
... the clubhouse. Mrs.
... Smith, Mrs. Harrison
... Mrs. John Ewing Blaine
...nna Blaine will serve as
... A dinner at 7 p. m. will
... program.

...ins High Honors

...serman represents one of
...nal violinists among the
...erican artists and is the
...any fellowships, includ-
...illiard Graduate School
... scholarships. She
...uate of the Cincinnati
...y of Music, where she
...ungest artist to achieve
... honor diploma in violin
...elor of music degree at
...17.
...serman has appeared ex-
... concerts and as soloist
...ony orchestras here and
... as well as in numerous
...over the National Broad-
...lumbia and Mutual net-
...ently she was presented
...veted medal of the Ohio
... New York, and last year
...e convention was chosen
...rate the valuable collec-
...ins for the Wurlitzer Co.

...ummer in Paris

...ss Wasserman had an
...st spring with Georges
...nous violinist, orchestra
...d composer, Mr. Enesco
...ressed with her playing
...ve her a scholarship in
...r course in Paris. She
... seven of a class of 40 to
...sonal instruction several
...eek, the others gaining
...tion by listening to the
...t the close of the term
... wrote a letter in praise
...asserman's musicianship
... execution.
...serman is coaching in
... this year with Erno Ba-
...ent pianist, accompanist

Chattanooga Free Press 1/13/39

College Books Violinist

CLEVELAND, Tenn., Jan. 13.—Bob Jones College is presenting Joyce Wasserman, violinist, as another of its season's celebrity and artists' series Monday night, Jan. 16, in the Margaret Mack Auditorium at the college.

Miss Wasserman is one of America's younger violinists, who has appeared in a number of concerts in the East and Middle West for the past seasons. She has been heard in radio programs, both over individual stations and over the National and Columbia networks. Miss Wasserman has the distinction of being the youngest musician to have achieved the highest honor diploma in violin and the bachelor of music degree from the Cincinnati Conservatory of Music, which was at the age of 17.

She was a fellowship holder of the Julliard Graduate School, and among other scholarships was the recipient of those of Schmidlapp and Fleischman.

Miami Herald 3/24/40

Miss Wasserman to Play

An interesting young artist, Joyce Wasserman, violinist, will be presented by the Mana-Zucca Club on Tuesday afternoon, with Lisa Maranz, Russian pianist, as the assisting artist.

Miss Wasserman is considered one of the sensational younger violinists who has achieved great praise from press and public for her outstanding musical and artistic ability. A holder of many fellowships, including the Juilliard Graduate School and Fleischman scholarship, she is a graduate of the Cincinnati Conservatory of Music and there had the distinction of being the youngest artist ever to have achieved the highest honor diploma and a Bachelor of Music degree conferred upon her at the age of 17.

She has appeared extensively in concerts and as soloist with symphony orchestras here and in Europe, and in numerous broadcasts. Recently she was presented the coveted medal of the Ohio Society of New York.

The program will be:

1. Preludium and Allegro — Pugnani-Kreisler
Air on G String — Bach
La Vida Breve — De Falla-Kreisler
2. Out of the East — Kroll
Canebrake — Gardner
Andantino (from Sonata) — Mana-Zucca
Frolic — Mana-Zucca
3. Piano solos (Selected) — Lisa Marana
4. Symphony Espanol — Lalo
Eleanor Linton at the piano.

Miami News 3/24/40

Joyce Wasserman, a distinguished young violinist who h... won laurels at home and abroad will be the guest artist ...day afternoon at 4 o'clock, at the Mana-Zucca Music club. ...serman is a graduate of the Cincinnati Conservatory of Mu... winner of fellowships in the Juilliard Graduate School... Fleischman Scholarship, and the Wooley International Sch...

Assisting on the program will be the interesting Russi... Lisa Maranz.

Eleanor Linton will be accompanist on the program w... follows:

1. Preludium and Allegro, Pugnani-Kreisler; Air on G St... La Vida Breve, De Falla-Kreisler.

2. Out of the East, Kroll; Canebrake, Gardner; Andan... Sonata), Mana-Zucca; Frolic, Mana-Zucca.

3. Piano Solos (Selected), Lisa Marantz.

4. Symphony Espagnol, Lalo.

Mt. Vernon Argus 3/5/40

Virginia Bartow, Joyce Wasserman To Give Joint Recital On Thursday

Joyce Wasserman, violinist, and Virginia Bartow, soprano, accompanied respectively by Edward Sporar and Evelyn Austin, will present a joint recital in the main building of Brantwood Hall School at 8:30 o'clock Thursday evening.

Miss Wasserman, one of the most talented of the younger violinists, recently won the Wooley International Scholarship which entitled her to study with Thibaut in Paris, but the war prevented her from going abroad.

She appeared as one of the featured artists at a dinner given for Lowell Thomas at the Advertising Club in New York City on Thursday, Feb. 29, and in April she will go on tour as soloist with the Armco Concert Band.

The violinist is a graduate of the Cincinnati Conservatory of Music, studied at the Julliard School of Music in New York City, and in the master class of Georges Enesco in Paris.

Miss Bartow, who studies with Adelaide Gescheidt in New York, is singing today with the Blue Hill Troupe at the Princeton Club in New York City.

Mrs. William Heeran of Brantwood Hall is ticket chairman for the recital, which is open to the public.

The first group on the program, sung by Miss Bartow, will include Schubert's "An Die Musik" and "Das Lied im Grunen," as well as Strauss' "Traum Durch Die Dammerung" and "Zueignung." Miss Wasserman will follow with "La Folia" by Corelli.

Miss Bartow's second group will feature "Contemplation" by Widor; Debussy's "Fantoches"; "L'Ete" (Koechlin) and Bizet's "Ouvre ton Coeur."

Miss Wasserman will play "Serenade Capricieuse" by Granville English; William Kroll's "Out of the East"; "Canebrake" (Samuel Gardner); "Subway" by Herbert Haufreucht, and "Frolic" (Mana-Zucca).

Miss Bartow will follow with Worth's "Midsummer"; "A Fairy Went A-Marketing" (Goodhart); Bantock's "Silent Strings"; "Little Finnish Folk Song" (Vehanen), and "Ecstasy" by Rummel.

The concluding group on the program, featuring Miss Wasserman, consists of "Preludium and Allegro" (Pagnini-Kreisler); Bach's "Air on G String"; "Gavotte" (Mozart-Auer); Smetena's "Aus der Heimat," and "Danse Espagnol (La Vida Brave)" (de Falla-Kreisler).

Some of Esther's news clippings 1939-1940.

ing Artist gaged for cital Here

Wasserman to Re-
n From East for
Winter Concert

MAY DEARNESS

NNATI friends of Miss
ier Joyce Wesserman,
l young Cincinnati
who has lived in
rk for a number of
re delighted to learn
s young artist expects
n here late in Febru-
give a concert for one
rominent music clubs.
asserman has been heard
ber of recitals through the
has given many radio pro-
She is a graduate of the
i Conservatory of Music
17 years of age, she re-
Bachelor of Music degree,
est student to receive this
the school and also the
onor diploma in violin.

* * *

udied With Masters

Cincinnati, Miss Wasser-
went to New York on a
at the Juilliard Graduate
th Paul Kochansky. She
scholarships with Remo
Vlado Kolitch, Hyman
nd Erno-Balogh and was
nt of the Schmidlapp and
nn Scholarships.
ary Bennett, widely-known
l singer and voice teacher,
in some joint programs
Wasserman last year in
. Miss Bennett spent the
ere taking special musical
h Douglas Stanley, dis-
l voice teacher and scien-
his month Miss Bennett
to Cincinnati for a vaca-
her family. She will re-
e until Labor Day and
return east to continue
al studies again with Mr.
Last season she had a
f singing engagements in
and is looking forward
on some joint programs
year with Miss Wasser-

* * *

Miss Wasserman's most
honors was to be chosen
trate a Stradivarius and
of other rare and some
uments at the sixth an-
ention of the National As-
of Music Merchants held
York. She played before
of visitors assembled from
of the country for this
engagement this month
ital which she gave at the
Plaza Hotel for the Con-
merican Poets. Mrs. Cor-
Pkine, founder and pres-
the organization, selected
serman for this solo ap-
and is planning to present
other recital in September.
visit to Cincinnati this
iss Wasserman expects to
iends at the Conservatory
which will open its new
pt. 9. When the summer
losed early this month,
the faculty members left
or a month's vacation be-
ming their classes next

Norfolk Virginian Pilot 2/12/38

Symphony Guest Artist

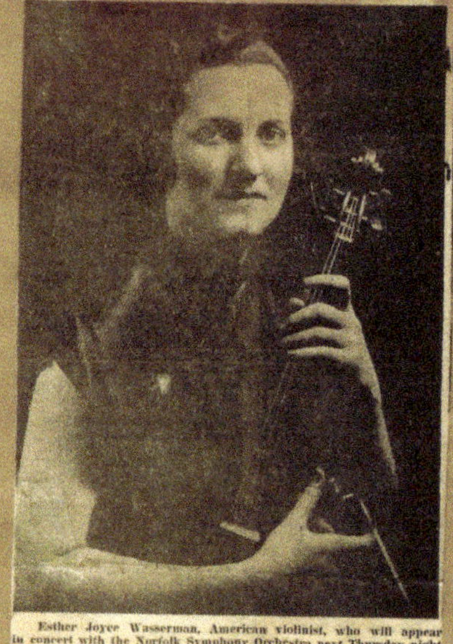

Esther Joyce Wasserman, American violinist, who will appear in concert with the Norfolk Symphony Orchestra next Thursday night at 8:15 o'clock in the City Auditorium.

Miss Wasserman Guest Artist With Symphony February 17

Norfolk Orchestra Likely to Play to Packed House at City Auditorium Next Week in Third Concert of Present Season

With Esther Joyce Wasserman, violinist, as guest artist, the Norfolk Symphony Orchestra will render its third concert of the season Thursday night, February 17, at 8:15 o'clock in the City Auditorium.

As her concerto, Miss Wasserman has chosen Lalo's "Symphonie Espagnole," a spirited, tuneful work originally written in five movements but reduced to the customary three for the purposes of the Norfolk concert.

Director Henry Cowles Whitehead has rounded out the program with orchestral renditions of Tschaikowsky's glorious Fifth Symphony and transcriptions from two of Wagner's operas—the Swan Song and Farewell from "Lohengrin" and the Good Friday Spell from "Parsifal."

If the generous, almost surprising public response to the first two concerts is continued at this performance the City Auditorium (which Director Whitehead says is admirably suited to symphonic programs) will be packed next Thursday night. A record-breaking sale of season tickets served as a prelude to audiences at the first concerts, breaking all records for the 18-year-old orchestra.

Miss Wasserman, a native and resident of Cincinnati, is a graduate of the Cincinnati Conservatory of Music and a pupil of Paul Kochanski at the Juilliard Graduate School, New York. She has been heard in concert over the National and Columbia broadcasting systems and has given many private and public performances.

Her appearance in Jackson Heights, N. Y., evoked the following commendation:

"Esther Wasserman, a young violinist, delighted the audience. She played with a rare velvety texture of tone, facile technique and with great breadth and depth. Her playing moved for its fine sincerity and nobility of line and feeling."

Norfolk Virginian Pilot 2/16/38

Violinist Arrives To Participate in Symphony Concert

Miss Esther Joyce Wasserman, talented young violinist who will appear as guest artist with the Norfolk Symphony Orchestra tomorrow night at 8:15 o'clock in the Municipal Auditorium, arrived in Norfolk yesterday morning and participated in her first rehearsal with the symphony last night.

A native of Cincinnati and a graduate of both the Cincinnati Conservatory of Music and the Juilliard School, Miss Wasserman now makes her home in New York. Her concerto with the Norfolk orchestra will be Lalo's "Symphonie Espagnole," a spirited work in Spanish rhythms.

The remainder of the program tomorrow night, as announced by Director Henry Cowles Whitehead, will include Tschaikowsky's Fifth Symphony and transcriptions of scenes from two Wagnerian operas—the Swan Song and Farewell from "Lohengrin," and the Good Friday Spell from "Parsifal."

Approximately 65 musicians compose the orchestra, which has been rehearsing diligently for this concert.

During her visit, Miss Wasserman is the guest of Mr. and Mrs. C. Wiley Grandy, at their home on Botetourt street. Mr. Grandy is president of the Norfolk Orchestral Association.

Bronxville Review Press 2/22/40

Joyce Wasserman, violinist, and Virginia Bartow, soprano, will be heard in joint recital at Brantwood Hall Thursday, March 7, at 8:30 p. m.

Miss Wasserman has held many fellowships, including one from the Juilliard Graduate School of Music in New York City. She is a graduate of the Cincinnati Conservatory of Music, where she was the youngest artist ever to have achieved the highest honor diploma in violin, and she received a Bachelor of Music degree at the age of seventeen.

She has appeared in concerts and as soloist with symphony orchestras here and in Europe, as well as in numerous radio broadcasts over coast-to-coast networks. She studied in France and for a short time was in the master class of George Enesco, violinist and conductor.

Miss Bartow is a pupil of Adelaide Gescheidt in New York City and previously studied in Europe.

Norfolk Ledger Dispatch 2/15/38

VIOLINIST HERE NEXT THURSDAY

Joyce Wasserman To Be Soloist With Symphony Orchestra

LALO 'SYMPHONIE' WILL BE PLAYED

Joyce Wasserman, violinist, who achieved the highest honor diploma and bachelor of music degree at the Cincinnati Conservatory of Music, at the age of 17, will be guest soloist with the Norfolk Symphony Orchestra in its third concert of the current season Thursday night at 8:15 o'clock at the City Auditorium.

She will be heard with the orchestra under the direction of Henry Cowles Whitehead in Lalo's "Symphonie Espagnole," of which three movements will be played.

Miss Wasserman has been heard extensively in concert and over the radio. She was a fellowship holder of the Juilliard Graduate School under the late Paul Kochanski, and also held scholarships with Remo Bolognini, Vlado Kolitsch, Hyman Shapiro and Erno Bologh. She received the Schmidlapp and Fleischman scholarships.

The orchestra's program will include Tschaikowsky's Fifth Symphony, one of the most universally liked of the composer's larger works; the "Good Friday Spell" from "Parsifal" and the "Abscheid" or "Swan Song" from "Lohengrin" by Wagner.

A capacity audience is expected for the concert.

Some of Esther's news clippings 1937-1940.

Esther Wasserman 171

Cincinnati Post 2/23/38

To Present Violin Recital

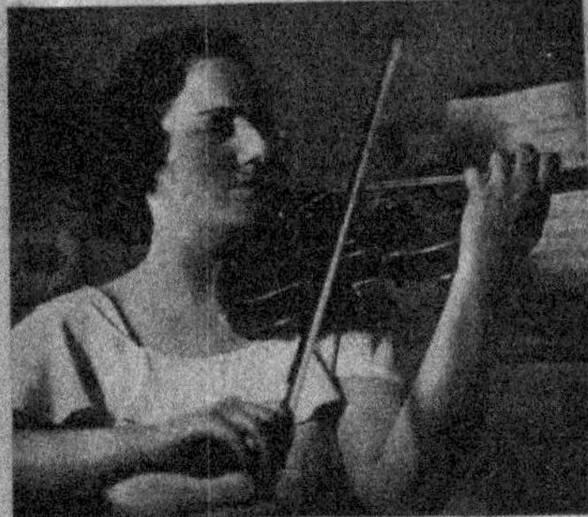

Miss Esther Joyce Wasserman

Mt. Auburn Music Club Concert Wednesday Night

Miss Esther Joyce Wasserman, gifted young violinist and former resident of Cincinnati, will be welcomed here Wednesday to give a recital that evening for the Mt. Auburn Music Club at the residence of Miss Bertha Baur on Highland avenue.

Mrs. Charles F. Sherrick (Violet Summer), president of the club, announces that guest tickets are available for this purpose to begin at 8:15 o'clock. Compositions by Corelli-Leonard, Bach, Lalo, Samuel Richards Gaines, Kreisler, Stravinsky, Granville English, Bloch and de Falla-Kreisler comprise the program.

This will be Miss Wasserman's first appearance in Cincinnati since her outstanding musical successes in the east. She has played extensively in the middle west and east and has been heard in numerous radio programs, including the Music at Twilight Hour, Federation of Music Clubs Hour, Dr. Stephen Wise Service from Carnegie Hall, the Golden Rule Mothers Foundation Hour, the Cincinnati Conservatory Hour, the Armco Hour, the Music Masters Symphonic program, the New York Civic Orchestra and the Federation of Churches program.

Miss Wasserman was graduated with highest honors from the Cincinnati Conservatory of Music and continued her studies with the late Paul Kochanski on a fellowship at the Juilliard Graduate School in New York. She also won the Schmidlapp and Fleischman scholarships and additional scholarships with Remo Bolognini, Vlado Kolitsch, Hyman Shapiro and Erno Balogh. The young artist has given first performances of compositions by Selsmit-Doda, Jan Kubelik, Granville English and Samuel Richard Gaines.

Early this month, Miss Wasserman was guest soloist with the Long Island Symphony Orchestra. Last Thursday she played with the Norfolk Symphony Orchestra. From her Cincinnati concert she will return east to appear in joint concerts with Steven Kennedy, lyric baritone, and Joan De Nault, contralto.

Cincinnati Post 2/19/38

Young Artist To Play Here

The Mt. Auburn Music Club, of which Mrs. Charles F. Sherrick (Violet Summer) is president, will open its concert Wednesday evening to friends of the organization, guest tickets being available from any of the members.

Miss Esther Joyce Wasserman, gifted young violinist and former Cincinnatian who has resided for a number of years in New York, will be the visiting artist for this recital for which Miss Bertha Baur is opening her attractive residence on Highland avenue.

Miss Wasserman's program will begin at 8:15 o'clock and will include compositions by Corelli-Leonard, Bach, Lalo, Samuel Richards Gaines, Kreisler, Stravinsky, Granville English, Bloch and De Falla-Kreisler.

The violinist is a graduate of the Cincinnati Conservatory of Music and was the youngest student to receive the highest honor diploma in violin and a Bachelor of Music Degree at the age of 17. She has continued her studies at the Juilliard Graduate School in New York through fellowships with Paul Kochansky and other distinguished artists. Miss Wasserman's most recent success was an outstanding concert which she gave a few days ago in Norfolk, Va.

Cincinnati Times Star 2/22/38

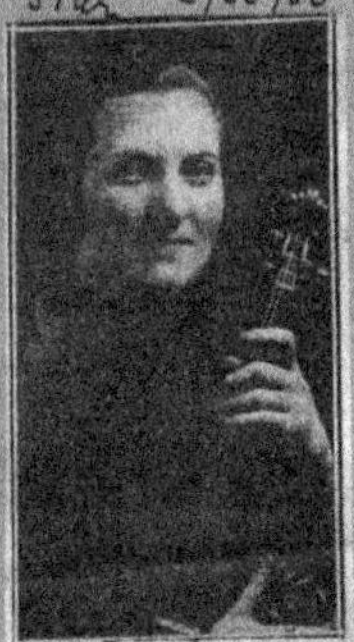

ESTHER JOYCE WASSERMAN

The Mt. Auburn Music Club, Violet Summer Sherrick, president, will present Esther Joyce Wasserman in a recital on February 23 at 8:15 o'clock at the residence of Miss Bertha Baur, south hall, Cincinnati Conservatory of Music. Guest tickets will be available at the door.

Miss Wasserman is a native Cincinnatian who has achieved distinction in New York city. This is her first appearance in Cincinnati since her eastern successes. She has appeared in a number of concerts in the Middle West and East and has been heard over the National Broadcasting and Columbia network, WOR, and the New York television stations on such programs as Golden Rule Mothers' Foundation hour, Music at Twilight hour, Federation of Music Clubs' hour, Dr. Stephen Wise Service from Carnegie Hall, Cincinnati Conservatory hour, Vladimir Bakaleinikoff, conducting; Armco hour, Frank Simon conducting; Music Masters' Symphonic hour, Henry Aaron conducting; New York Civic Orchestra, Eugene Plotnikoff, conducting; Federation of Churches program, etc.

She was a fellowship holder of the Julliard Graduate School under the late Paul Kochanski; also held scholarships with Remo Bolognini, Vlado Kolitsch, Hyman Shapiro and Erno Bologh, and was a recipient of the Schmidlapp and Fleischmann scholarships.

Cincinnati Times Star 1/9/39

VIOLIN RECITAL—

Miss Joyce Wasserman, who will be presented by the Music Department of the Cincinnati Woman's Club in a recital at 8:30 o'clock Thursday evening, represents one of the sensational violinists among the younger American artists. She is a holder of many fellowships, including the Julliard Graduate School, and the Fleischman scholarship. She is a graduate of the Cincinnati Conservatory of Music, where she has the distinction of being the youngest artist ever to have achieved the highest honor diploma in violin, and a Bachelor of Music Degree conferred upon her at the age of seventeen.

Joyce Wasserman has appeared extensively in concerts and as soloist with symphony orchestras, here and in Europe, as well as in numerous broadcasts over the National Broadcasting, Columbia and Mutual networks. Recently she was presented with the coveted medal of the Ohio Society of New York, and last year at the music convention was chosen to demonstrate the valuable collection of violins for the Wurlitzer company.

Miss Wasserman's musicianship is of a very high order—her playing is filled with the glow of youth, with a firm, sure tone and a variety of warmth and color. She compasses the delicacy of a woman with the strength of a man, and in all her work she evidences good taste reflecting the absorption in her work and her serious innate love of the music.

Last spring, in an audition with George Enesco, the very outstanding and well-known violinist, orchestra director and composer, he was so impressed with Miss Wasserman's playing that he gave her a scholarship in his summer course in Paris. She was one of seven of a class of 40 to receive personal instruction several time a week. This group of 40 gained their instruction listening to lessons of these seven.

At the close of this term Mr Enesco wrote a fine letter in praise of her musicianship, talent and splendid execution.

She is in New York, coaching with Erno Balogh, well-known pianist, accompanist and coach.

Cincinnati Times-Star 1/3/40

IN NEW YORK—

Cincinnatians will be interested to learn that since Miss Joyce Wasserman's passport was invalidated and her European scholarship and concerts postponed for this season, that this young artist is having a very busy and successful season in her native land.

Recently she appeared as soloist at the Beethoven Association in New York in a program of original compositions of Granville English. She was again soloist for the Ohio Society of New York at their fifty-fourth annual rally, at which Governor Bricker was guest of honor. Included in her program for the Ohio Society was a short suite of compositions by the tremendously gifted composer from Cleveland, O., Herber Haufreucht. The compositions are entitled "Tobzik's Lullabye," "Subway Music," "Sentimental Theme" and "Happy Music."

Miss Wasserman and Mr. Haufreucht were fellow students at the Julliard Graduate School.

The Pleiades Society of New York, which is an old traditional organization patronizing the fine arts, also honored Miss Wasserman with a solo appearance in their Sunday night concerts.

Christmas caroling is quite an event of the Studio Club of New York. Miss Wasserman participated in the Christmas caroling and was delighted to share the honors with the amazing young maestro, Buddy Swan, in the renditions of the "Rosary," "Ave Maria" and "Silent Night." They also appeared in a Christmas broadcast.

In January Miss Wasserman will [illegible] before embarking on her spring concert tour, which will include a concert on the Mana Zucca Artist Series in Miami, Fla., March 12. Miss Wasserman will be accompanied at the piano by the composer for two of the numbers in her program when she plays Andante and "Frolic" of Mana Zucca in this concert.

Besides her busy concert activity, Joyce Wasserman has created several radio programs this season and has been working with the newly organized Quartet International, which will be heard in concerts in the near future.

Some of Esther's news clippings 1937-1940.

New York, April 1947

Miss Joyce Renée has studied with me, and is a young artist of real talent, who has already demonstrated her ability in successful public appearances. I feel that she is worthy of being helped in every way, so that she may establish herself in a distinguished solo career. I am willing to suggest her for European appearances.

Georges Enesco

Miss Joyce Wasserman est une violoniste très sérieuse, dont l'art est d'une haute tenue et la connaissance de son instrument parfaite. En plus elle a de la personnalité et beaucoup de feu. Les succès qu'elle récolta sont des plus mérités.

Georges Enesco

Signed

Position or Title membre correspondant de l'Institut des Beaux-Arts de France

Address 26 Rue de Clichy Paris France

Date ce 24 Avril 1939

Eugene Enesco's handwritten notes extolling Joyce's talent and recommending her for performances.

GEORGES ENESCO

INTERNATIONALLY FAMOUS

CONDUCTOR—COMPOSER—VIOLINIST

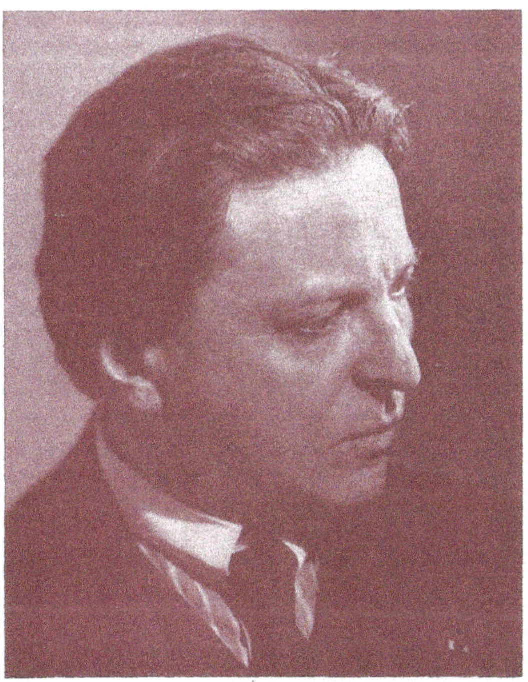

McMILLIN THEATRE
BROADWAY & 116th STREET
Sat. Eve. FEB. 15 - 8:30 p.m.
Tickets:
$1.20, $1.80, $2.10, $2.40 (Incl. Tax)
Auspices: Institute of Arts & Sciences
Columbia University UNiversity 4-3200

PROGRAM SANFORD SCHLUSSEL at the Piano

I.

a. Grave .... Fr. Bach-Kreisler
b. Andante, Minuet and Rondo .... Mozart

II.

Sonata No. 2, in D minor .... Schumann
Ziemlich langsam—Lebhaft — Sehr lebhaft
Leise, einfach — Bewegt

Intermission

III.

a. Poeme .... Chausson
b. Minstrels .... Debussy
c. Bagatelle (in Romanian Style) .... Scarlatescu
d. Zigeunerweisen (Gypsy Airs) .... Sarasate

CONCERT MANAGEMENT ARTHUR JUDSON, Inc.
DIVISION OF COLUMBIA CONCERTS, INC.
113 West 57th Street • New York 19, N. Y.

Program for Eugene Enesco concert in New York City.

GEORGES ENESCO, ***internationally famous composer, conductor and violinist will make a limited American tour in the course of his first visit here in seven years.***

Roumania's distinguished musical representative, whose whereabouts and activities during the war were hidden in a cloud of rumor until his former pupil Yehudi Menuhin brought back reassuring news of him from Europe last autumn, returns to the United States this season under the auspices of Columbia Concerts. Triply talented, Enesco is known and honored in all three capacities in this country. As composer his Roumanian Rhapsody in A major is one of the most popular works in the orchestral repertoire. As conductor he has been seen on the podium of every major American orchestra from coast to coast. As violinist he has toured the length and breadth of the land.

Enesco was last here in 1938-39 when his engagements included two weeks as guest conductor of the New York Philharmonic-Symphony and an appearance at the World's Fair as representative of his country. He cancelled a tour the next year because of illness; the following season the war prevented his coming. For the next few years communication with Roumania was cut off and Enesco's fate was a matter of international conjecture and concern. However, in the fall of 1945, when Menuhin was abroad, the violinist discovered his idolized former teacher unscathed and active in his own country, living at his country home in Sinaia, in the mountains outside Bucharest.

Born in the Moldavian Hills of Roumania in 1881, Enesco absorbed as a child the simplicity and sincerity which is an integral part of his nature.

At seven he was enrolled in the Vienna Conservatory, from which he was graduated with the highest honors. At the age of seventeen, he was launched upon a brilliant career as a violin virtuoso, which has taken him into the four corners of the world. Wherever he plays he wins the ready admiration of his audiences for his technical abilities and penetrative interpretations.

Enesco's debut as a composer came in 1898 when his "Poeme Roumain" was featured at the Concerts Colonne. "The Symphonie Conertante", his first outstanding work, was given its first hearing in 1908. One of his more recent musical creations is the magnificent four-act lyrical tragedy, "Oedipus Rex" which had its premiere in March, 1938 at the Paris Opera.

Reports from Roumania indicate that Enesco has been composing during the war and intends to bring his new works with him when he arrives in this country.

After his last appearance as conductor with the New York Philharmonic-Symphony Orchestra in 1939, Olin Downes, critic of the Times said: "He is, beyond doubt or peradventure, one of the greatest musicians of his day".

Enesco biography from program for concert.

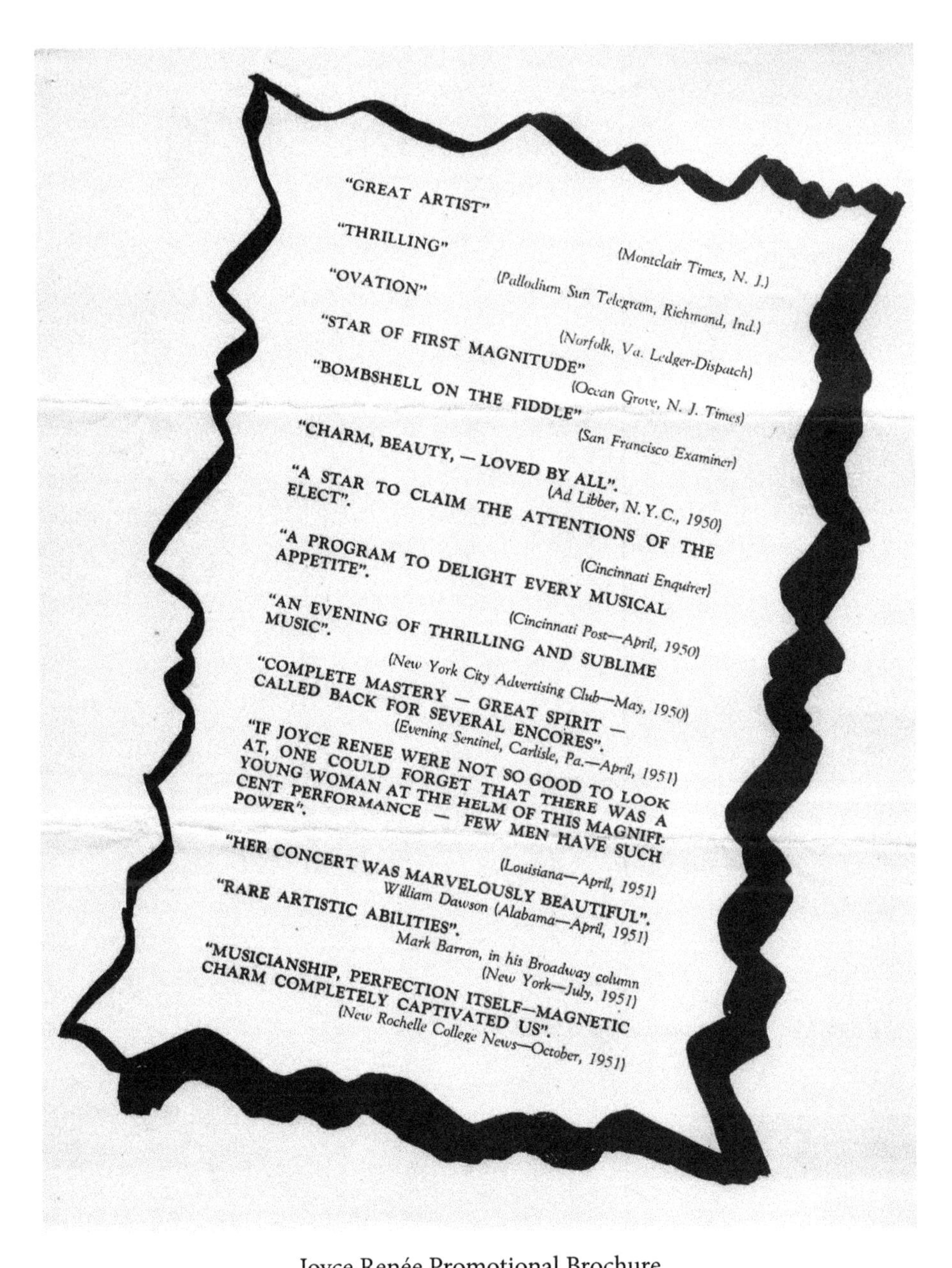
"GREAT ARTIST"
(Montclair Times, N. J.)

"THRILLING"
(Palladium Sun Telegram, Richmond, Ind.)

"OVATION"
(Norfolk, Va. Ledger-Dispatch)

"STAR OF FIRST MAGNITUDE"
(Ocean Grove, N. J. Times)

"BOMBSHELL ON THE FIDDLE"
(San Francisco Examiner)

"CHARM, BEAUTY, — LOVED BY ALL".
(Ad Libber, N. Y. C., 1950)

"A STAR TO CLAIM THE ATTENTIONS OF THE ELECT".
(Cincinnati Enquirer)

"A PROGRAM TO DELIGHT EVERY MUSICAL APPETITE".
(Cincinnati Post—April, 1950)

"AN EVENING OF THRILLING AND SUBLIME MUSIC".
(New York City Advertising Club—May, 1950)

"COMPLETE MASTERY — GREAT SPIRIT — CALLED BACK FOR SEVERAL ENCORES".
(Evening Sentinel, Carlisle, Pa.—April, 1951)

"IF JOYCE RENEE WERE NOT SO GOOD TO LOOK AT, ONE COULD FORGET THAT THERE WAS A YOUNG WOMAN AT THE HELM OF THIS MAGNIFICENT PERFORMANCE — FEW MEN HAVE SUCH POWER".
(Louisiana—April, 1951)

"HER CONCERT WAS MARVELOUSLY BEAUTIFUL".
William Dawson (Alabama—April, 1951)

"RARE ARTISTIC ABILITIES".
Mark Barron, in his Broadway column
(New York—July, 1951)

"MUSICIANSHIP, PERFECTION ITSELF—MAGNETIC CHARM COMPLETELY CAPTIVATED US".
(New Rochelle College News—October, 1951)

Joyce Renée Promotional Brochure

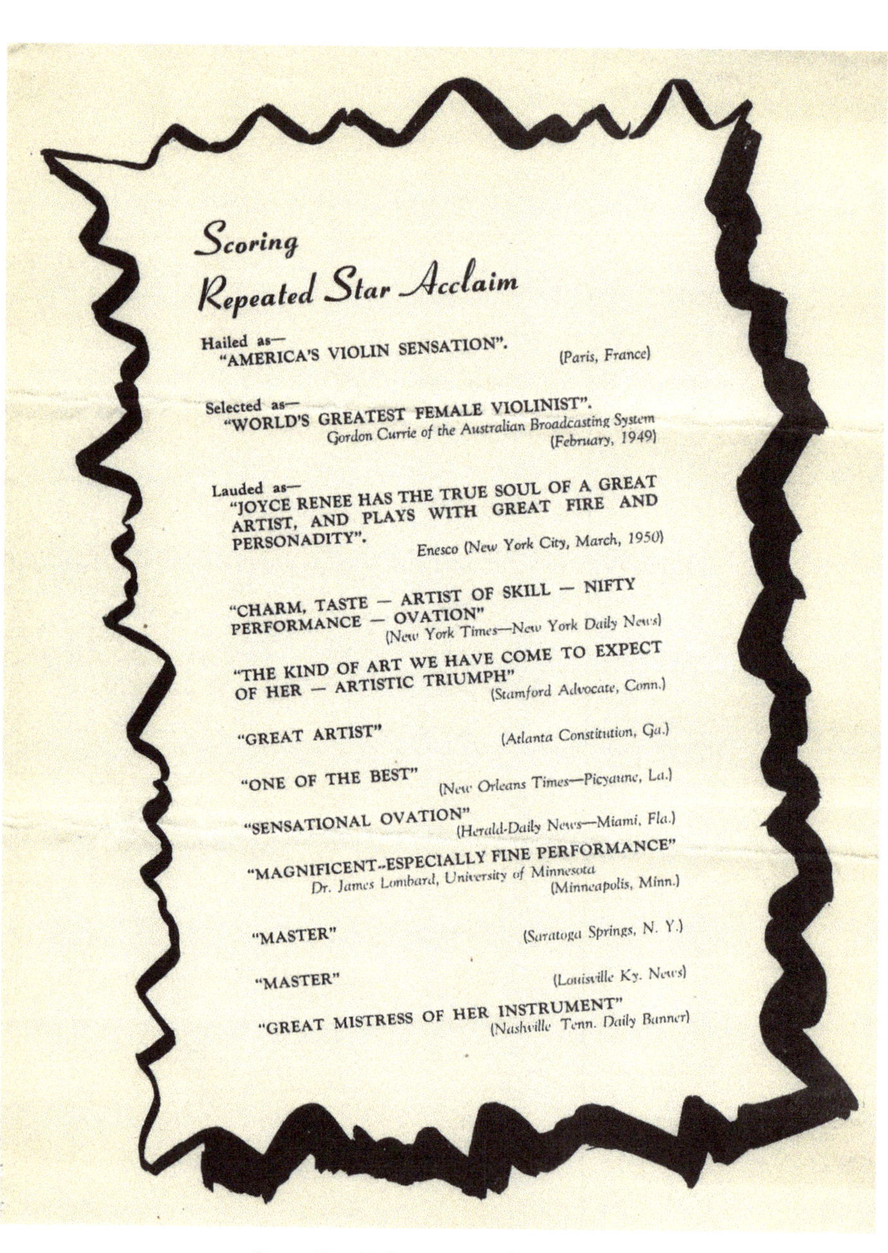

Scoring Repeated Star Acclaim

Hailed as—
"AMERICA'S VIOLIN SENSATION". (Paris, France)

Selected as—
"WORLD'S GREATEST FEMALE VIOLINIST".
Gordon Currie of the Australian Broadcasting System (February, 1949)

Lauded as—
"JOYCE RENEE HAS THE TRUE SOUL OF A GREAT ARTIST, AND PLAYS WITH GREAT FIRE AND PERSONADITY".
Enesco (New York City, March, 1950)

"CHARM, TASTE — ARTIST OF SKILL — NIFTY PERFORMANCE — OVATION"
(New York Times—New York Daily News)

"THE KIND OF ART WE HAVE COME TO EXPECT OF HER — ARTISTIC TRIUMPH"
(Stamford Advocate, Conn.)

"GREAT ARTIST" (Atlanta Constitution, Ga.)

"ONE OF THE BEST" (New Orleans Times—Picyaune, La.)

"SENSATIONAL OVATION" (Herald-Daily News—Miami, Fla.)

"MAGNIFICENT-ESPECIALLY FINE PERFORMANCE"
Dr. James Lombard, University of Minnesota (Minneapolis, Minn.)

"MASTER" (Saratoga Springs, N. Y.)

"MASTER" (Louisville Ky. News)

"GREAT MISTRESS OF HER INSTRUMENT" (Nashville Tenn. Daily Banner)

Joyce Renée Promotional Brochure

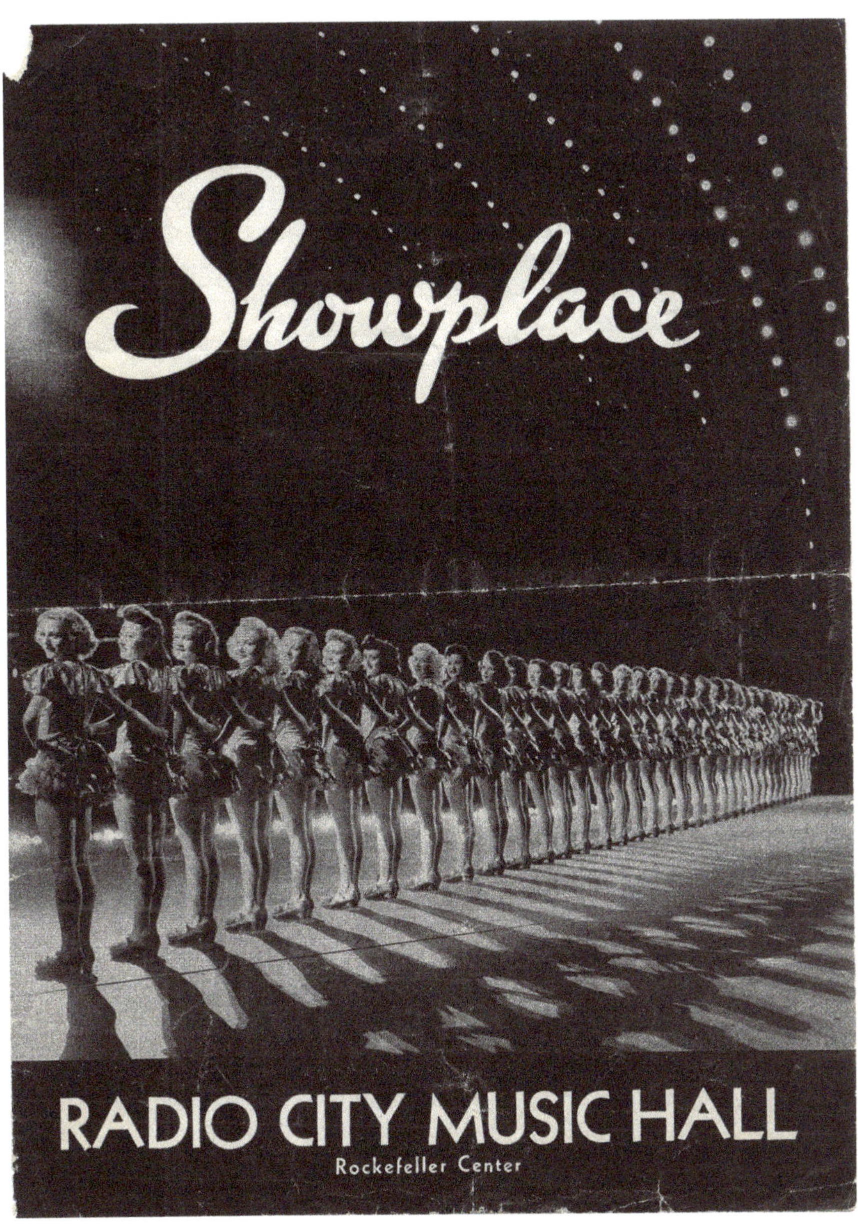

Cover of program for Sept. 12, 1946, show at Radio City Music Hall.

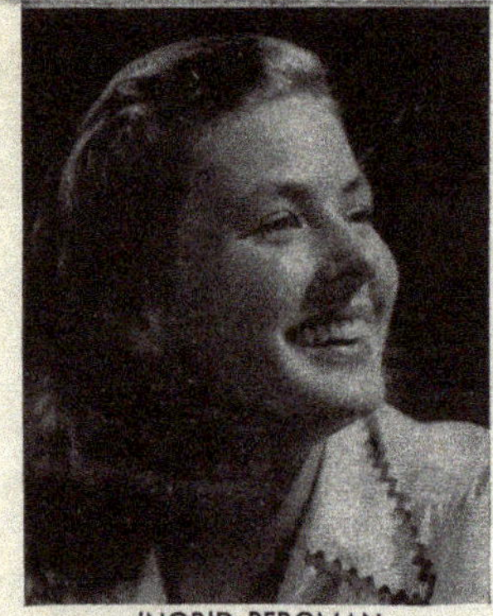

INGRID BERGMAN

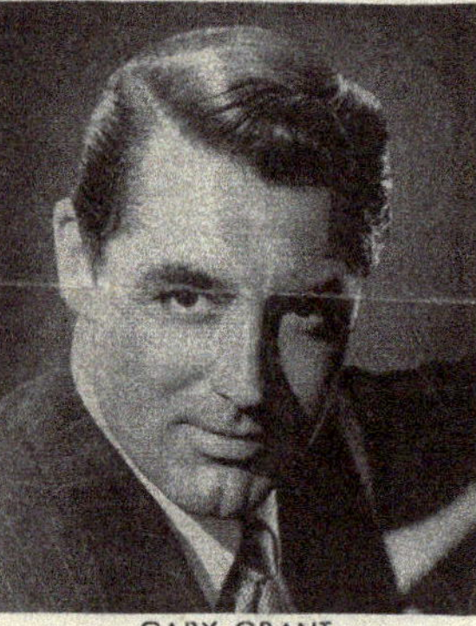

CARY GRANT

RADIO CITY MUSIC HALL **PROG**

G. S. EYSSELL, MANAGING DIRECTOR — WEEK BEGINNING THURS

1. MUSIC HALL GRAND ORGAN
Richard Leibert, Leo Weber,
Harry Campbell

2. MUSIC HALL SYMPHONY ORCHESTRA
CHARLES PREVIN, Director
Jules Silver, Otto Frohn
Associate Conductors
Overture to "Tannhäuser"—Wagner

3. "COLORAMA"
Produced by Leon Leonidoff
Settings by Bruno Maine
Costumes designed by William Livingston, Marco Montedoro—executed by H. Rogge
Lighting effects by Eugene Braun
Special lyrics by Albert Stillman

A. "Painting the Town"
Music Hall Glee Club
(Charles Previn, Director; Kay Holley, Associate)
Featuring: Estelle Sloan, Dancer, as "Marie"
William Judd, Soloist
Joyce Renee as "Laura"
Brunhilda Roque as "Chiquita Banana"

B. "Color Scheme"
Charles Tyrrell
Music Hall Rockettes
(Dances by Russell Markert)

C. "Old Master"
Bob Williams
Assisted by Fred Schneider

FIRE NOTICE: The exit, indicated by a red light and sign, nearest to the seat you occupy, is the shortest route to the street. In the event of fire or other emergency please do not run—WALK TO THAT EXIT.
FRANK J. QUAYLE, Fire Commissioner.

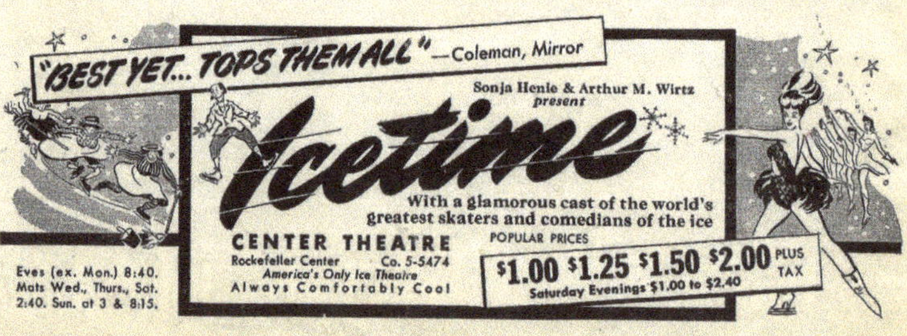

Performers for program at Radio City Music Hall, including Joyce.

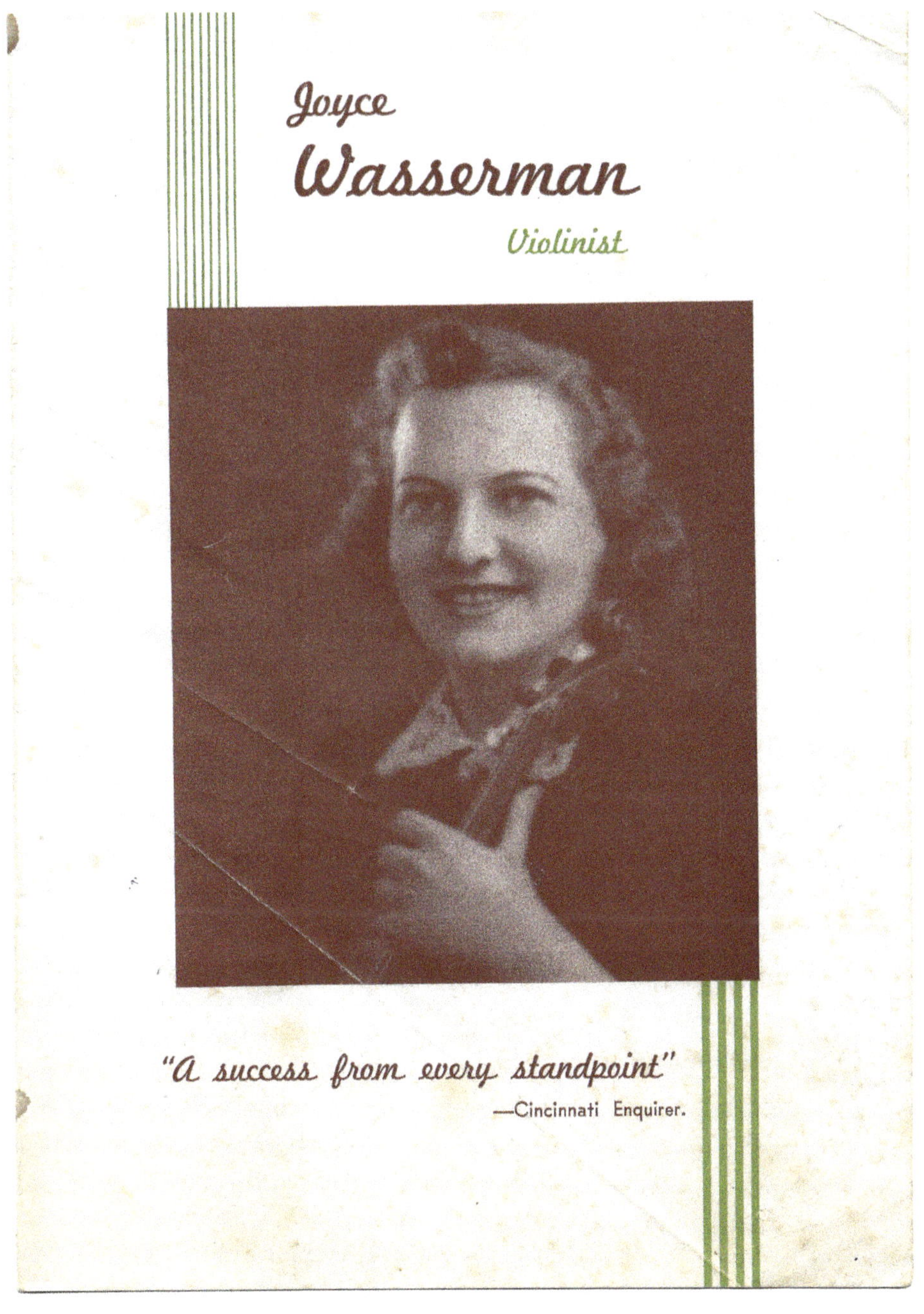

Promotional brochure about Joyce prepared by
George Leyden Colledge Management in New York City

Joyce Wasserman

represents one of the sensational violinists among the younger artists. A holder of many fellowships, including the Juilliard Graduate School, and the Fleischman Scholarship. She is a graduate of the Cincinnati Conservatory of Music, where she has the distinction of being the youngest artist ever to have achieved the highest honor diploma in violin, and a Bachelor of Music Degree conferred upon her at the age of seventeen.

Joyce Wasserman has appeared extensively in concerts and as soloist with symphony orchestras, here and in Europe, as well as in numerous broadcasts over the National Broadcasting, Columbia and Mutual networks. Recently she was presented with the coveted medal of the Ohio Society of New York, and last year at the music convention, was chosen to demonstrate the valuable collection of violins for the Wurlitzer Company.

Miss Wasserman's musicianship is of a very high order—her playing is filled with the glow of youth, with a firm sure tone and a variety of warmth and color. She compasses the delicacy of a woman with the strength of a man, and in all her work, she evidences good taste reflecting the absorption in her work and her serious innate love of Music. Wherever she appears, the press and public are unanimous in their praise of her outstanding musical and artistic ability.

Promotional brochure about Joyce prepared by
George Leyden Colledge Management in New York City

"A large audience received the entire program with the utmost enthusiasm. The breadth and sweep of the first movement, the melodious quality of the second, and the brilliance of the Finale of the Mendelssohn Concerto demonstrated the singing tone of the wide variety of violin technique of the performer. She displayed a wide range of moods in the short numbers. Gifted, well trained, and versatile, Miss Wasserman should, and no doubt will, go far—and probably famously—in her chosen career. She swung into her program with verve, ease, and a rhythmic aplomb, that seemed to mark her as one of those rare souls to whom Music becomes a passion, and which offers those who listen, an intent sensation of a vivid personality at the helm, and which makes for musical, artistic and personal success upon the artist's rostrum!"—*Enquirer, Cincinnati*

"She handled a difficult program with astonishing ease, poise and flexibility."
—*Times Star, Cincinnati*

"Played with facile technique, vigor, velvety texture of tone, and sound interpretation. Miss Wasserman was given an ovation following the final rondo movement of Lalo's 'Symphonie Espagnole.'" —*Ledger Dispatch, Norfolk*

"She is an artist of exceptional ability, with fine technique and style of presentation." —*Post Star, Glens Falls, N. Y.*

"Miss Wasserman is a master of the violin."
—*The Saratogian, Saratoga Springs, N. Y.*

"The young artist helped make the occasion memorable. She is a beautiful mature artist." —*Journal, Middletown, Ohio*

"We were impressed with her playing—she has that certain something—a very fine artist who should go a long way in her chosen profession."
—*Reginald Billen, Louisville, Ky.*

"Miss Wasserman charmed her audience at the Bob Jones College as she presented a masterful performance. She played the most difficult passages and runs with an ease and certainty that marked her as an artist of the highest order."
—*Daily Banner, Cleveland, Tenn.*

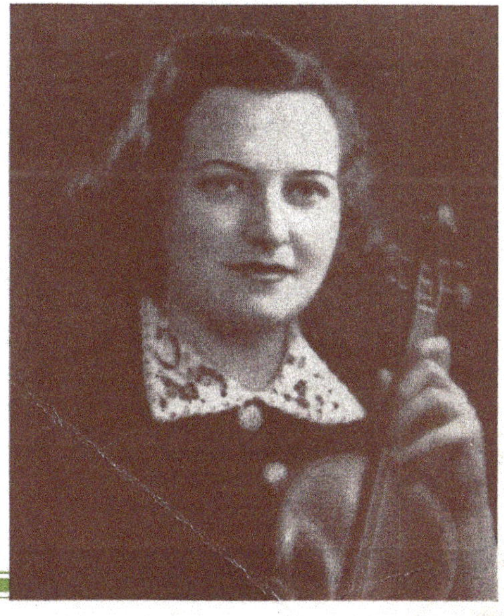

Promotional brochure about Joyce prepared by
George Leyden Colledge Management in New York City

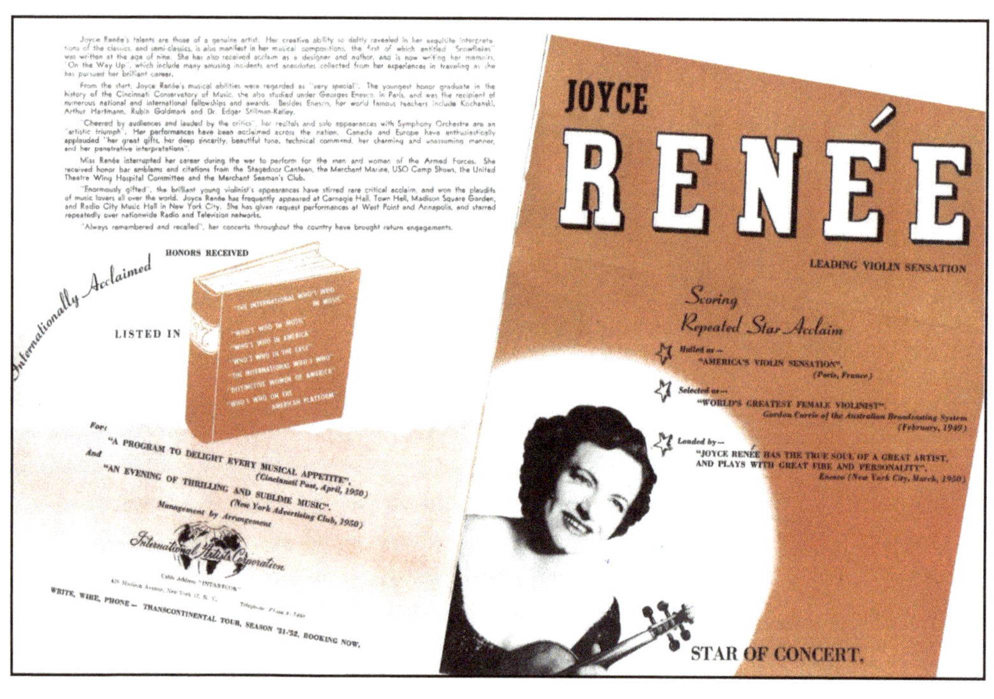
Joyce Renée's talents are those of a genuine artist. Her creative ability so deftly revealed in her exquisite interpretations of the classics and semi-classics, is also manifest in her musical compositions, the first of which entitled "Snowflakes" was written at the age of nine. She has also received acclaim as a designer and author, and is now writing her memoirs, "On the Way Up", which include many amusing incidents and anecdotes collected from her experiences in traveling as she has pursued her brilliant career.
From the start, Joyce Renée's musical abilities were regarded as "very special". The youngest honor graduate in the history of the Cincinnati Conservatory of Music, she also studied under Georges Enesco, in Paris, and was the recipient of numerous national and international fellowships and awards. Besides Enesco, her world famous teachers include Kochanski, Arthur Hartmann, Rubin Goldmark and Dr. Edgar Stillman-Kelley.
"Cheered by audiences and lauded by the critics", her recitals and solo appearances with Symphony Orchestra are an "artistic triumph". Her performances have been acclaimed across the nation. Canada and Europe have enthusiastically applauded "her great gifts, her deep sincerity, beautiful tone, technical command, her charming and unassuming manner, and her penetrative interpretations".
Miss Renée interrupted her career during the war to perform for the men and women of the Armed Forces. She received honor bar emblems and citations from the Stagedoor Canteen, the Merchant Marine, USO Camp Shows, the United Theatre Wing Hospital Committee and the Merchant Seaman's Club.
"Enormously gifted", the brilliant young violinist's appearances have stirred rare critical acclaim, and won the plaudits of music lovers all over the world. Joyce Renée has frequently appeared at Carnegie Hall, Town Hall, Madison Square Garden, and Radio City Music Hall in New York City. She has given request performances at West Point and Annapolis, and starred repeatedly over nationwide Radio and Television networks.
"Always remembered and recalled", her concerts throughout the country have brought return engagements.
Internationally Acclaimed
HONORS RECEIVED
LISTED IN
"THE INTERNATIONAL WHO'S WHO IN MUSIC"
"WHO'S WHO IN MUSIC"
"WHO'S WHO IN AMERICA"
"WHO'S WHO IN THE EAST"
"THE INTERNATIONAL WHO'S WHO"
"DISTINCTIVE WOMEN OF AMERICA"
"WHO'S WHO ON THE AMERICAN PLATFORM"
For:
"A PROGRAM TO DELIGHT EVERY MUSICAL APPETITE",
(Cincinnati Post, April, 1950)
And
"AN EVENING OF THRILLING AND SUBLIME MUSIC",
(New York Advertising Club, 1950)
Management by Arrangement
International Artists Corporation
WRITE, WIRE, PHONE — TRANSCONTINENTAL TOUR, SEASON '51-'52, BOOKING NOW.
JOYCE
RENÉE
LEADING VIOLIN SENSATION
Scoring
Repeated Star Acclaim
Hailed as —
"AMERICA'S VIOLIN SENSATION",
(Paris, France)
Selected as —
"WORLD'S GREATEST FEMALE VIOLINIST",
Gordon Currie of the Australian Broadcasting System
(February, 1949)
Lauded by —
"JOYCE RENÉE HAS THE TRUE SOUL OF A GREAT ARTIST, AND PLAYS WITH GREAT FIRE AND PERSONALITY",
Enesco (New York City, March, 1950)
STAR OF CONCERT,

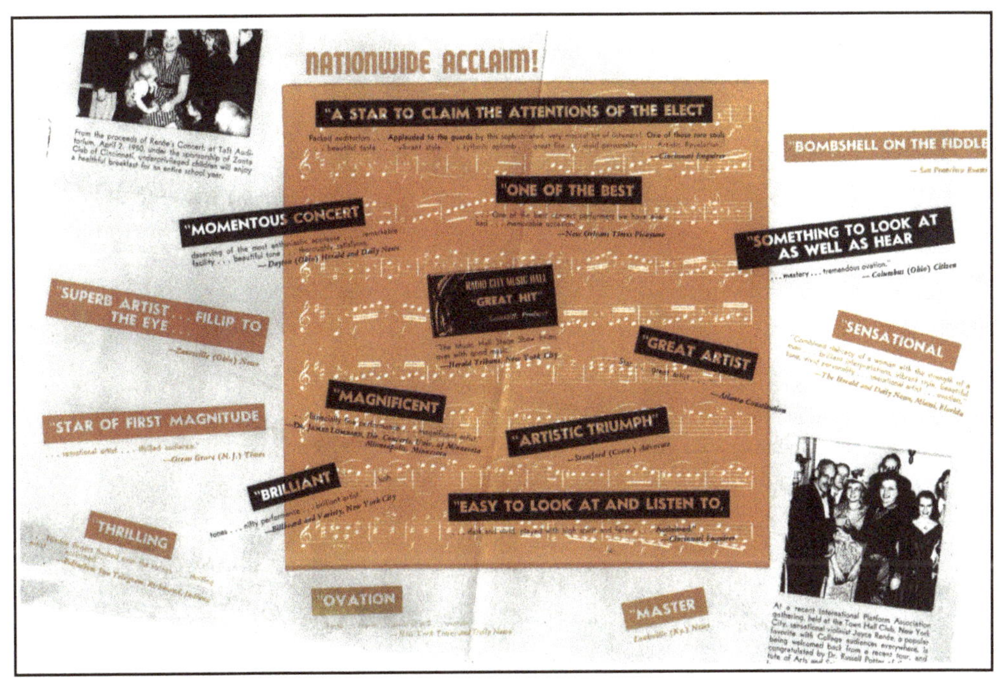

Joyce Renée promotional brochure.

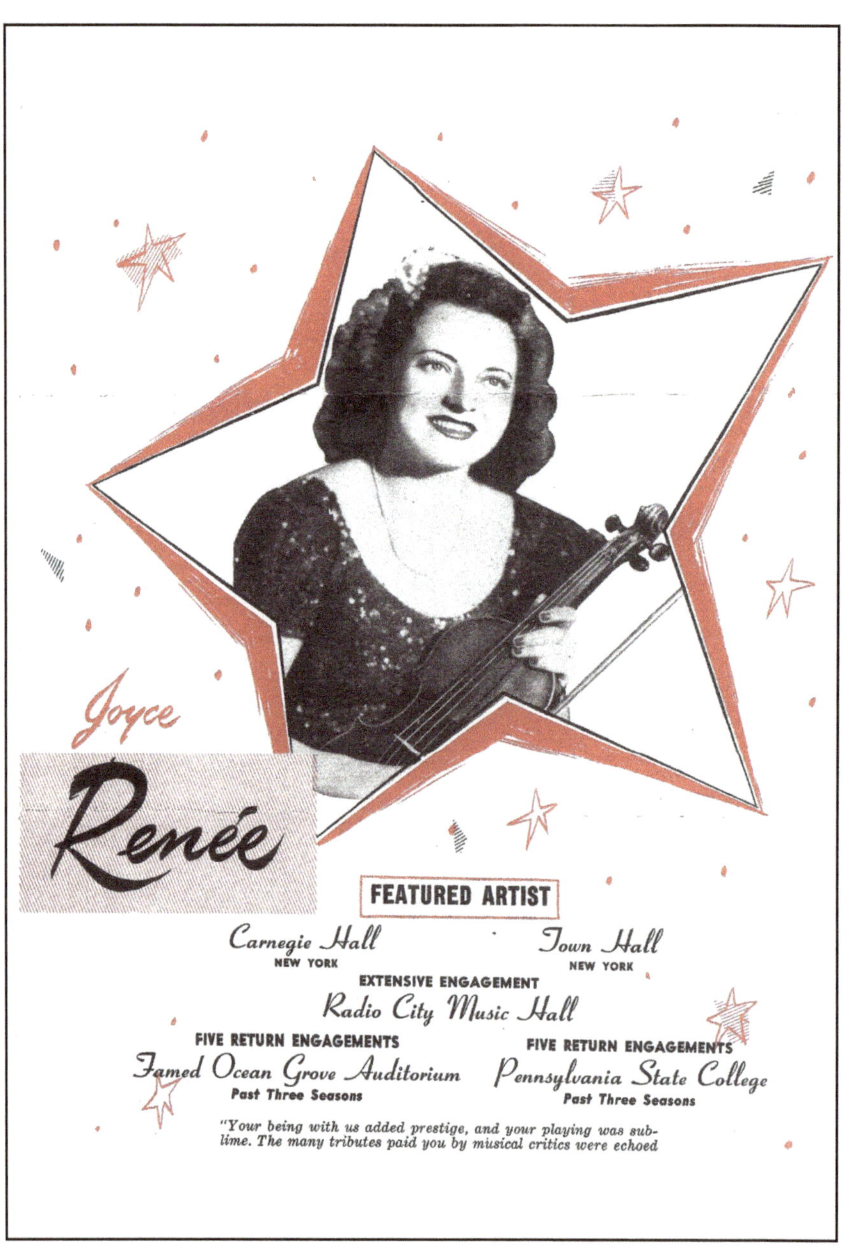
Joyce
Renée
FEATURED ARTIST
Carnegie Hall
NEW YORK
Town Hall
NEW YORK
EXTENSIVE ENGAGEMENT
Radio City Music Hall
FIVE RETURN ENGAGEMENTS
Famed Ocean Grove Auditorium
Past Three Seasons
FIVE RETURN ENGAGEMENTS
Pennsylvania State College
Past Three Seasons
"Your being with us added prestige, and your playing was sub-
lime. The many tributes paid you by musical critics were echoed

Typical Nationwide Tributes

"One of those rare souls . . . success from every viewpoint . . . verve . . . ease . . . rhythmic aplomb . . . vivid personality . . . packed auditorium . . . applauded to the gaurds! . . ."
— **Cincinnati (Ohio) Enquirer**

"Virtuoso violinist of skill . . . ovation . . ."
— **New York Daily News**

"Nifty . . ."
— **The Billboard**

"Astonishing . . ."
— **Times Star, Cincinnati, Ohio**

"Tasteful performance . . ."
— **New York Times**

"Especially fine performance . . . played magnificently . . ."
— **Dr. James Lombard, Minneapolis**

"Charmed audience . . . masterful performance . . ."
— **Nashville (Tenn.) Daily Banner**

"High spot of the season . . . ovation . . ."
— **Norfolk (Va.) Ledger-Dispatch**

"Thoroughly satisfying . . ."
— **Dayton (O.) Herald**

"Gifted artist . . . sure and thorough command of technique, coupled with a robust tone of exceptional quality . . . charming and artistic interpretations."
— **Musical America, New York**

"Star of first magnitude . . . sensational artist . . . thrilled audiences past three seasons."
— **Ocean Grove (N.J.) Times**

"Bombshell on the fiddle . . ."
— **Herb Simmons, war correspondent, San Francisco, Cal.**

"One of the best concert performers we have ever had . . ."
— **New Orleans (La.) Times Picayune**

"Brilliant interpretation . . . vibrant style . . . vivid personality . . . beautiful tone . . . ovation . . ."
— **Miami (Fla.) Daily News**

"Star . . . great artist . . ."
— **Atlanta (Ga.) Constitution**

"Master of the violin . . ."
— **The Saratogian, Saratoga Springs, N. Y.**

"Nimble fingers flashed over strings . . . acclaimed . . ."
— **Palladium Sun-Telegram, Richmond, Ind.**

"Her performance justified her artistic standing . . ."
— **New York World-Telegram**

"Superb artist . . . fillip to the eye . . ."
— **Zanesville (Ohio) News**

"Has that certain something . . ."
— **Louisville (Ky.) News**

Joyce Renée promotional brochure.

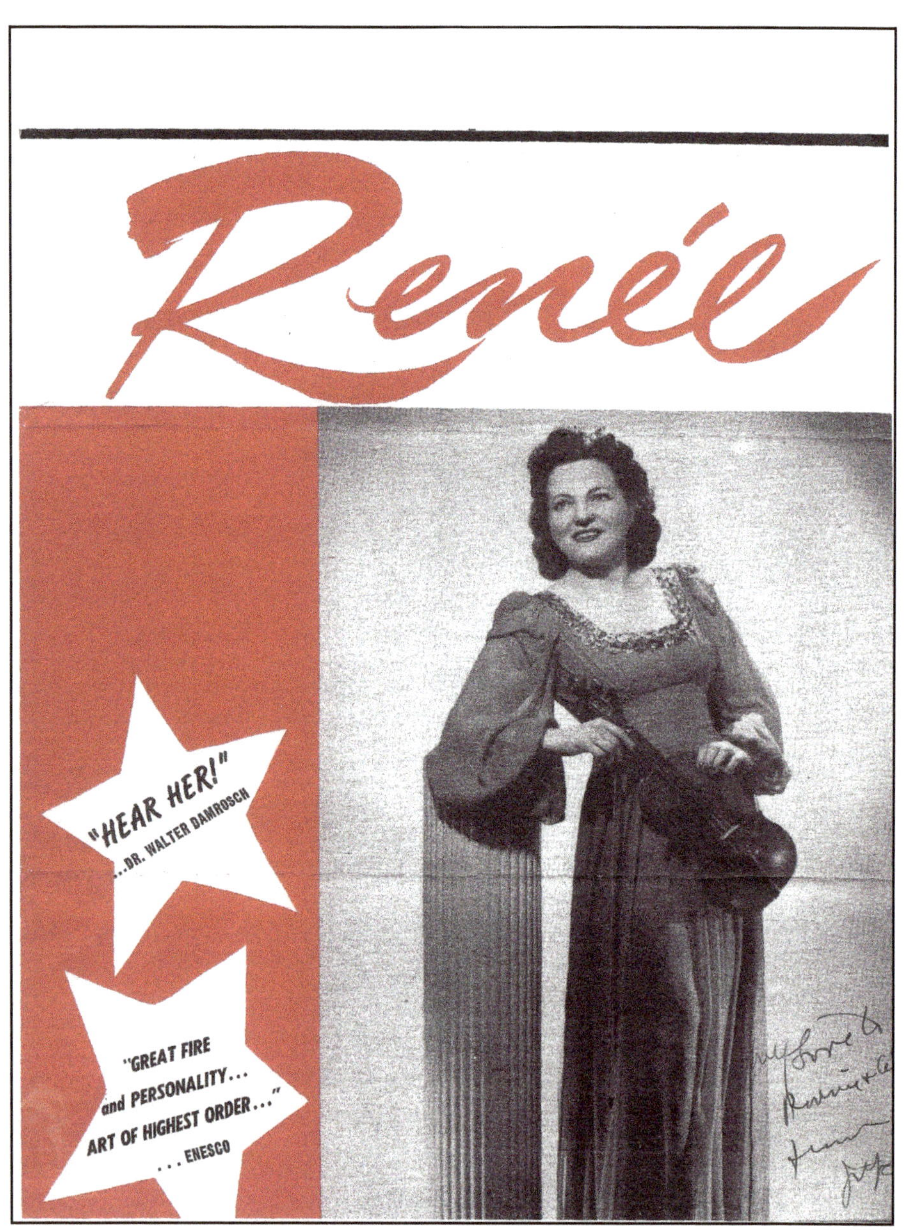

Cover of promotional brochure with Joyce's inscription to her brother Allan and his fiancée Renate ("Ronnie")

Joyce Renée

INTERNATIONALLY ACCLAIMED

APPEARANCES:
EUROPE,
CANADA,
AND IN THE UNITED STATES

At Carnegie Hall, Town Hall, Madison Square Garden, Radio City Music Hall, Ocean Grove (N.J.) auditorium, and other noted concert halls and auditoriums. Request performances at West Point and Annapolis. Frequent guest artist with leading symphony orchestras throughout America. Her club and college appearances include the New York Advertising Club, Cincinnati Women's Club, Daughters of the American Revolution, Xavier College, University of Minnesota, Wells College, Pennsylvania State College and other leading institutions. ***Recipient of national and international awards.***

RADIO ACTIVITIES

Starred repeatedly over three major radio networks . . . "Music at Twilight," "Works of the Masters," "American Festival Series," American Federation of Music Clubs program, "Community Chest Drive," "American Rolling Mills program, The Red Cross series, Homefront Favorites. The Stromberg-Carlson Show, Barbara Lee Program, and on several television shows.

PERFORMED FOR ROYALTY

and is a frequent guest on "Night of Stars". Joyce Renée has appeared on programs with such notable personages as Mrs. Eleanor Roosevelt, General Drum, Admiral Woodward, Lowell Thomas, Madame Chiang-Kai-Shek, the late Wendell Willkie, Edward G. Robinson, Kate Smith and a host of others.

Miss Renée's world famous teachers include Enesco, Kochanski, Arthur Hartmann and Rubin Goldmark.

COLORFUL PERSONALITY

Joyce Renée is artistically gifted in many ways. She is a composer, author and successful designer.

JOYCE RENÉE IS ONE OF THE MOST CONSISTENTLY RE-ENGAGED ARTISTS OF CONCERT . . . RADIO . . . STAGE

Programs played by Joyce Renée include the beloved, popular classics, semi-classics, American compositions, and varied concerto repertoire for symphony orchestras.

Now Booking — 1948-49 Season

Joyce Renée permanent address HOTEL LINCOLN, N. Y. C.
OR 765 GREENWOOD AVE. • CINCINNATI 29, OHIO

MANAGEMENT
Personal Representative:
LEE MAY BOSSE
12 Fifth Avenue - New York 11, Y. Y.
TEL. GRamercy 3-4358.
WIRE—WRITE—PHONE

Promotional brochure.

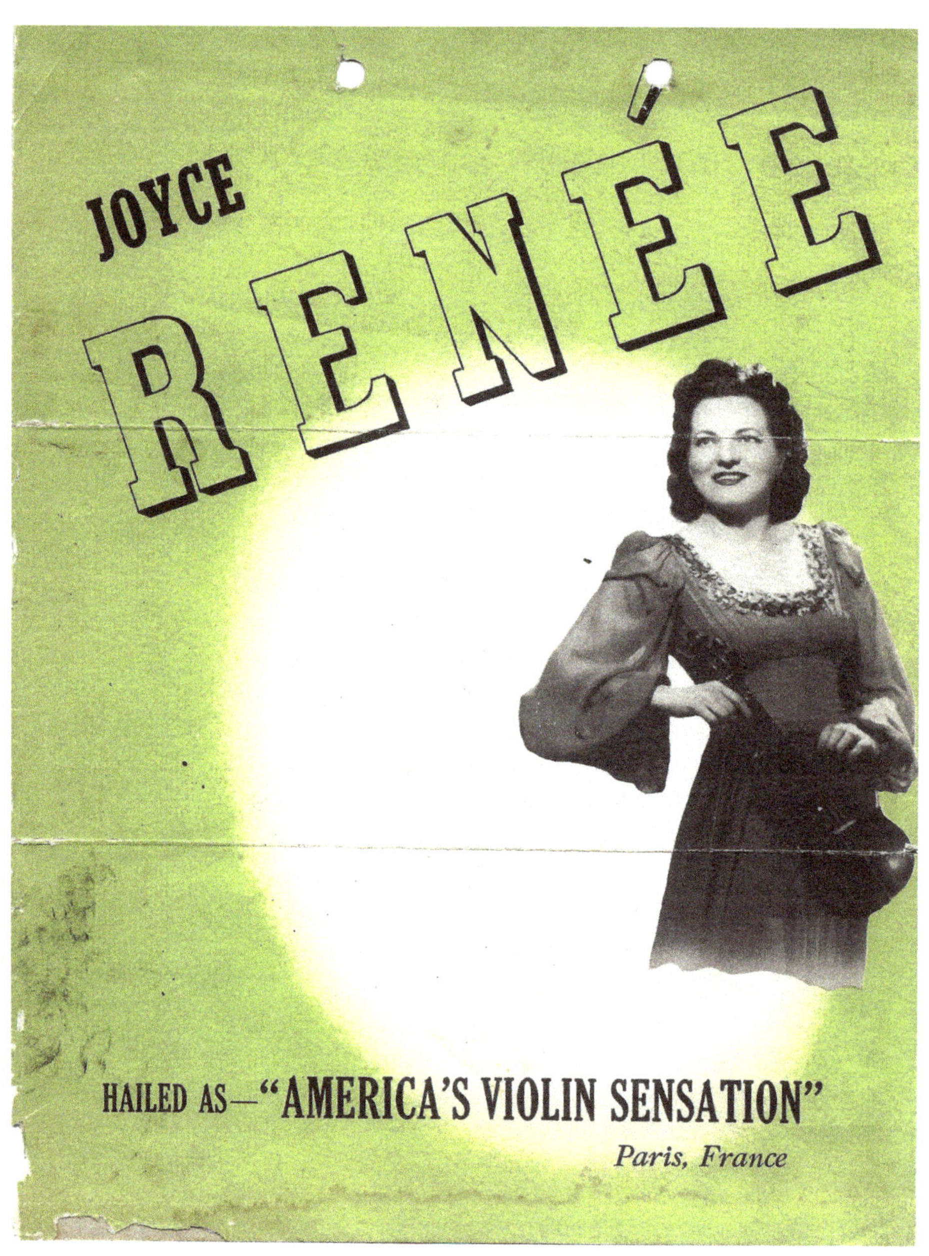
JOYCE
RENÉE
HAILED AS—"AMERICA'S VIOLIN SENSATION"
Paris, France

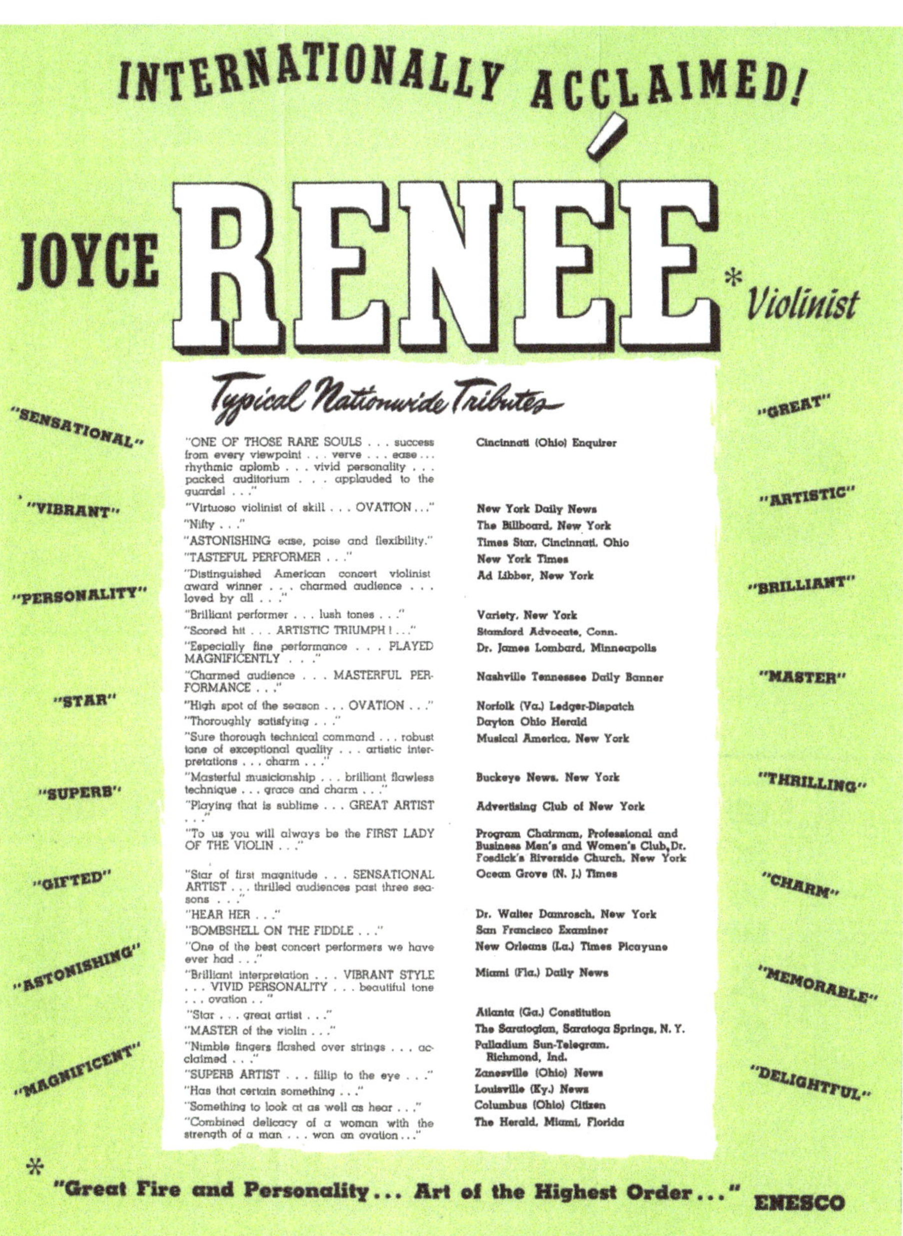

Joyce Renée promotional brochure.

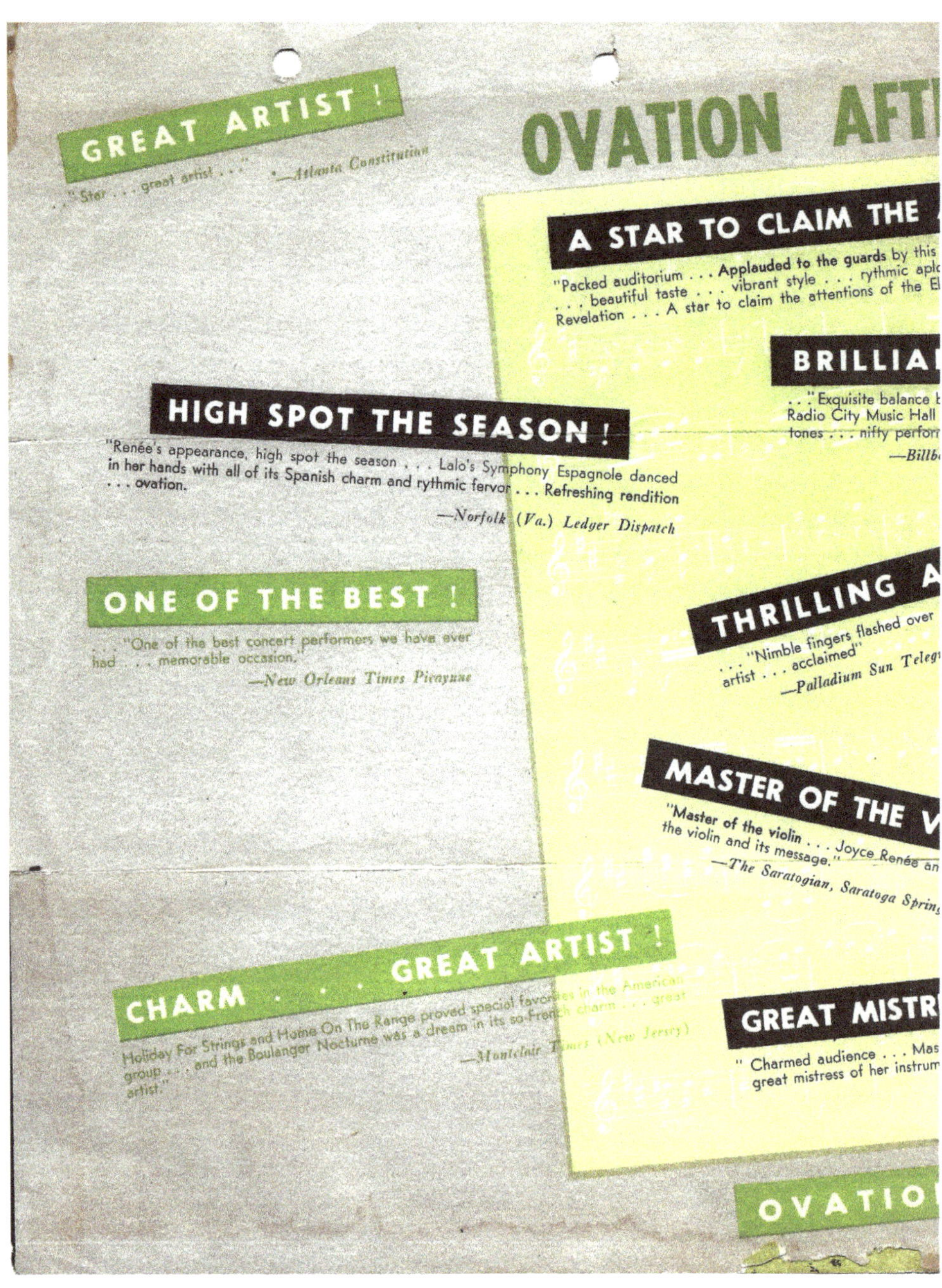

GREAT ARTIST !
. . "Star . . . great artist . . ." —Atlanta Constitution
OVATION AFT
A STAR TO CLAIM THE
"Packed auditorium . . . Applauded to the guards by this
. . . beautiful taste . . . vibrant style . . . rythmic aplo
Revelation . . . A star to claim the attentions of the E
BRILLIA
. . ." Exquisite balance
Radio City Music Hall
tones . . . nifty perfor
HIGH SPOT THE SEASON !
"Renée's appearance, high spot the season . . . Lalo's Symphony Espagnole danced in her hands with all of its Spanish charm and rythmic fervor . . . Refreshing rendition . . . ovation.
—Norfolk (Va.) Ledger Dispatch
ONE OF THE BEST !
. . . "One of the best concert performers we have ever had . . . memorable occasion."
—New Orleans Times Picayune
THRILLING A
. . . "Nimble fingers flashed over
artist . . . acclaimed"
—Palladium Sun Teleg
MASTER OF THE V
"Master of the violin . . . Joyce Renée an
the violin and its message."
—The Saratogian, Saratoga Sprin
CHARM . . . GREAT ARTIST !
Holiday For Strings and Home On The Range proved special favorites in the American group . . . and the Boulanger Nocturne was a dream in its so-French charm . . . great artist."
—Montclair Times (New Jersey)
GREAT MISTR
" Charmed audience . . . Mas
great mistress of her instrum
OVATIO

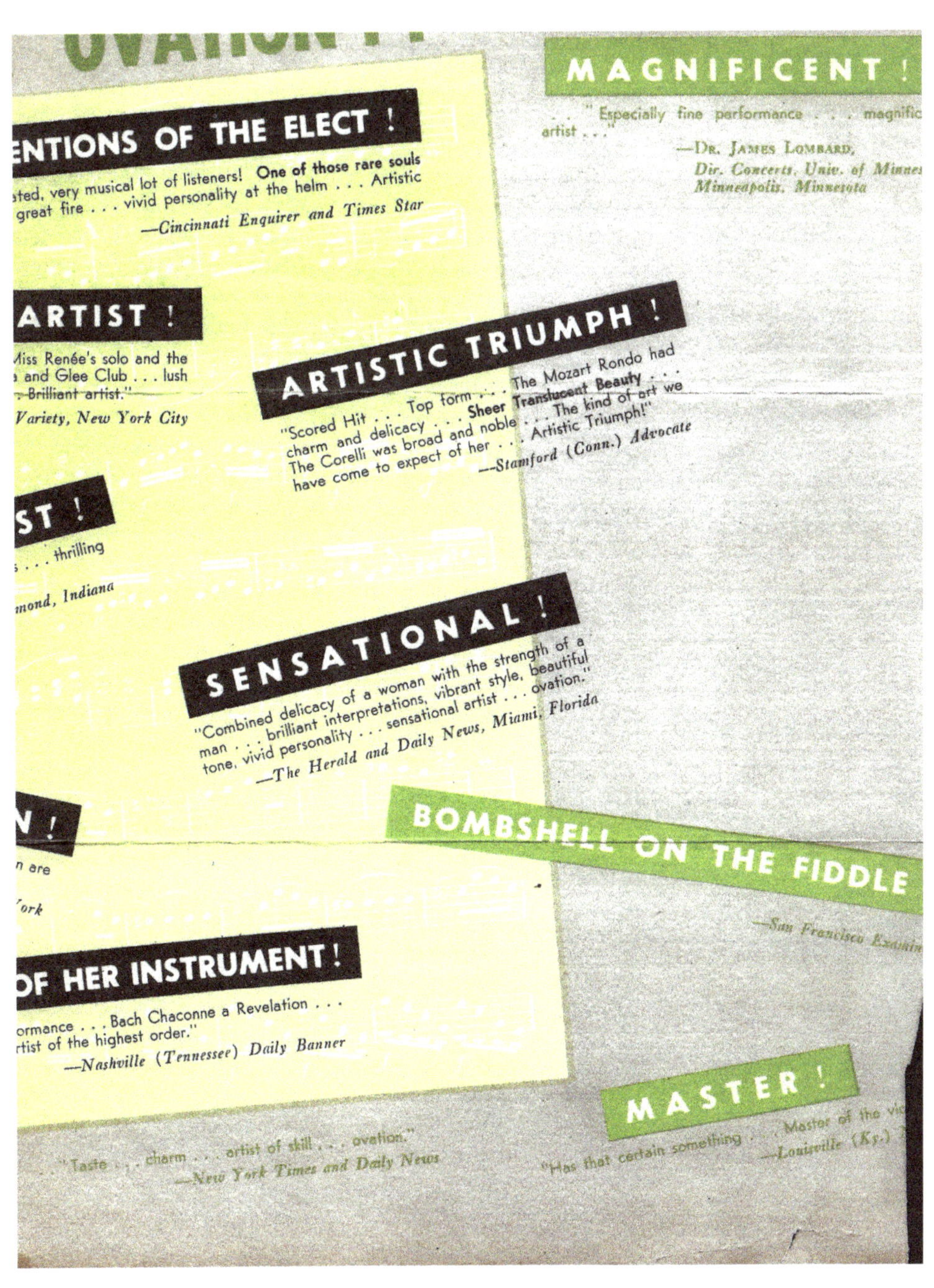

Joyce Renée promotional brochure.

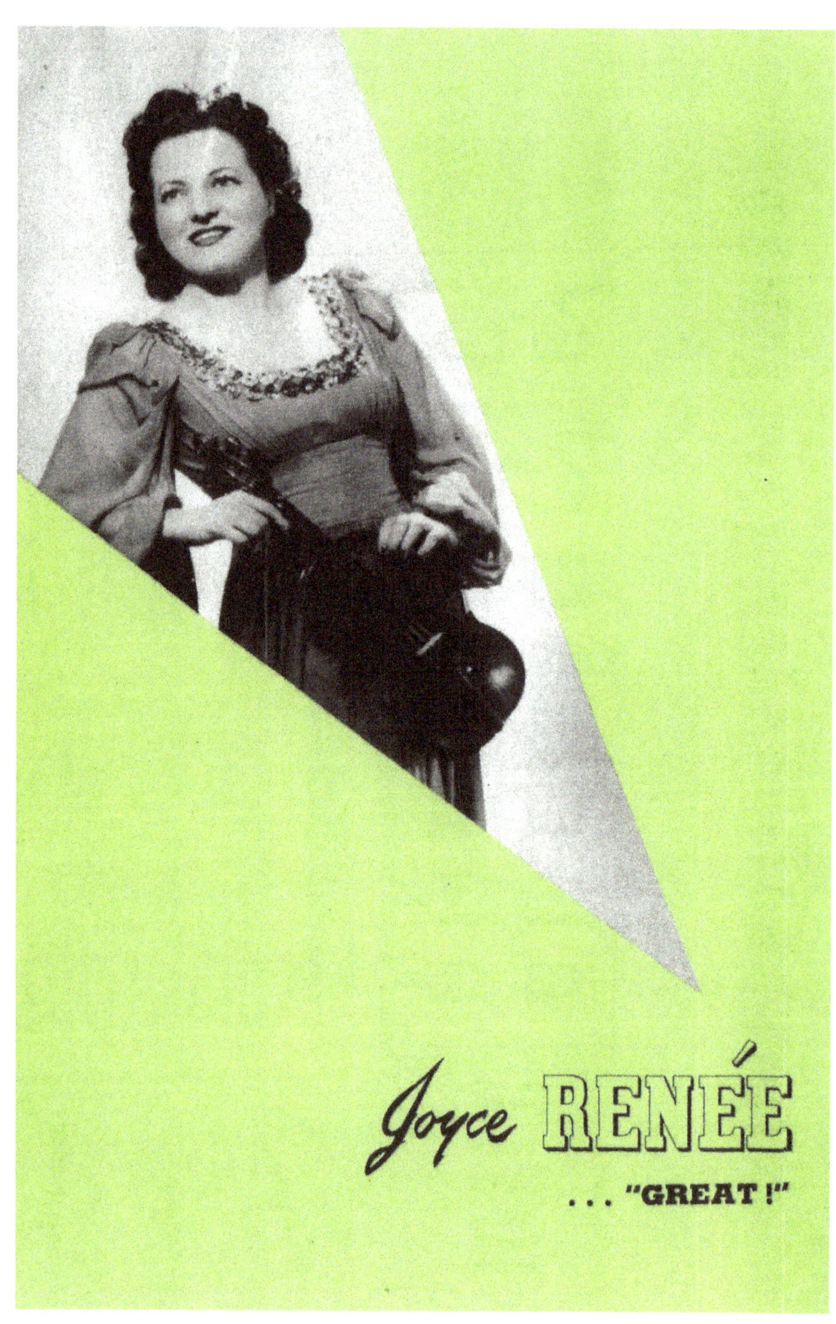
Joyce RENÉE
... "GREAT!"

HELD OVER

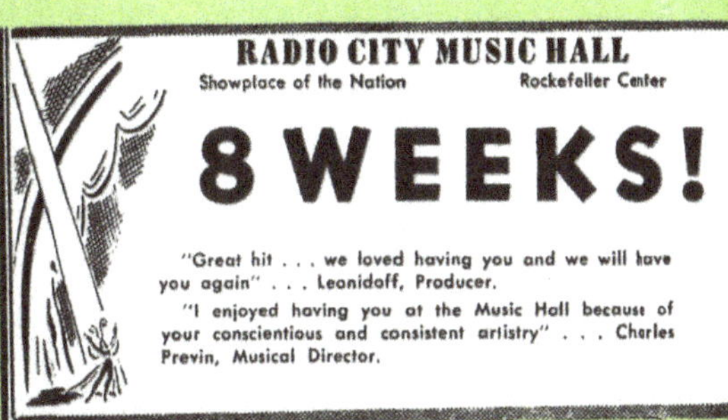
RADIO CITY MUSIC HALL

Showplace of the Nation Rockefeller Center

8 WEEKS!

"Great hit . . . we loved having you and we will have you again" . . . Leonidoff, Producer.

"I enjoyed having you at the Music Hall because of your conscientious and consistent artistry" . . . Charles Previn, Musical Director.

The Recipient of National and International awards, the distinguished American violinist, JOYCE RENÉE, appears frequently at Carnegie Hall, Town Hall, and Madison Square Garden, in New York City, and has given request performances at West Point, and Annapolis.

"Cheered by audiences and lauded by the critics," her recitals and solo appearances with symphony orchestra are an "artistic triumph." Her perfomances have been acclaimed throughout the United States. Canada and Europe have praised her great gifts, her deep sincerity, beautiful tone, technical command, and her penetrative interpretations."

A familiar figure in the Broadcasting Studios, JOYCE RENÉE is starred "repeatedly" on the major networks and on Television. Recently, GORDON CURRIE, distinguished Australian Broadcasting correspondent selected JOYCE RENÉE for inclusion in his book of World Famous Personalities, as the "World's Greatest Female Violinist."

Her world famous teachers include ENESCO, KOCHANSKI, ARTHUR HARTMANN, RUBIN GOLDMARK and DR. EDGAR STILLMAN-KELLEY.

"ALWAYS REMEMBERED AND RECALLED"

5 Return engagements at famed Ocean Grove Auditorium in N. J. within 3 seasons.

5 Return Engagements at State Teacher's College, Pennsylvania . . . Bloomsburg, within 3 seasons.

After 33 successive appearances on tour, as soloist with Dr. Frank Simon and his famous Radio Band. Dr. Simon praised her "great artistry and brilliant performances."

After 2 Tours as soloist with Joseph Cherniavsky and his Orchestra Mr. Cherniavsky enthusiastically acclaimed her great gifts . . . "MARVELOUS . . . JOYCE RENÉE ALWAYS BRINGS DOWN THE HOUSE."

JOYCE RENEE IS ONE OF THE MOST CONSISTENTLY RE-ENGAGED AND BEST LOVED ARTISTS OF CONCERT . . . RADIO . . . STAGE.

Management **Booking Now**

By Arrangement
CONCERT DIVISION, MUSIC CORP. of AMERICA
745 Fifth Avenue, N. Y. C.

Joyce Renée promotional brochure.

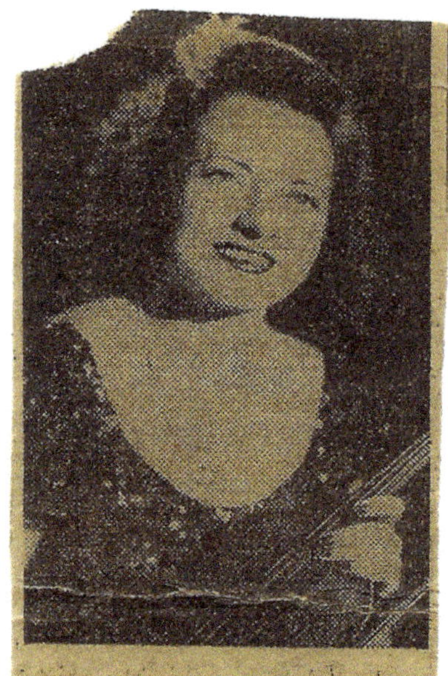

Joyce Renee

Miss Joyce Renee has been awarded a Town Hall appearance in New York City for early January.

Her most recent reported appearances include West Point, Ocean Grove auditorium, solo broadcasts for the Stromberg Carlson Radio commercials, and NBC broadcasts on the west coast.

During the war, Miss Renee made two coast-to-coast tours of camps and hospitals in this country, and recently spent five weeks, greeting returning Pacific veterans on the west coast.

She is a recipient of Honor Bar Emblems from the Stage Door Canteen, and Merchant Seamen's Club and citations from the Merchant Marine and Hospital committees.

Georges Enesco is quoted as saying of her playing: "Her art is of the highest order and her knowledge of the instrument perfect. She has personality and great fire."

Following the Town Hall engagement, Joyce Renee will fill return engagements of colleges and universities in the south.

JOYCE RENEE.......................... *Sensational American Violinist*
Leading Soloist with many Symphony Orchestras

7. Violin Solo by Miss Renee — **"SYMPHONY ESPAGNOLE"**, by Lalo (1823-1892)

In this selection, Composer Lalo departed from prevailing convention and created a work in which both the violin solo part, and an intricate, abundant. semi-independent orchestral accompaniment are successfully blended to form a beautiful entity.

"PRAELUDIUM": Bach-Kreisler

In his long and fruitful life Johann Sebastian Bach contributed a large library of solos for the violin. Fritz Kreisler has selected one of these from Bach's Sonata No. 6 and added a piano accompaniment. From this arrangement, a background of band instrumentation was transcribed for desired richness in presentation.

VIOLINIST

Joyce Renee, violinist, will play at Tougaloo College church Thursday at 8:15 p.m. as one of the artists on the college's lyceum program. Miss Renee is a graduate of Cincinnati Conservatory of Music.

Miss Clark Has Reunion With Famous Teacher

Miss Lucy Clark returned to her home in Martinsville Monday evening after a reunion with a former teacher, Georges Enesco, who was in Indianapolis over the week end as guest conductor of the Indianapolis Symphony orchestra at its Saturday night and Sunday afternoon concerts.

Miss Clark and Miss Joyce Renee of New York and Cincinnati, both pupils of Enesco in his master violin classes in Paris, had luncheon Monday at the Lincoln hotel with Enesco, Jacques Thibaud, soloist with the Symphony Saturday and Sunday, and the latter's accompanist, Marinus Flipse.

Enesco, famed Romanian conductor, violinist and composer, and Thibaud, French violinist, arrived in the United States Christmas week for a winter concert tour.

Saturday evening Miss Clark was the overnight guest of Mrs. Leonard Strauss and Sunday evening, she and Miss Renee were guests of Mrs. Herbert Wagner.

Joyce Renée news clippings.

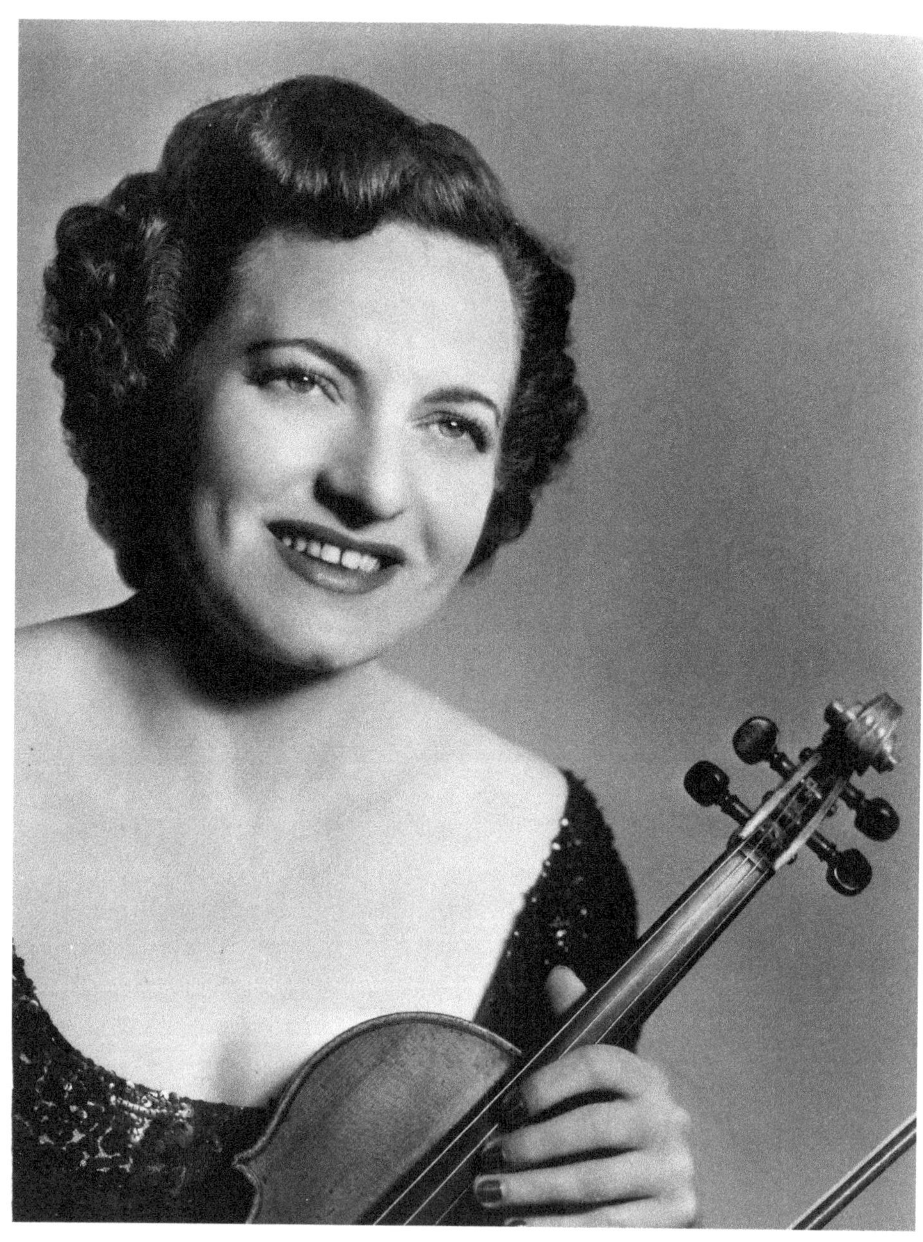

Joyce with her violin, or "fiddle" as she sometimes called it.

Little Town Series Club
presents
JOYCE RENÉE, Violinist

Program

I

Sonata No. 6 (in E Major) . . . . Handel
Adagio
Allegro
Largo
Allegro

II

Preludium and Allegro . . . . Pugnani-Kreisler

Air on G String . . . . Bach

Gavotte . . . . Mozart

Chanson et Pavane . . . . Couperin-Kreisler

III
(American Group)

Out of the East . . . . William Kroll

Subway . . . . Haufreucht
(Dedicated to Miss Renée)

Home on the Range . . . . Arranged by Joyce Renée
(Traditional Cowboy Melody)

Ghost Dance . . . . Ellis Levy

IV

Songs My Mother Taught Me . . . . . . Dvorak-Persinger

Aus der Heimat . . . . Smetana

Nocturne . . . . Lili Boulanger

Jota . . . . De Falla-Kochanski

Old Refrain . . . . Kreisler

Dance Espagnole . . . . De Falla-Kreisler
(From "La Vida Breve")

Joyce Renée, Program for Concert as part of Little Town Concert Series.

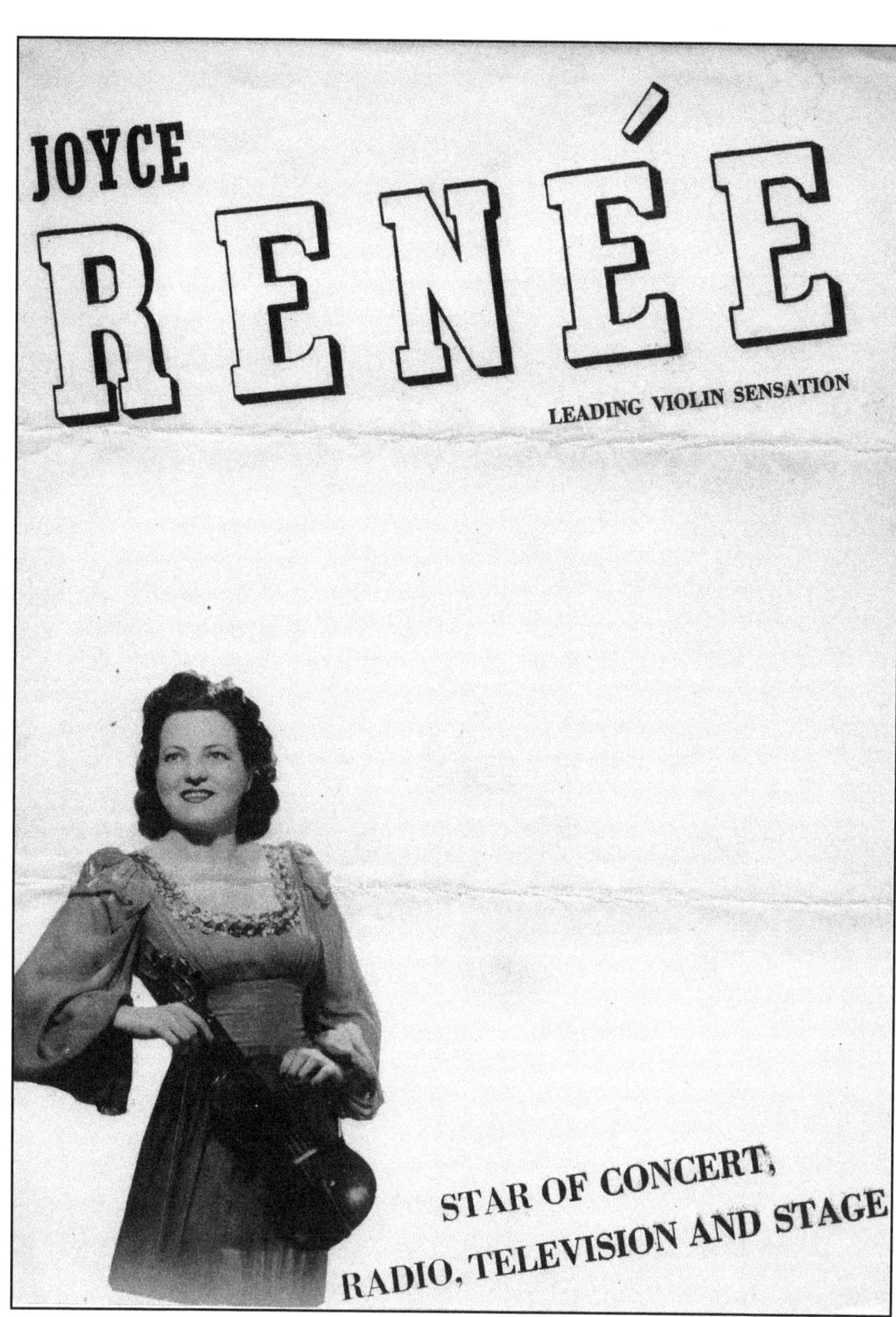

Joyce Renée, publicity cover.

UNIVERSITY OF MINNESOTA
SUMMER SESSION

presents

JOYCE RENÉE

VIOLINIST

LAURA FORDE GIERE—Accompanist

Wednesday Evening August 6, 1947	Music Auditorium 8:15 p.m.

PROGRAM

I.

Sonata No. 6 (in E Major) - - - - - - - - - - *Handel*
(For violin and piano)

Adagio
Allegro
Largo
Allegro

Preludium and Allegro - - - - - - - - *Pugnani-Kreisler*

II.

Chaconne - - - - - - - - - - - - - - - - *Bach*
(For violin alone)

III.

Songs of Home - - - - - - - - - - - - - *Smetana*
Gavotte - - - - - - - - - - - - - - - - - *Mozart*
Nocturne - - - - - - - - - - - - - - *Lili Boulanger*
Ghost Dance - - - - - - - - - - - - - - *Ellis Levy*

IV.

Jota - - - - - - - - - - - - - - *De Falla-Kochanski*
Old Refrain - - - - - - - - - - - - - - - - *Kreisler*
Subway (Dedicated to Miss Renée) - - - - *Haufreucht*
Dance Espagnole (from "La Vida Breve") - - *De Falla-Kreisler*

Joyce Renée, program for concert at the University of Minnesota, Aug. 6, 1947.

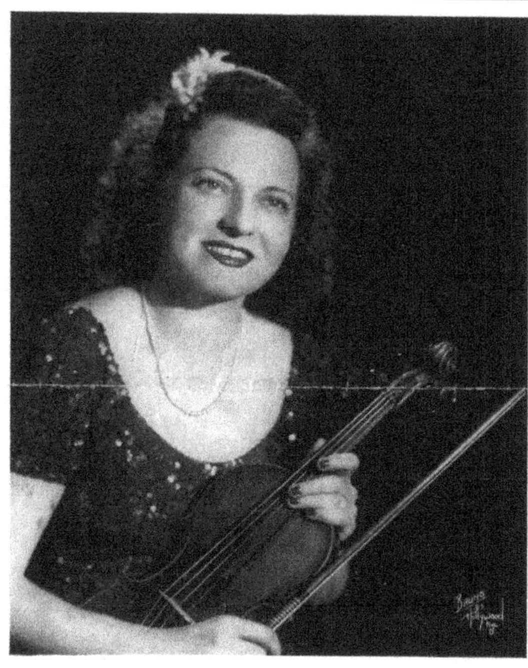

Joyce Renée

..."Has Personality and Great Fire"

GEORGES ENESCO

Composer - Conductor

MUSICAL VERSATILITY

Supreme talent and a winning personality are only two of the many assets of violinist Joyce Renee, who, at the age of seventeen, had the musicianship and experience of a seasoned veteran.

HONORS

The holder of both national and international awards including the Juilliard Graduate School, Schmidlapp, Fleischmann and Woolley International Scholarships, Miss Renee is a graduate of the Cincinnati Conservatory of Music, where she earned a Bachelor of Music degree, and was the youngest artist ever to have achieved the highest honor diploma in violin.

Additional honors bestowed on her are a medal presented by the late Wendell Willkie, two medals from the Ohio Society of New York, honor bar emblems from the Stage Door Canteen, merchant seaman's club, as well as citations from the Merchant Marine and USO camp shows.

MUSICAL GLOBE TROTTER

For a young artist Miss Renee has covered a lot of territory. She has been heard at Carnegie Hall, Madison Square Garden, and Town Hall in New York City; at the great auditorium in Ocean Grove, New Jersey; at West Point; in colleges and universities across the country, and has been soloist with symphony orchestras throughout the United States and Europe.

RADIO ACTIVITIES

In addition, she has appeared repeatedly over three major radio networks, playing as soloist on such programs as "Music at Twilight," "Works of the Masters," the American Federation of Music Clubs program, the "American Festival Series," the "American Rolling Mills" program, the "Stromberg Carlson Commercials", and several television shows.

Joyce Renée publicity biography.

THE CLIMB TO PROMINENCE

In her climb to prominence this gifted violinist has played before all kinds of audiences from the Bowery Mission to Carnegie Hall, and has performed every kind of music from the St. Louis Blues to the Brahms violin concerto. During her studies, at the Juilliard Graduate School, she earned her way by doing an early-morning stint over a "milkman's program" on a local radio station.

PLAYED WORLD'S GREATEST VIOLINS

All violinists cherish the privilege of playing on fine instruments, and Joyce Renee is no exception. She has sampled the tonal beauty of the violins in the famous Henry Ford collection, at Dearborn, Michigan, and demonstrated instruments from the rare Wurlitzer collection before the Music Merchandizers Convention in New York. Her greatest thrill came recently, when she played the famous Aranyi Stradivarius from the Sturchio collection, the earliest Stradivarius in existence.

MOST VALUED TRIBUTE

Miss Renee has received highly favorable criticism from critics everywhere. But the tribute she values most of all was that paid her by composer-conductor Georges Enesco, with whom she studied in Paris. Enesco said of her playing, "Her art is of the highest order, and her knowledge of the instrument perfect. She has personality and great fire, and the success she has reaped are highly deserved."

Another tribute, typical among the many favorable press notices she has received is one that appeared in the Cincinnati Enquirer, "Joyce Renee, who is easy to look at, swung into her program with verve, ease and a rhythmic aplomb that seemed to mark her as one of those rare souls to whom music becomes a passion. Her playing offers listeners an intent sensation of a vivid personality at the helm, and makes for musical, artistic and personal success."

TYPICAL TRIBUTES FROM THE PRESS

"A SUCCESS FROM EVERY VIEWPOINT — high spirit and fervor — Large audience received entire program with the utmost enthusiasm."
Cincinnati Enquirer, Cincinnati, O.

"Astonishing ease, poise, and flexibility."
Cincinnati Times-Star, Cincinnati, O.

"Young artist featured at Town Hall — disciplined, reserved, tasteful performance."
New York Times, N. Y.

"Virtuoso violinist of skill — won ovation."
Daily News, New York

"Renee's performance justified her artistic standing."
New York World-Telegram, N. Y.

"Masterful musicianship — brilliant flawless technique — grace and charm."
Buckeye News, New York

"Nifty."
Billboard, New York

"Star Concoction — great artist."
Atlanta Constitution, Atlanta, Ga.

"Beautiful tone, fluent technique, vibrant style, vivid personality."
Daily News, Miami, Florida

"Outstanding ability — one of best concert performers we have ever had."
Times,—Picayune, New Orleans, La.

"Scored hit — rich warm tone — brilliant technique — artistic triumph."
Stamford Advocate, Stamford, Conn.

"A favorite of service men and returnees."
San Francisco Examiner, Calif.

"Bombshell on the Fiddle."
Herb Symmons, (War Correspondent)
San Francisco, Calif.

"Sensational artist — Thrilled Ocean Grove audiences past two seasons."
Ocean Grove Times, New Jersey

"Lilting tunes of brilliant violinist bring joy".
The Seattle Star, Seattle, Wash.

"High spot the season—The violinist given an ovation".
Ledger Dispatch, Norfolk, Va.

"Something to look at as well as hear — fine musicianship — enthusiastically received."
Columbus Citizen, Columbus, Ohio

"Has that certain something."
Louisville News, Kentucky

FEATURED EXTENSIVE ENGAGEMENT RADIO CITY MUSIC HALL, N. Y.

"Consistent Artistry"
Chas. Previn,
Musical Director,
Radio City Music Hall

THE REDPATH BUREAU

1316 Kimball Bldg., Chicago 4, Illinois
Tel. Harrison 8723

24 West 45th Street, New York 19, N. Y.
Tel. MUrray Hill 7-7073

Joyce Renée publicity biography and press quotes.

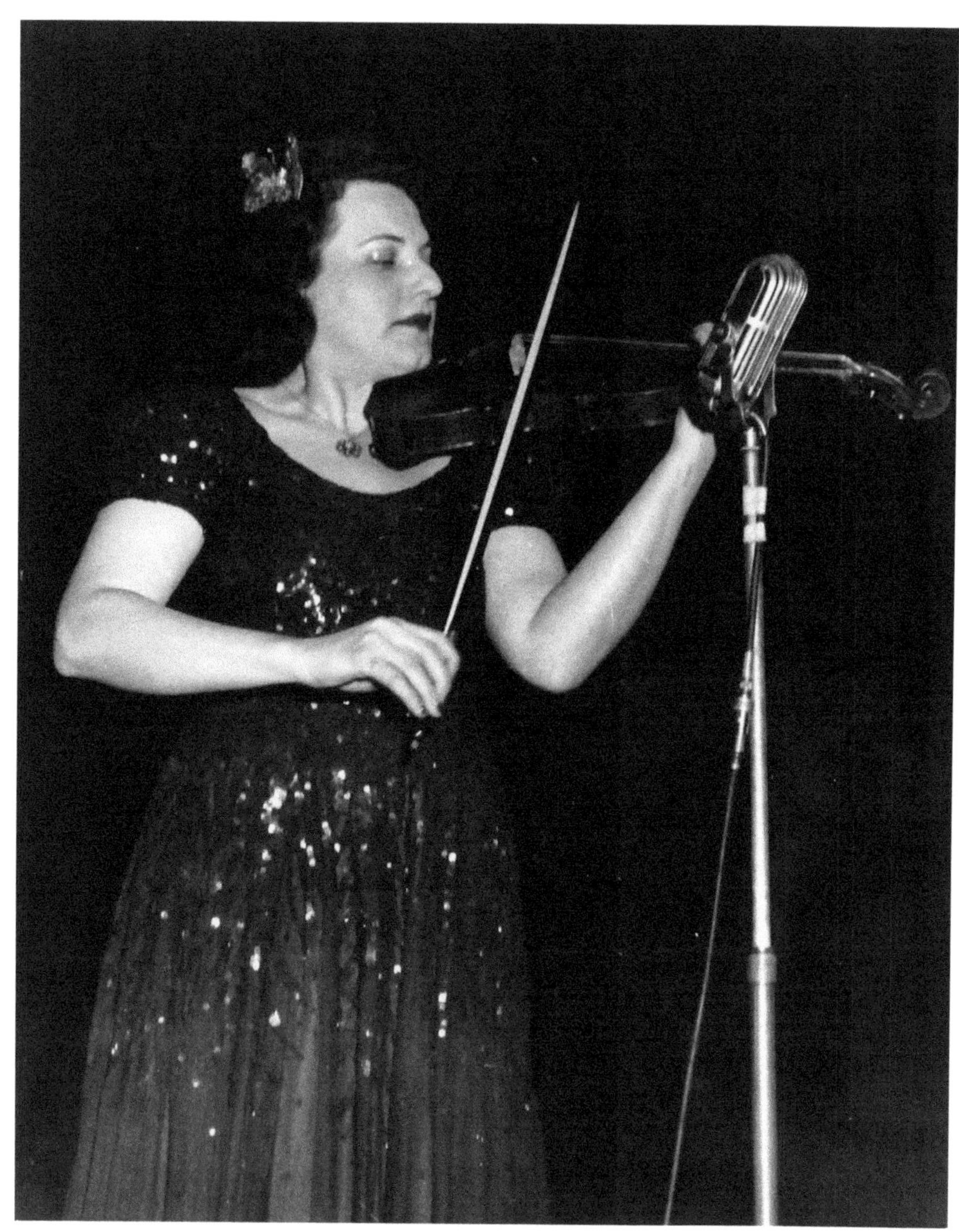

Joyce playing in concert.

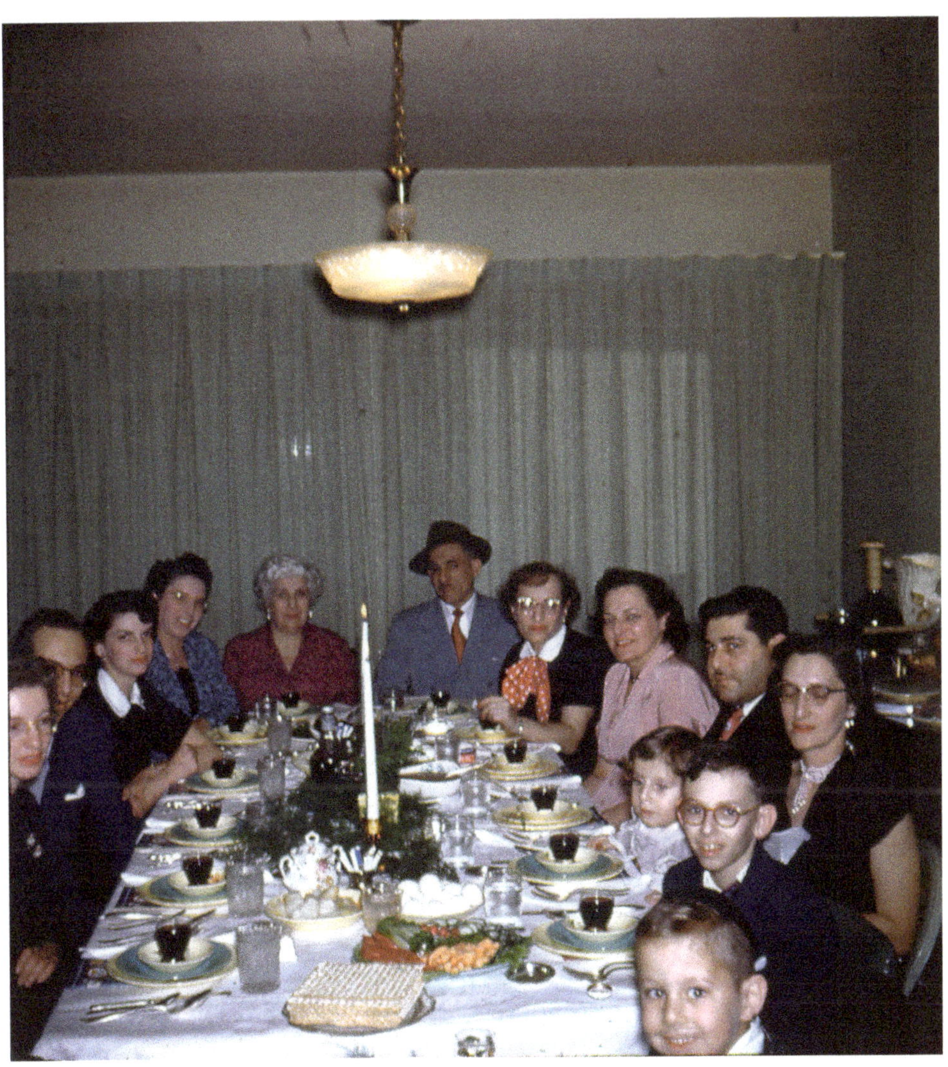

Seder at Anna Wasserman home. L-R: Erica Houser, Sandy Cohen, Renate Wasserman, Trudy Houser, Anna ("Granny") Wasserman, Joe Cohen, Rose Aronoff, Joyce, Nate Aronoff, Rose Aronoff, Cookie Aronoff (on Rose's lap), Mark Cohen, Michael Aronoff.

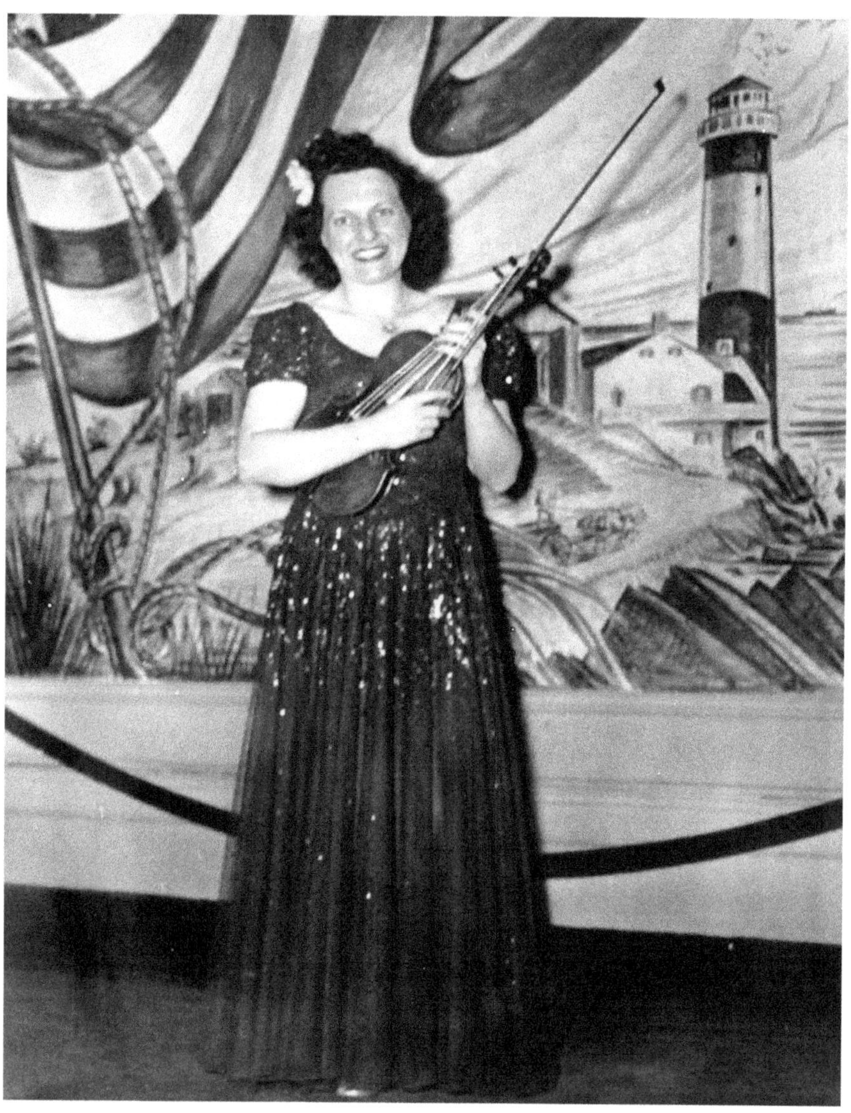

Joyce played at dozens of USO shows, military bases, and hospitals to entertain returning and injured troops.

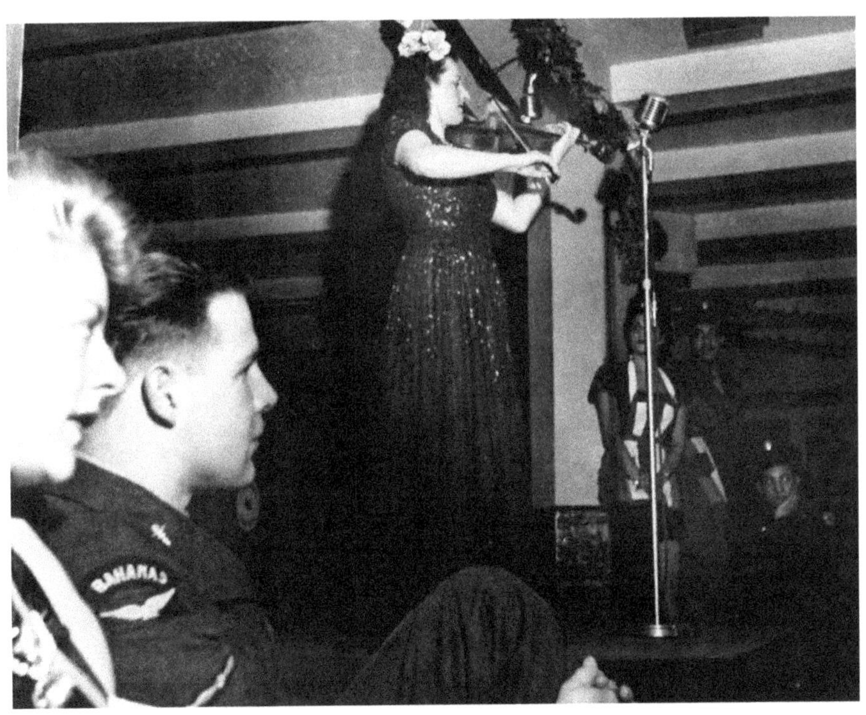

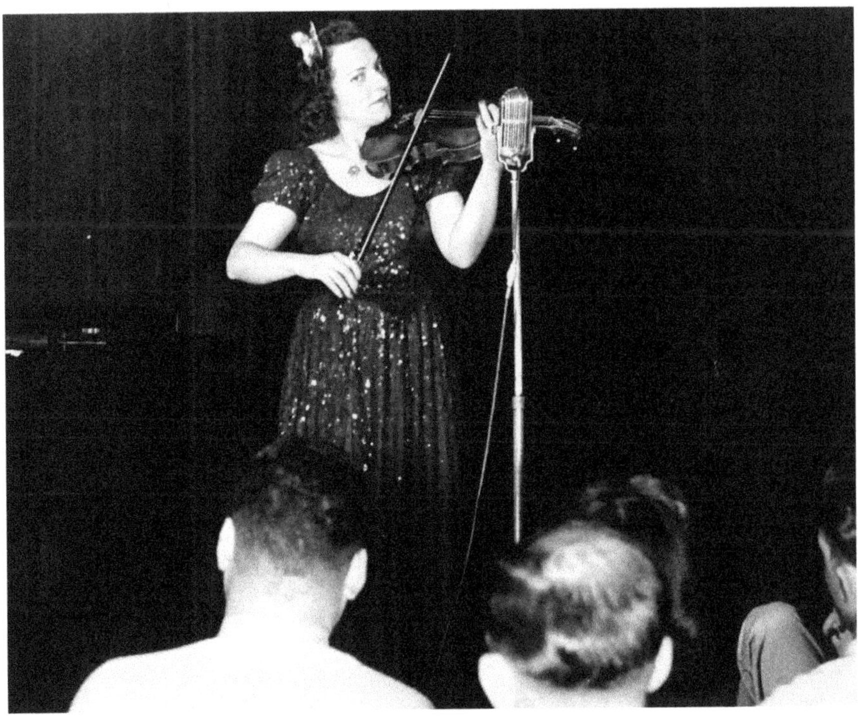

Joyce playing for servicemen.

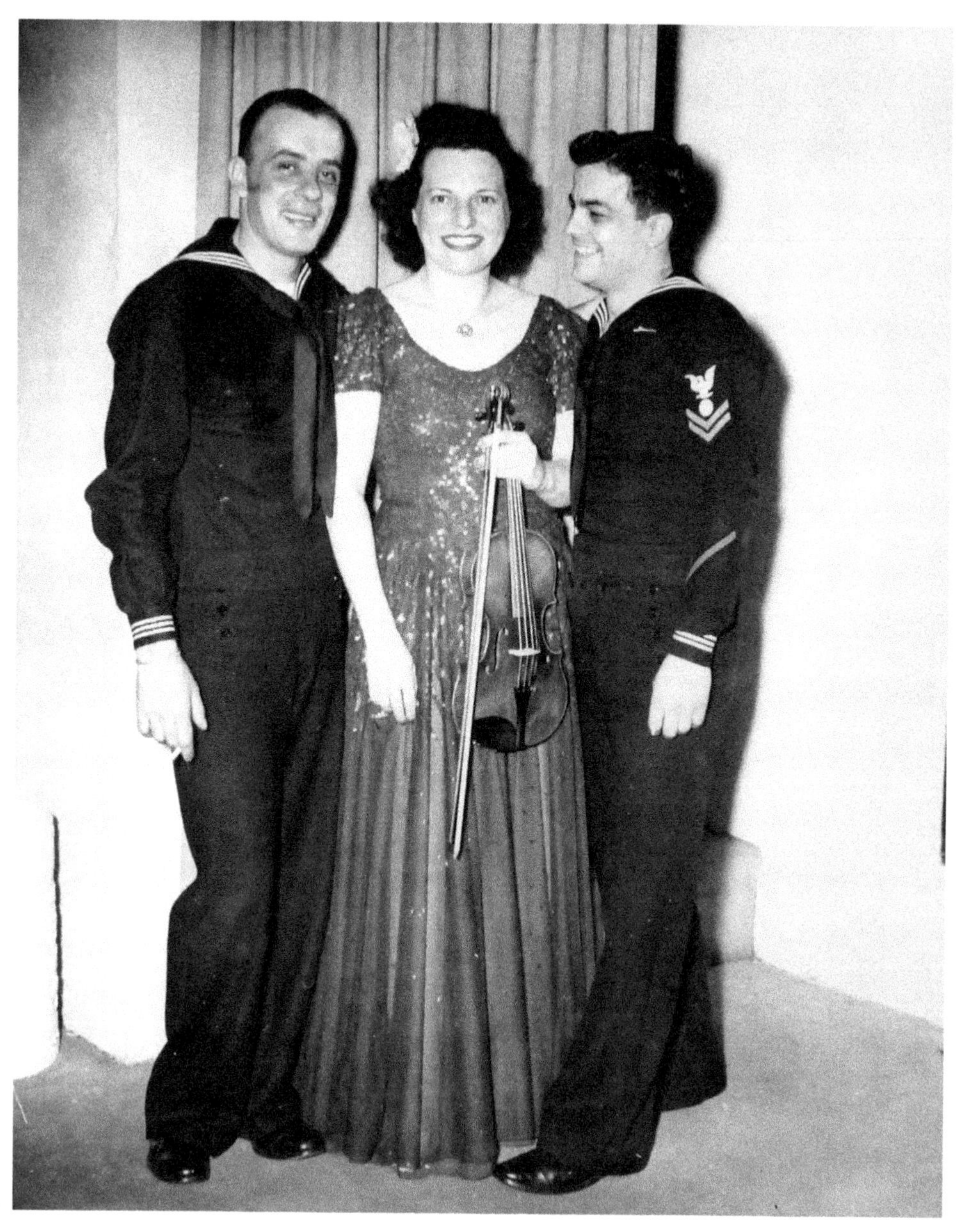

Joyce with U.S. Naval servicemen.

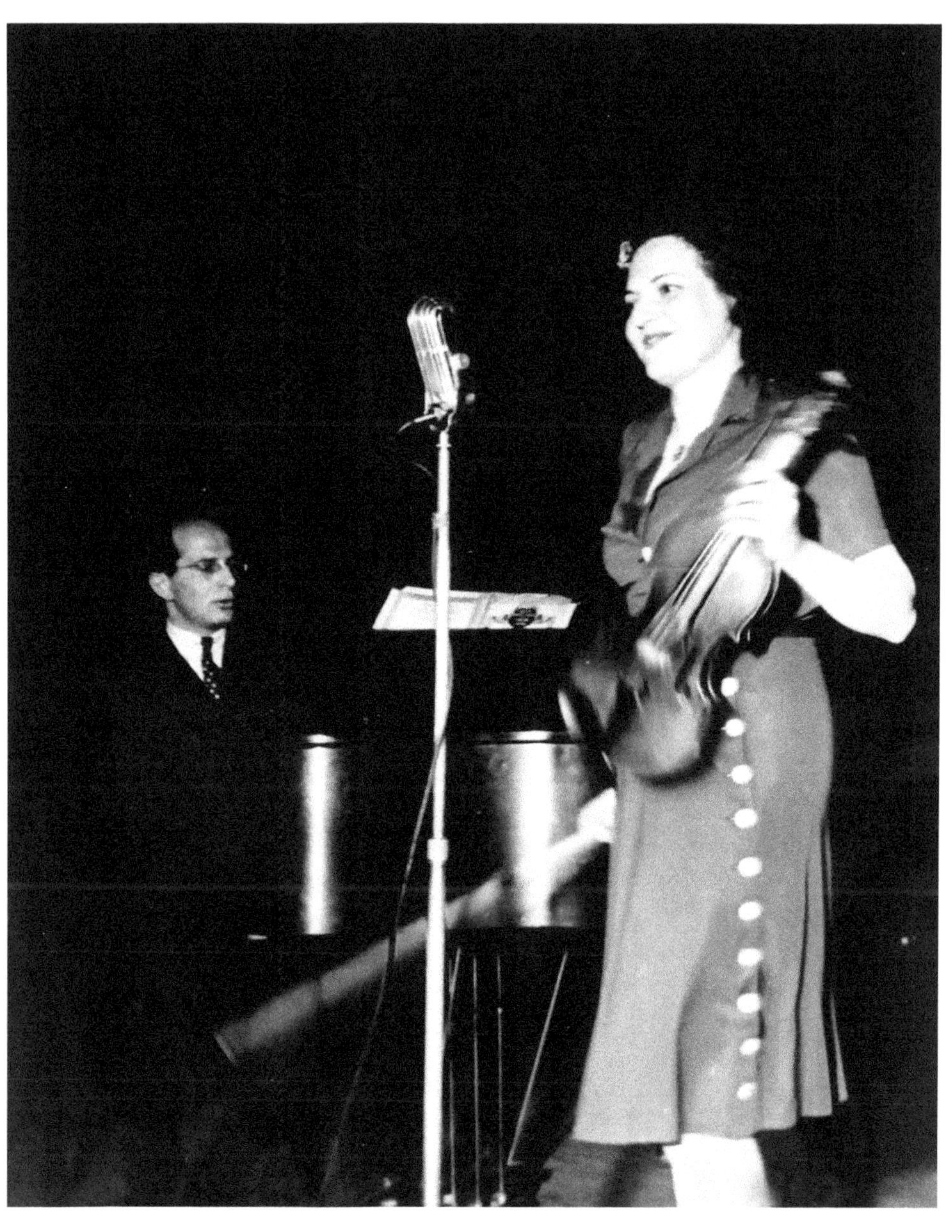

Joyce preparing to play with pianist accompanying her.

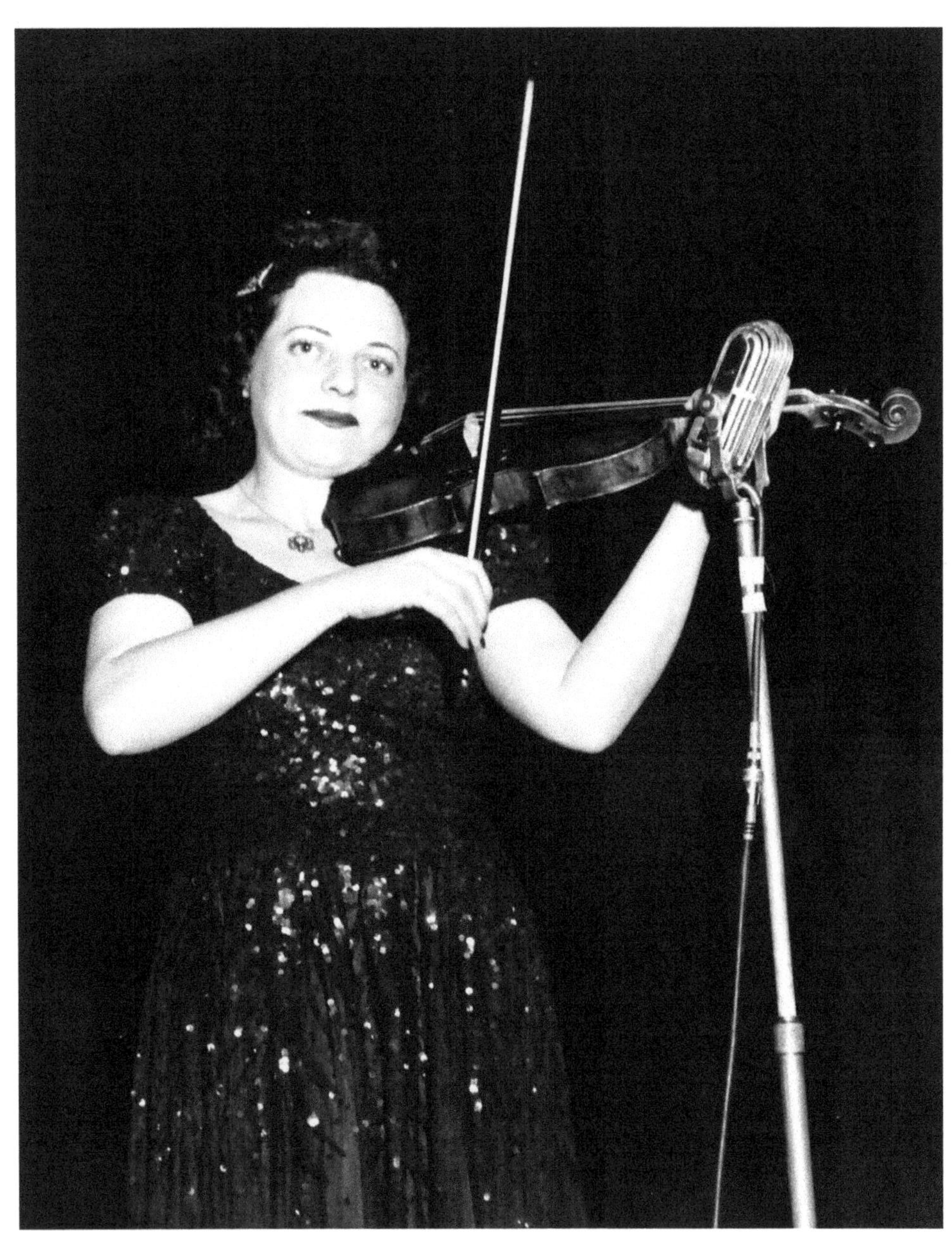

Joyce preparing to play.

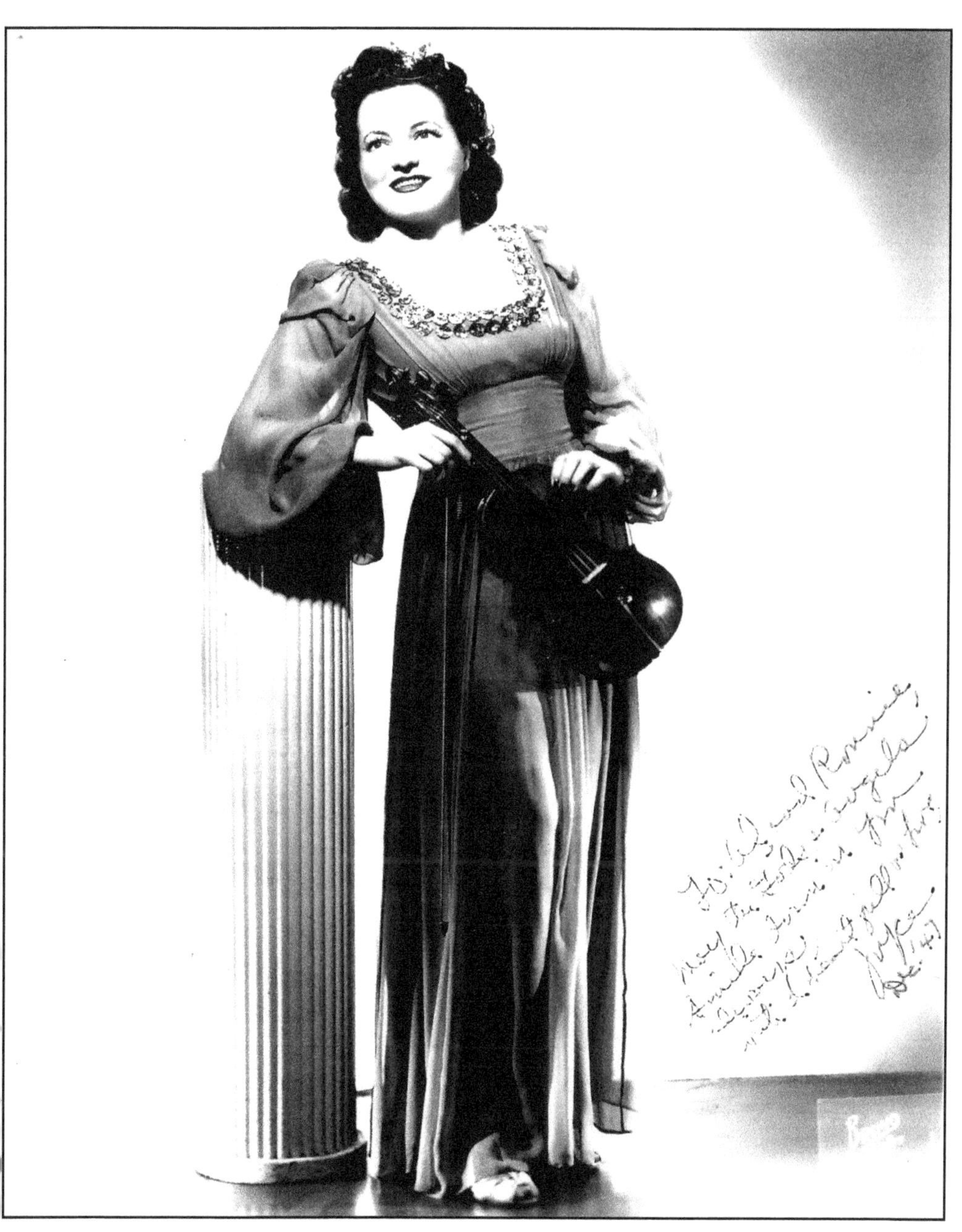

Joyce publicity shot with her December 1947 dedication to her brother Allan and his wife Ronnie.

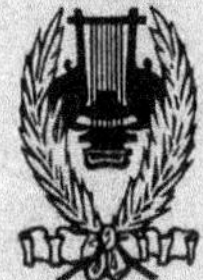

THE IMMANUEL CHOIR

BIRGER E. AMBROSE, DIRECTOR

presents

Annual Concert

Saturday Evening, April 12, 1947

at 8 o'clock prompt

[*Tickets including tax $1.00*]

IMMANUEL METHODIST CHURCH

REVEREND IVAR F. PEARSON, MINISTER

DEAN STREET NEAR FIFTH AVENUE BROOKLYN, NEW YORK

•

Our traditional social and fellowship will follow the Concert in the Vestry. Refreshments will be served by our ever faithful ladies of the Womens Society for Christian Service at a nominal charge.

Your kind interest and attendance at this our Annual Concert will be sincerely appreciated by members of the Immanuel Choir.

COME AND ENJOY THIS VERY ATTRACTIVE CONCERT

REMEMBER—The Concert begins promptly at eight o'clock with the playing of organ chimes.

Immanuel Choir Program, Cover

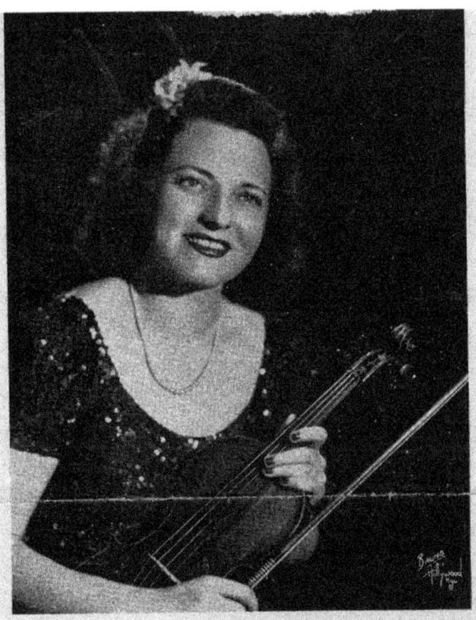

JOYCE RENEÉ, Violinist

Joyce Reneé, brilliant American violinist, who at 17 was the youngest honor Bachelor of Music Degree graduate, in the history of the Cincinnati Conservatory of Music, and who also won numerous National and International Fellowships, including the Juilliard Graduate School, the Schmidlappe, Fleischman, and Woolley International Fellowships, has had many honors bestowed upon her. Pembroke College named a Recording Club for her. The Ohio Society of New York awarded her three coveted medals, and she was given four honor bar emblems for her distinguished war work. Several honorary societies have elected her to membership, and there are many contemporary compositions dedicated to her.

This season, Miss Reneé appeared before a million and a half people at the Great Radio City Music Hall in New York. She performed for millions of men and women in the Armed Forces, besides the countless thousands who have heard her in appearances at Carnegie Hall and Town Hall, New York, in successive return engagements at West Point, the Great Ocean Grove Auditorium in New Jersey, Universities, Clubs, as soloist with symphony orchestras in the United States and Europe, and in broadcasts on the East and West Coasts.

LEOLA C. ANDERSON, Organ Soloist

Studied piano and organ with Anna A. Knowlton in Jamestown, New York. Studied piano several seasons in Chautauqua Summer Schools with Gordon Stanley and Wendel Diebel. May 1946 Graduate Juilliard School of Music in piano with Muriel Kerr. Presently in Organ and Church Music Department studying organ with Lillian Carpenter. Formerly organist Pilgrim Memorial Congregational Church, Jamestown, N.Y. and Director of Music First Congregational Church, Maplewood, New Jersey. At present, organist Immanuel Methodist Church, Brooklyn, N. Y.

IRENE STRONG HUNTLEY, Guest Organist

and SOLOISTS OF THE IMMANUEL CHOIR

Edith Ann Peterson, *Soprano* Robert W. Schelin, *Tenor* Walton Scott, *Baritone*

Immanuel Choir Program, Back

Hotel Lincoln

"THE HOUSE OF HOSPITALITY"

44TH TO 45TH STREETS
AT EIGHTH AVENUE
NEW YORK 19, N.Y.

JOHN L. HORGAN
GENERAL MGR
NEIL S. ALLEN
BUSINESS MGR

CIRCLE 6-4500
1400 ROOMS WITH BATH AND SHOWER, RADIO AND SERVIDOR

MARIA KRAMER
PRESIDENT

Dear Ronnie,

You were such an angel to fix me that lovely box of cookies, and I am still enjoying them. Thank you very, very much, Ronnie dear. It was certainly an unexpected and delightful surprise, and you were very sweet and thoughtful to send them to me.

I have always adored Al, and I couldn't have wished for him to have picked a lovelier girl, and I'm happy that you have him too, 'cause he's pretty "special," absent-mindedness and all."

When I can get around to it, I'll mail you something I bought — 'seems quite the vogue in new fall showings (costume jewelry), and when you can get around to it, pleeease send me your address, 'cause Al hasn't yet.

Lots of love to both of you, and your charming mother and sister, too.

Joyce

July 1947 letter from Joyce to Renate "Ronnie" Houser, her brother Allan's fiancée.

VIOLINIST HONORED

The noted American concert violinist Miss Joyce Renée, of New York City, who has won the plaudits and acclaim of music lovers all over the world, was recently elected to honorary membership in Phi Delta Alpha Medical Fraternity at its convention in Chicago. This honor is one of a long list accorded the artist, who is the youngest honor graduate in the history of the Cincinnati Conservatory of Music, and a former Paris artist student of Georges Emesco. These included the Fleischmann, Schmidlapp, Juilliard and Woolley International Fellowships and an Institute Instrumental award in Paris. She has also received three medals from the Ohio Society of New York, one of which was presented by the late Wendell Wilkie, and a Walters Town Hall award.

During the war, when she forgot about her career, to perform for the men and women of the Armed Forces, she received Honor Bar Emblems and Citations from the Stage Door Canteen, the Merchant Marine, U.S.O. Camp Shows, the Merchant Seaman's Club and the United Theatre Wing Hospital Committee, and was invited to appear at West Point and Annapolis; Pembroke College has a recording club named for her and at Ursuline College, in New Orleans, Sister Mary Agatha, dedicated a daily Novena for Miss Renée's art.

"For her high professional competence and her cultural contributions to an enriched America," she has again been selected by the committee on listings for "Who's Who on the International Platform"; and invited for inclusion in "Who's Who in Music," "Who's Who in America," "Who's Who in the East," "The International Who's Who," and the publication, "Distinctive Women of America," and recently Gordon Currie, the Australian Broadcasting Correspondent, selected Joyce Renée for inclusion in his book of illustrations on "World Famous Personalities," as the world's greatest female violinist.

One of four great American young artists chosen by the Concert Division of Music Corporation of America, New York City, to appear in their "Great American Young Artist Concerts," Miss Renée is a colorful personality. She is a successful designer, composer and author. During the war, her sweater designs, "Your Heart's in the Navy," "Your Heart's in the Army," "Your Heart's in the Marines," "Your Heart's in the Air-Corps," were put out by "Royal." Her first hobby venture in the designing field immediately established her as having designing gifts to be taken seriously.

As a composer, her first piece called "Tale", was written at the age of nine, and she has since won several composition awards and frequently includes her own arrangements in concert and radio programs.

As an author, her first prize came from the "Sec'tary Hawkins Club" at the age of six, and she is now working at "On the way up," a kind of memoires including a lot of amusing incidents and anecdotes, gathered on the way up and during her many travels.

Miss Renée's world famous teachers include Enesco, Arthur Hartmann, and the late Paul Kochanski, Rubin Goldmark and Dr. Edgar Stillmann-Kelley.

In her climb to prominence, this gifted artist has played before all kinds of audiences from the Bowery Mission to Carnegie Hall, and has performed every kind of music from the "St. Louis Blues" to the "Brahms" violin concerto.

During her studies at the Juilliard Graduate School she earned her way by doing an early morning stint over a "Milkman's Program," on a local radio station.

A musical globe trotter, Miss Renée has been acclaimed in her appearances through-out the United States, Canada and Europe.

All violinists cherish the privilege of playing fine instruments. Joyce Renée has sampled the tonal beauty of the violins in the famous Henry Ford collection at Dearborn, Michigan; demonstrated instruments from the rare Wurlitzer collection before the Music Merchandiser's Convention in New York, and performed on the fabulous violins from the wonderful Emil Herrmann collection. Her greatest thrill came recently, when she played the famous Aranyi Stradivarius, the earliest "Strad" in existence.

In all of her concerts, Joyce Renée uses a certain kind of mute, made for her by one of her friends. The mute is made of a chemical substance that looks like glass, and it gives the soft violin tones a magnificent purity.

A popular favorite of college audiences and music lovers all over the world, her enthusiasm for music and people is contagious, but Joyce Renée says "My audiences give me that enthusiasm."

Joyce Renée, September 21, 1949 press release regarding recent honor.

POST, SATURDAY, JUNE 23, 1951.

Versatile

Cincinnati Violinist At Work on Memoirs

BY EARL WILSON
Post Broadway Columnist

NEW YORK: Her next concert tour won't get under way for a while, so Joyce Renee, the talented Cincinnati violinist, is fiddling the time away on a typewriter.

She's writing a book she'll call "On the Way Up," a series of anecdotes collected since she came out of the Cincinnati Conservatory of Music at 17, the youngest honor graduate in the school's history.

One of her favorites is the story of how she met Georges Enesco, the famous French violin virtuoso, and became his student in Paris.

"I wanted so much to meet him," Joyce said, "but didn't know how to go about it. I thought if I wrote to him, someone else would see the letter first and into the waste basket it would go.

"One evening I went into a little restaurant near Carnegie Hall. There were some musicians talking at the next table," she continued.

"One of them asked, 'Where is Enesco stopping now?' Another musician answered, saying he was at a certain hotel here. The next morning," she said, "I phoned the hotel and spoke to Enesco himself and he agreed to hear me play.

"Eventually I went to Paris to be his pupil," she said. "I had to sell my fiddle to pay for the trip."

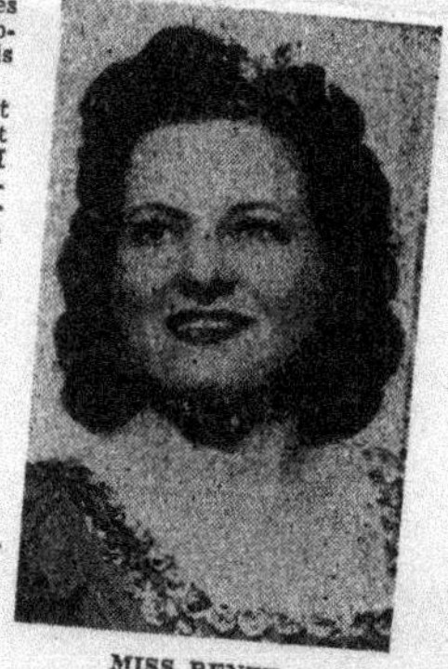

MISS RENEE

At nine she was playing violin solos on Dr. Frank Simon's Armco programs over WLW and the Blue network. Since that time she's appeared in some of the biggest concert halls here and in Europe.

In Cincinnati she has given many concerts in Taft Auditorium, the Cincinnati Woman's Club Auditorium, and South Hall, Xavier. She's appeared in New York at Carnegie Hall, Town Hall, and Radio City Music Hall, and at a Madison Square Garden benefit on the same stage with Mrs. Eleanor Roosevelt and Edward G. Robinson.

Part of Joyce's book will be devoted to her experiences at the Conservatory.

"There were about 50 other students waiting to play for the final examinations ahead of me," she told me. "I didn't want to sit indoors until my turn came, so I put my violin and music down on my seat and took a walk in Burnet Woods. It was such a beautiful day," she said.

"But the others got through faster than I thought they would. A searching student," she said, "found me and rushed me back to the examination hall.

"When I got there I found my violin but not my music," she said. "So I played without music."

Joyce collects violins as a hobby, and prizes a little silver Strad given to her by the late Mrs. John Withrow, wife of the man whose name was given to Withrow High School.

She's had plenty of troubles with violins. A string once snapped in the middle of a performance at Radio City. While she was playing on the radio program, "Music At Twilight," the fiddle came apart in her hands.

"There isn't much you can do standing there with your hands full of violin parts," she said. "I walked off."

"Before I'm through playing I suppose there'll be more to write about. That's why I'm planning two sequels," she said. "The next book I'll write will be 'On Top' and the second—'On the Way Down.'"

Broadway Column

By MARK BARRON

NEW YORK—From her name and from her voice, you would think that Joyce Renee is the most French Madamoiselle you could meet anywhere removed from the Champs Elyssees, or removed from Avenue D'Orleans or the Louvre.

It is true that she has a great deal of French background, but Mlle. Renee is truly American. She was the youngest honot graduate in the history of the Cincinnati Conservatory of Music. But, in Paris, she studied with Georges Enesco, one of the masters, and she also studied with such famous teachers as Kochanski, Arthur Hartmann, Rubin Goldmark and Dr. Edgar Stillman-Kelley.

Mlle. Renee has also been acclaimed for her violin solos in Carnegie Hall, Madison Square Garden, Radio City Music Hall and at West Point and Annapolis.

During the war she did what many other musical artists did. She gave up her professional career while she performed for soldiers and hospitalized veterans. For her shows she received citations from the Srage Door Canteen, the Merchant Marine, USO Camp Shows, the United States Theater Wing Hospital Committee and the Merchant Seaman's Club.

Mlle. Renee is an artist of the violin, but this Cincinnati girl uses her talent to benefit the underprivileged. In her native Cincinnati, for instance, the proceeds from her concerts are given to children who may not get all the nourishment they need.

Other than being a brilliant violinist, Miss Renee's talents have won her reknown as a musical composer. The first of her compositions happened at an early age, when she wa sa mere nine years old. At that time she was looking out the window at a snowfall and wrote a symphony called "Snowflakes", being a quiet interpretation of snow flakes falling gently to the ground. She was only nine years old at the time, but her sensitive mind reflected the feeling of this happenchance of nature and the one way she could express it was in gentle music.

Since then she has written many other songs, and improvises on her violin chords of musical numbers which are suggested, apparently, from her mind as a composer. Mlle. Renee is a gifted composer, an artist of rare skill and effervescent personality.

News reports regarding Joyce Renée.

OCTOBER 2, 1951

Violinist To Be Honored By Music Fraternity

New honors soon are to be accorded Cincinnati's noted violinist, Joyce Renee, it was learned Monday. The youngest honor graduate in history of the Cincinnati Conservatory of Music, who was hailed in Paris as "America's Violin Sensation," in 1949, has been selected as a patron of Phi Beta, honorary fraternity of music ad speech, it was announced Monday.

Last year Miss Renee, a graduate of Hughes High School, was honored with membership in Zonta International and organization of top professional, executive and business women throughout the world.

Since graduation Miss Renee has received acclaim in the major conctrt halls in the United States and abroad.

October 2, 1951, press report of honor given to Joyce by the Phi Beta Honorary Music fraternity.

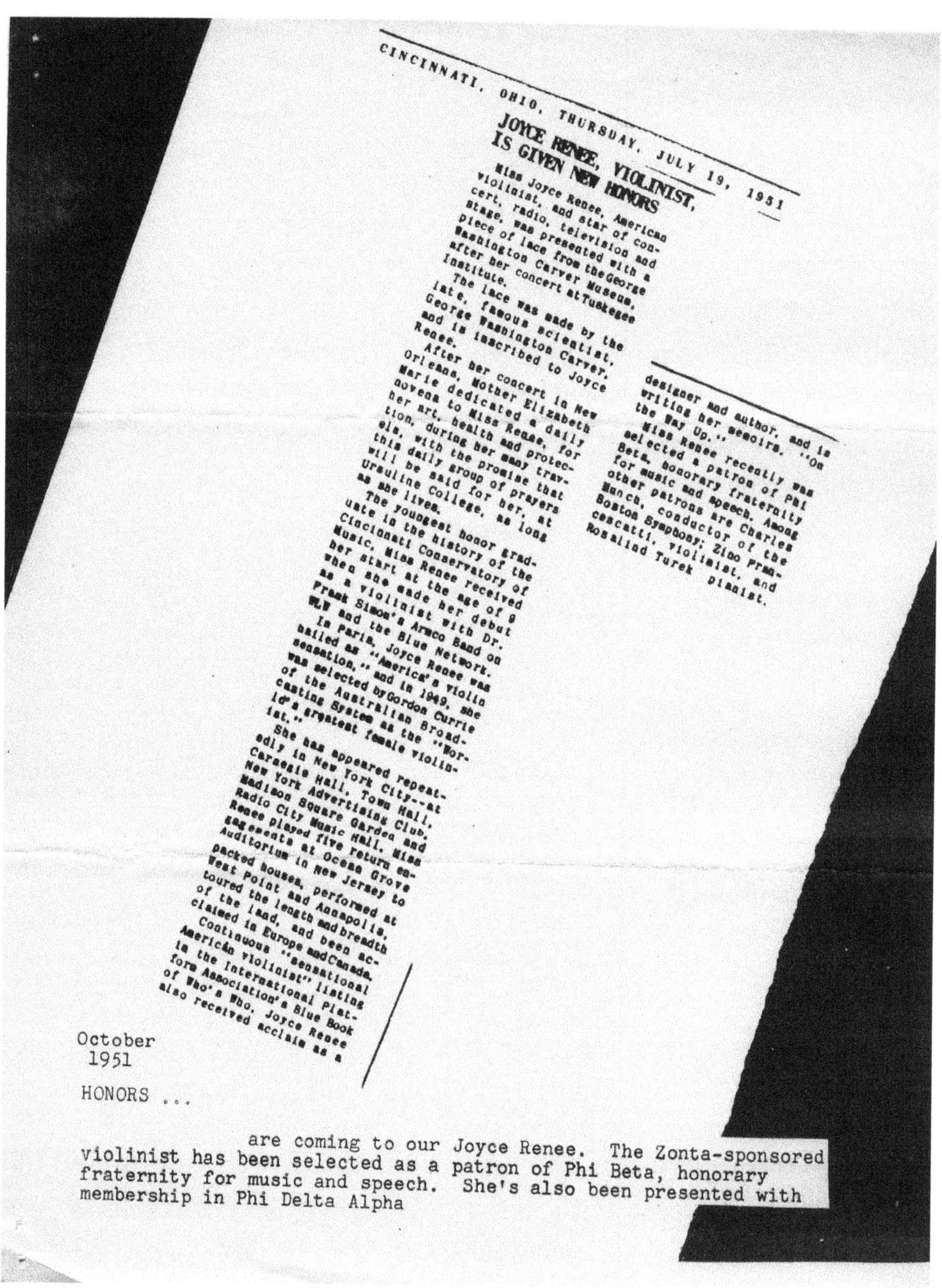

CINCINNATI, OHIO, THURSDAY, JULY 19, 1951

JOYCE RENEE, VIOLINIST, IS GIVEN NEW HONORS

Miss Joyce Renee, American violinist, and star of concert, radio, television and stage, was presented with a piece of lace from the George Washington Carver Museum, after her concert at Tuskegee Institute.

The lace was made by the late, famous scientist, George Washington Carver, and is inscribed to Joyce Renee.

After her concert in New Orleans, Mother Elizabeth Marie dedicated a daily novena to Miss Renee, for her art, health and protection, during her many travels, with the promise that this daily group of prayers will be said for her, at Ursuline College, as long as she lives.

The youngest honor graduate in the history of the Cincinnati Conservatory of Music, Miss Renee received her start at the age of 9 when she made her debut as a violinist with Dr. Frank Simon's Armco Band on WLW and the Blue Network.

In Paris, Joyce Renee was hailed as "America's violin sensation," and in 1949, she was selected by Gordon Currie of the Australian Broadcasting System as the "world's greatest female violinist."

She has appeared repeatedly in New York City--at Carnegie Hall, Town Hall, New York Advertising Club, Madison Square Garden and Radio City Music Hall. Miss Renee played five return engagements at Ocean Grove Auditorium in New Jersey to packed houses, performed at West Point and Annapolis, toured the length and breadth of the land, and been acclaimed in Europe and Canada.

Continuous "sensational American violinist" listing in the International Platform Association's Blue Book of Who's Who. Joyce Renee also received acclaim as a designer and author, and is writing her memoirs, "On the Way Up."

Miss Renee recently was selected a patron of Phi Beta, honorary fraternity for music and speech. Among other patrons are Charles Munch, conductor of the Boston Symphony; Zino Francescatti, violinist, and Rosalind Turek, pianist.

October 1951

HONORS ...

are coming to our Joyce Renee. The Zonta-sponsored violinist has been selected as a patron of Phi Beta, honorary fraternity for music and speech. She's also been presented with membership in Phi Delta Alpha

News reports regarding Joyce Renée.

College of New Rochelle

and

The Ursuline Guild

Present

JOYCE RENEE

hailed as

"America's Violin Sensation"

SUNDAY, OCTOBER 7th, — 8:15 P. M.

CHIDWICK HALL — Castle and West Castle Places

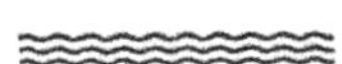

From the first, Joyce Renee's career has been phenomenal. The youngest honor graduate in the history of the Cincinnati Conservatory of Music and a former Paris Artist Student of Georges Enesco, Miss Renee has also won several National and International Fellowships including the Fleischmann, Schmidlapp, Julliard and Woolley International Fellowships, plus an Institute Instrumental award in Paris.

Soloist with symphony orchestras in the United States, Canada and Europe, Miss Renee interrupted her career during the war to perform for the Armed Forces. She received Honor Bar Emblems and citations from the Stage Door Canteen, the Merchant Marine, U.S.O. Camp Shows, the United Theatre Wing Hospital Committee and the Merchant Seamen's Club.

Enormously gifted, the brilliant young American violinist, Joyce Renee, has stirred rare critical acclaim and won the plaudits of music lovers all over the world. She has frequently appeared at Carnegie Hall, Town Hall, Madison Square Garden and was held over 8 weeks at Radio City Music Hall.

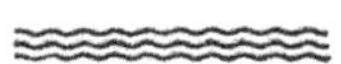

Program for Joyce's concert sponsored by the College of New Rochelle and The Ursuline Guild.

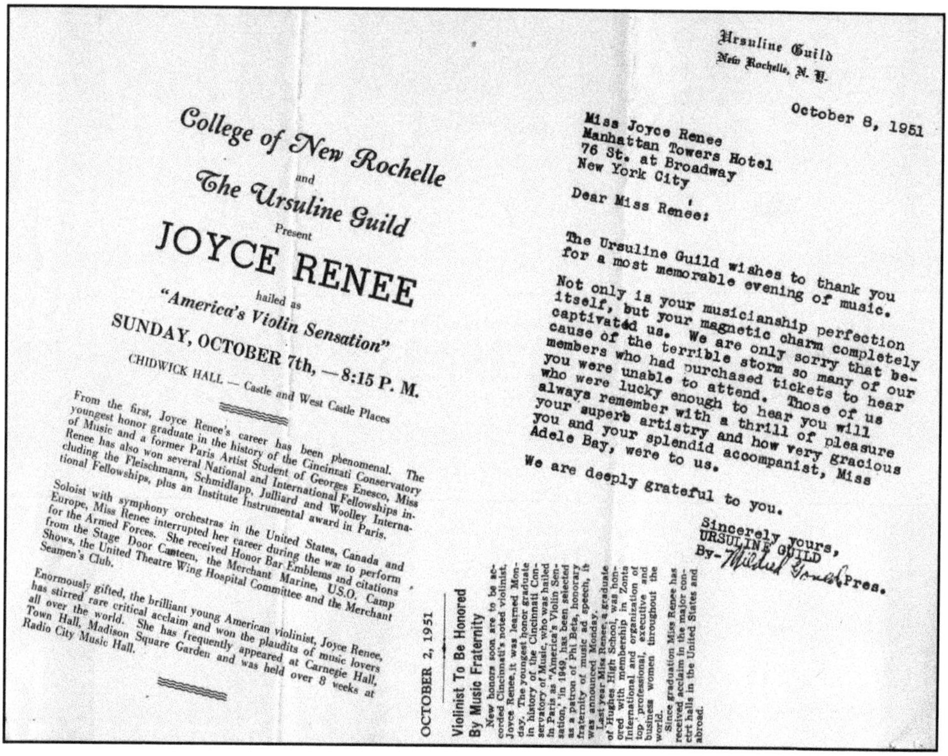

College of New Rochelle
and
The Ursuline Guild
Present

JOYCE RENEE

hailed as
"America's Violin Sensation"

SUNDAY, OCTOBER 7th, — 8:15 P. M.

CHIDWICK HALL — Castle and West Castle Places

From the first, Joyce Renee's career has been phenomenal. The youngest honor graduate in the history of the Cincinnati Conservatory of Music and a former Paris Artist Student of Georges Enesco, Miss Renee has also won several National and International Fellowships including the Fleischmann, Schmidlapp, Julliard and Woolley International Fellowships, plus an Institute Instrumental award in Paris.

Soloist with symphony orchestras in the United States, Canada and Europe, Miss Renee interrupted her career during the war to perform for the Armed Forces. She received Honor Bar Emblems and citations from the Stage Door Canteen, the Merchant Marine, U.S.O. Camp Shows, the United Theatre Wing Hospital Committee and the Merchant Seamen's Club.

Enormously gifted, the brilliant young American violinist, Joyce Renee, has stirred rare critical acclaim and won the plaudits of music lovers all over the world. She has frequently appeared at Carnegie Hall, Town Hall, Madison Square Garden and was held over 8 weeks at Radio City Music Hall.

Ursuline Guild
New Rochelle, N. Y.

October 8, 1951

Miss Joyce Renee
Manhattan Towers Hotel
76 St. at Broadway
New York City

Dear Miss Renee:

The Ursuline Guild wishes to thank you for a most memorable evening of music.

Not only is your musicianship perfection itself, but your magnetic charm completely captivated us. We are only sorry that because of the terrible storm so many of our members who had purchased tickets to hear you were unable to attend. Those of us who were lucky enough to hear you will always remember with a thrill of pleasure your superb artistry and how very gracious you and your splendid accompanist, Miss Adele Bay, were to us.

We are deeply grateful to you.

Sincerely yours,
URSULINE GUILD
By- [signature] Pres.

OCTOBER 2, 1951

Violinist To Be Honored By Music Fraternity

New honors soon are to be accorded Cincinnati's noted violinist, Joyce Renee, it was learned Monday. The youngest honor graduate in history of the Cincinnati Conservatory of Music, who was hailed in Paris as "America's Violin Sensation," in 1949, has been selected as a patron of Phi Beta, honorary fraternity of music ad speech, it was announced Monday.

Last year Miss Renee, a graduate of Hughes High School, was honored with membership in Zonta International and organization of top professional, executive and business women throughout the world.

Since graduation Miss Renee has received acclaim in the major concert halls in the United States and abroad.

News reports regarding Joyce Renée.

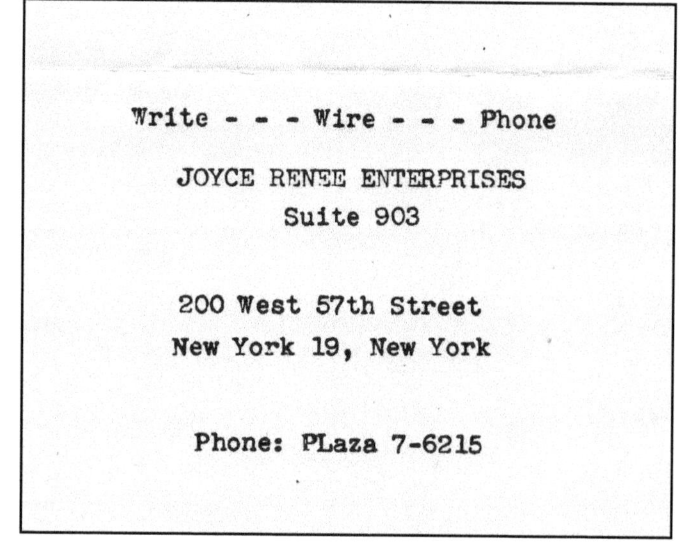

Write - - - Wire - - - Phone

JOYCE RENEE ENTERPRISES
Suite 903

200 West 57th Street
New York 19, New York

Phone: PLaza 7-6215

Joyce Renée Enterprises

Ursuline Guild
New Rochelle, N. Y.

October 8, 1951

Miss Joyce Renee
Manhattan Towers Hotel
76 St. at Broadway
New York City

Dear Miss Renee:

The Ursuline Guild wishes to thank you for a most memorable evening of music.

Not only is your musicianship perfection itself, but your magnetic charm completely captivated us. We are only sorry that because of the terrible storm so many of our members who had purchased tickets to hear you were unable to attend. Those of us who were lucky enough to hear you will always remember with a thrill of pleasure your superb artistry and how very gracious you and your splendid accompanist, Miss Adele Bay, were to us.

We are deeply grateful to you.

Sincerely yours,
URSULINE GUILD
By- Mildred Gould, Pres.

October 8, 1951, thank you note to Joyce from Mildred Gould, President of The Ursuline Guild.

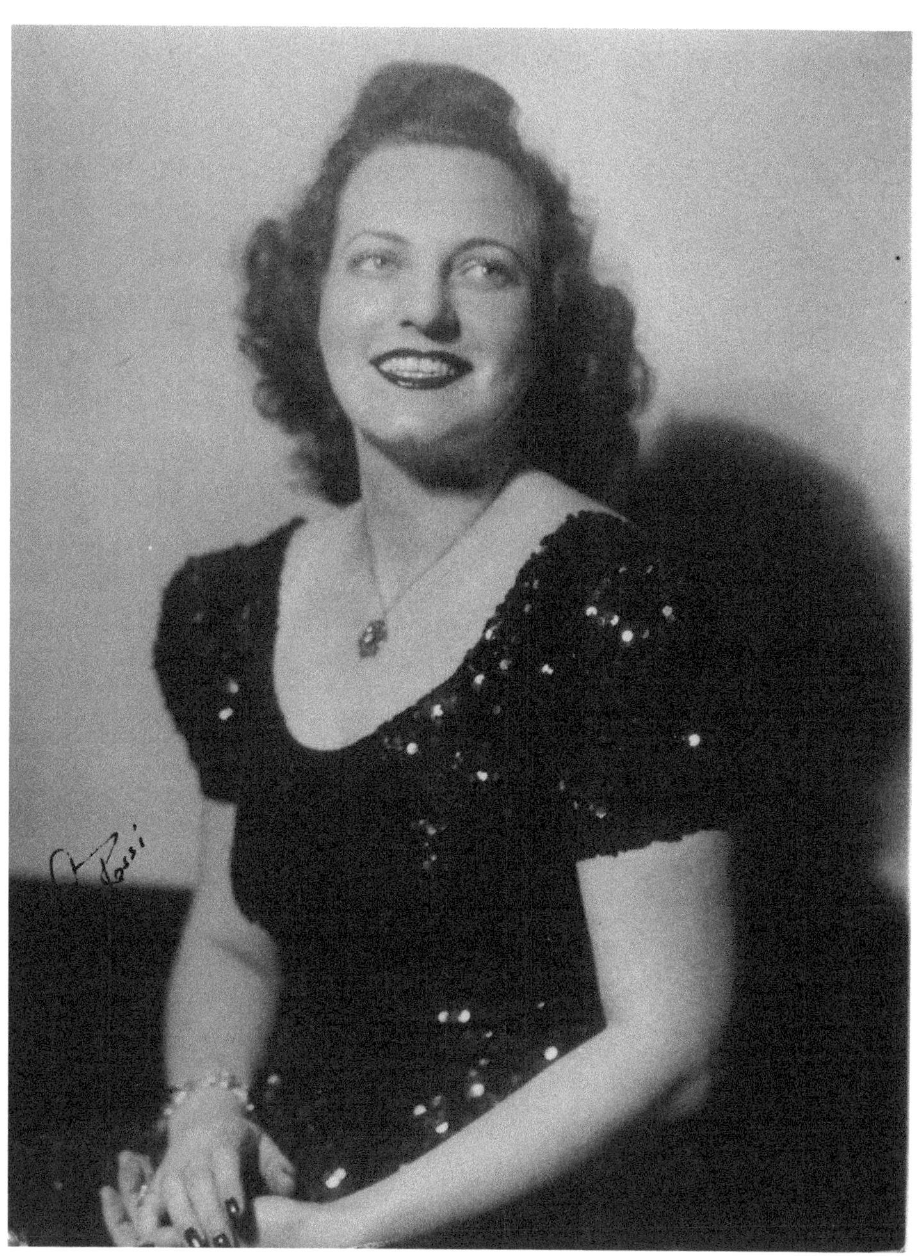

Publicity photo.

JOYCE RENÉE

Hailed as------
"AMERICA'S VIOLIN SENSATION"
(PARIS, FRANCE)

Selected as------
"WORLD'S GREATEST FEMALE VIOLINIST"
(Gordon Currie, of The Australian Broadcasting Commission)
March, 1949
"Joyce Renée's Fame should travel to the Four Corners of the World"
(Georges Enesco, New York City, March 1950)

A FEW NOTABLE ENGAGEMENTS ACROSS THE NATION

Carnegie Hall (2)
Town Hall, New York City (2)
Madison Square Garden, New York City (5)
Radio City Music Hall, New York City (held over 8 weeks, featured with orchestra)
("Great Hit" Leonidoff, producer)
Advertising Club of New York (5)
("Great and Thrilling Artist", Joe Paley, Chairman, January 1950)
Professional and Business Women's Club of The Riverside Church, New York City
(Great beyond words---to Riverside B's and P's, Joyce Renée, is The First Lady of The Violin", Mae Rau, Chairman)
Columbia University
Easter Festival for the Greater Federation of New York Churches
Ohio Society of New York (4)
Advertising Women's Club of New York
("Loved By All---that quality called Charm", Ad Libber, N. Y. C.)
Town Hall Club, New York City (2)
Women's Engineering Club of New York (2)
Mu Phi Epsilon (2)
United States Senator's Banquet, N. Y. C.
Men's and Women's Clubs of Temple Emanuel, N. Y. C. (3)
Phi Delta Gamma Convention
Bi-Centennial Concert for Shrewsbury Presbyterian Church, N. J.
(200th Anniversary)
Utah Club, N. Y. C.
Concert at Scottish Rite Cathedral, Newark, N. J.
Benefit Concert---Montclair Elk's Lodge, N. J.
Knights Of Templar, Montclair, N. J.
Cosmopolitan Club of Montclair, N. J.
Famed Ocean Grove Auditorium, New Jersey (5)
Wells College
State Teachers College, Bloomsburg, Pa. (5)
Mosque Auditorium, Harrisburg, Pa. (4)
Lewisburg College, Pa.
State Teachers College, Farmville, Va.

Joyce Renée multi-page career summary (page 1 of 5).

- 2 -

Ruskin Hall, Bronxville, New York
Center Theatre, Norfolk, Va.
Theatre and Arts Course, Hampton, Va.
Music Club, Louisville, Ky.
Kiwanis, Atlanta, Georgia
Library Concert Series, Stamford, Conn.
Theatre, Wooster, Mass.
Church Concert Series, Meridan, Conn.
Theatre, Danbury, Conn.
Mosque Auditorium, Altoona, Pa. (2)
West Point Military Academy
Auditorium, Great Neck, Long Island
Hayne's Town Hall Series in Clinton, Wadesboro, and Cramerton, N. C.
("Never have I seen audiences so completely spellbound", Evelyn Haynes, Manager)
Teachers College, Fayetteville, N. C.
Atlantic Christian College, Wilson, N. C.
University, Durham, N. C.
Pembroke College, N. C. (4)
Mana-Zucca Club, Miami, Fla.
Series, Dover, & Lisbon, Ohio
Radford College, Va.
Xavier University
Jones Auditorium, Xenia, Ohio
East Central Junior College, Decatur, Miss.
Auditorium, Tougaloo, Miss. (4)
University of Cincinnati
Hebrew Union College, Cincinnati, Ohio
Memorial Hall, Dayton, Ohio
Casino, Saratoga Springs, New York
Armco Summer Concerts, Middletown, Ohio (3)
Auditorium, Richmond, Indiana
Cleveland Heights Auditorium, Cleveland, Ohio
D. A. R. Convention
University, Houston, Texas
Mount Auburn Music Club, Cincinnati, Ohio
Cincinnati Woman's Club
University of Minnesota
Capitol University
Bob Jones College
Ursuline College of New Orleans (2)
Municipal Auditorium, Zanesville, Ohio
Annapolis Naval Academy
Dickinson College, Carlisle, Pa.
Buckhills Auditorium, Buckhills Falls, Pa.
Tuskeege Institute, Tuskeege, Ala.
Auditorium, Norfolk, Va.
Auditorium, Hotel, Hot Springs, Va.
Auditorium, Hotel, Richmond, Va.
High School Auditorium, Montclair, N. J.
High School Auditorium, Babylon, L. I.
Jackson Heights Music Club, Jackson Heights, L. I.
Auditorium, Riverside Church, N. Y. C.
Auditorium, Temple Emanuel, N. Y. C.
Stage Door Canteen, N. Y. C.

Joyce Renée multi-page career summary (page 2 of 5).

Taft Auditorium, Cincinnati, Ohio (Sponsored by Zonta Int'l., April, 1950 - The net proceeds from Miss Renée's concert will enable 34 underpriviledged children to have a healthful breakfast for an entire school year.)

The following is part of a letter to Miss Renée's managers, after the concert--"Her charming and unassuming manner endeared her to her audience at the very beginning--we nearly burst with pride at the reception and appreciation of her glorious talent--it is with grateful hearts that we ask you to accept our sincere appreciation for the Joyce Renée concert which was given at Taft Auditorium, April 2, by arrangement with you."

Zonta Club of Cincinnati
Louise Brooks, President.

Miss Renée, was featured soloist on tour with Dr. Frank Simon and his Famous Band ("Great," Dr. Frank Simon, Conductor)

Featured soloist on two tours with Joseph Cherniavsky and his orchestra (Joyce Renee always brings down the house," Joseph Cherniavsky, conductor)

Featured artist on coast to coast tours of Camps, Hospitals, Service and Officers Clubs, installations as well as aboard ships, Destroyers and Transports, and Canteens, for the Armed Forces, and she was selected by the U. S. Government to perform for returning Pacific Veterans, in Seattle, and San Francisco. Miss Renée also performed innumerable times for outgoing and returning veterans in and around the New York and New Jersey areas, at embarkation points, as well as installations and hospitals. With Lanny Ross, Miss Renée gave the first program at the Tilton General Hospital for the first returned wounded veterans from North Africa. A popular favorite of service men and women, she made innumerable appearances at the Stage Door and Merchant Marine Canteens and at The Merchant Seaman's Club in New York City.

Her frequent appearances to raise funds for worthy causes includes performances for The Allied Relief organizations, and Broadcasts for The Community Chest and The Red Cross and others.

RADIO ACTIVITIES

"Starred" over three major networks------------Miss Renée was featured on such programs as:

"American Rolling Mills" Programs (soloist with band)
"Chance of a Lifetime" Programs (soloist with orchestra)
U. S. Treasury Broadcasts (Band Rallys)
"Music at Twilight"
"Works of The Masters" (soloist with orchestra)
"American Music Festival" Series
"American Federation of Music Clubs" Programs
"Homefront Favorites" (soloist with band)
"Stromberg Carlson Orchestra Broadcasts" (Soloist with orchestra)
"Red Cross" Program
"Jergens" Program
"Treasury of Music" Series (soloist with orchestra)
"Celebrity Time"

Joyce Renée multi-page career summary (page 3 of 5).

Community Chest Broadcasts
"Norfolk Virginia Symphony Orchestra Concert Broadcast" (featured soloist)
"Federation of Churches" Program
"Golden Rule Mother's Hour" (soloist with orchestra)
"Barbara Lee Show"
"Latin Rythms" (soloist with orchestra)
"Annapolis Naval Academy Band Concert Broadcast" (featured soloist)
"West Point Military Band Concert Broadcast" (featured soloist)
And on several other programs, as well as Television Shows in the beginnings of Television.

HONORS

Youngest honor graduate in the history of the Cincinnati Conservatory of music, where she received a collegiate Honor Diploma, and a Bachelor of Music Degree. Held Juilliard Graduate School Fellowship, Schmidlapp and Fleischmann Scholarships, and was awarded the Woolley International Fellowship for study in Paris, as well as numerous other Scholarships including Scholarships with the late Georges Enesco in Paris, and in the United States. Selected to appear at the World's Fair for Ohio Day, and to perform the Kol Nidre for High Holyday Service conducted by the late Dr. Stephen Wise at Carnegie Hall, in New York City. A recording club is named for Miss Renée, at Pembroke, the all Indian College in North Carolina, and Tuskeege Institute presented her with a piece of Lace made by the late George Washington Carver. At Ursuline College in New Orleans, a daily novena was dedicated to Miss Renée, for her health, her art and her safety during her many travels. Many musical compositions have been dedicated to her and she has given world premiers of a number of musical selections.

In 1950, she was presented with the key to her home town, Cincinnati. Among her honored appearances were her performances at West Point and Annapolis, and the D. A. R. Convention. Miss Renée is listed in a number of Who's Who, and for many years was listed as "Sensational American Violinist" in Who's Who of The American Platform Association "Talent" publication.

HONORS AND AFFILIATIONS

HONORARY MEMBER OF PHI DELTA GAMMA, COLUMBIA UNIVERSITY ALUMNI CHAPTER, N.Y.C.
Honorary Life Member of Phi Delta Alpha
Member of Zonta International
Member of Three Arts Club + THREE ARTS SCHOLARSHIP FUND
Member of Studio Club
Member of International Platform Association
Member of American Musicological Society
Member of Phi Beta in New York City
Patroness of Phi Beta in Cincinnati
Member of Juilliard Alumni Association
Member of Cincinnati Conservatory Alumni Association
PATRON MU PHI EPSILON
PROFFESSIONAL MEMBER NATIONAL ASSOCIATION FOR COMPOSERS AND CONDUCTORS.
MEMBER OF PARNASSUS CLUB, N.Y.C.
MEMBER OF AMERICAN GUILD OF CONCERT ARTISTS, NYC
MEMBER OF GARDEN CLUB, CIN., O.

Joyce Renée multi-page career summary (page 4 of 5).

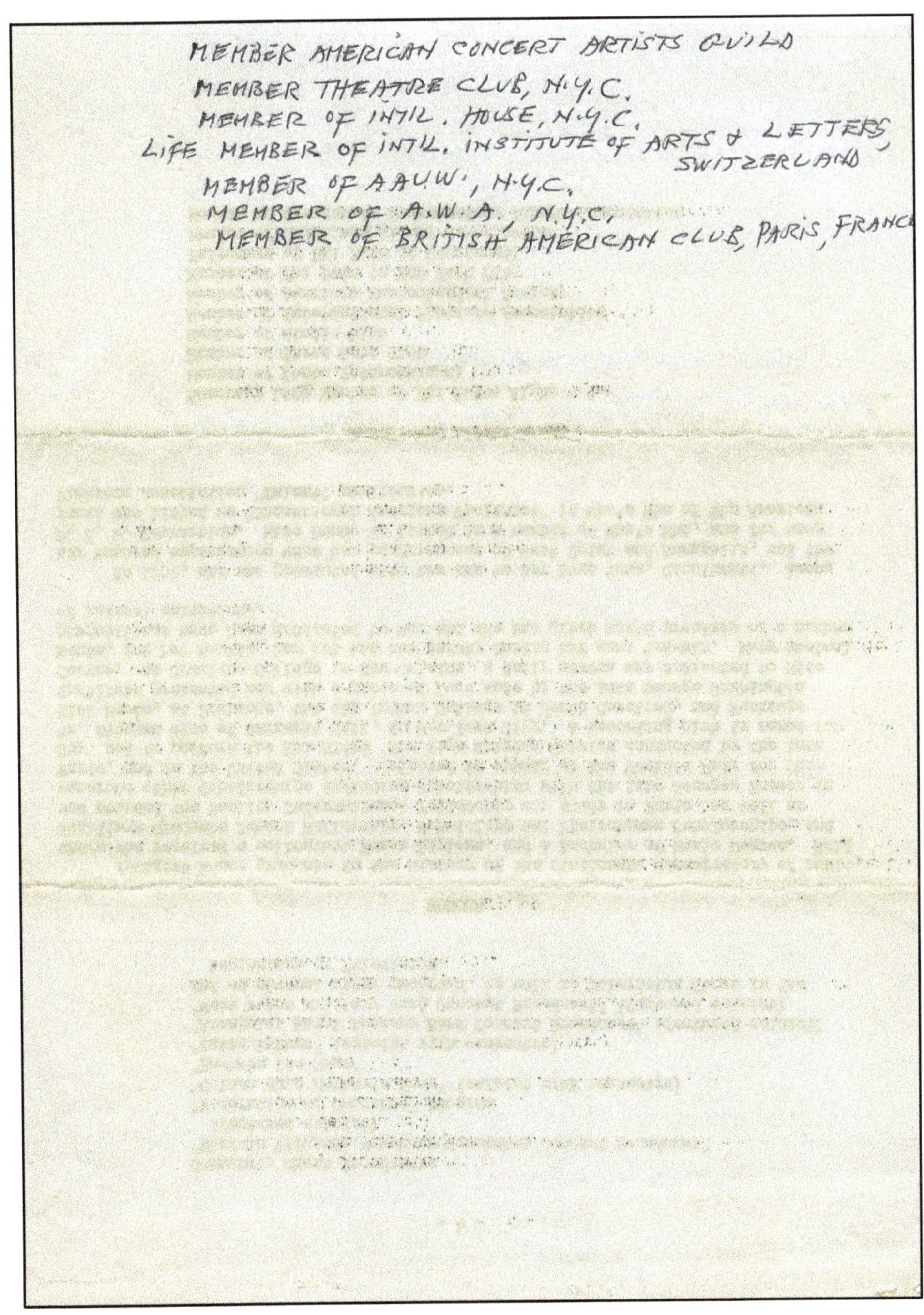

MEMBER AMERICAN CONCERT ARTISTS GUILD
MEMBER THEATRE CLUB, N.Y.C.
MEMBER OF INT'L. HOUSE, N.Y.C.
LIFE MEMBER OF INT'L. INSTITUTE OF ARTS & LETTERS, SWITZERLAND
MEMBER OF A.A.U.W., N.Y.C.
MEMBER OF A.W.A., N.Y.C.
MEMBER OF BRITISH AMERICAN CLUB, PARIS, FRANCE

Joyce Renée multi-page career summary (page 5 of 5).

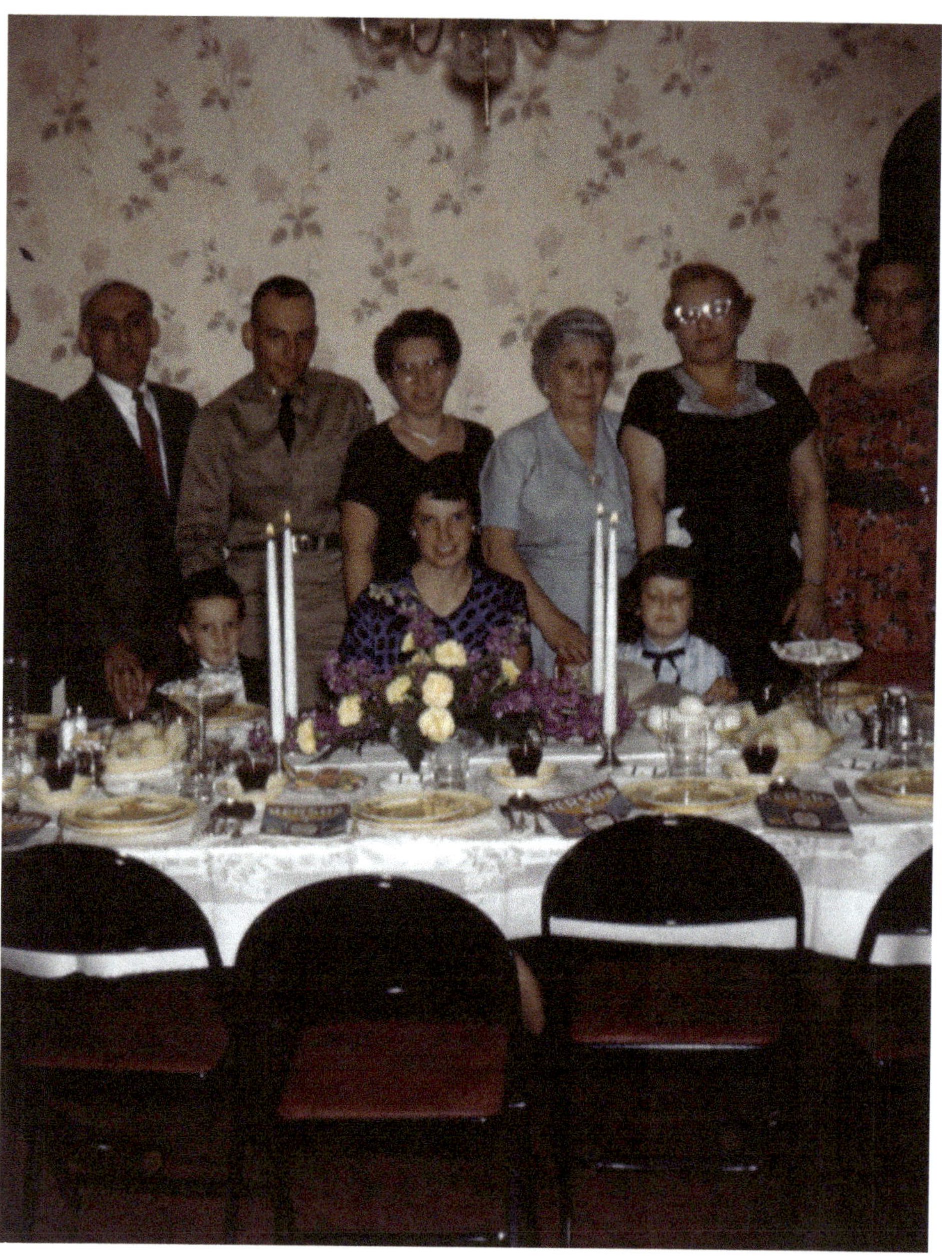

1959 Seder at Anna Wasserman home. Standing L-R: Mark, Joe and Sandy Cohen, Trudy Houser, Anna Wasserman, Hilda Cohen, Joyce; Seated: Steve (the author), Renate, and Marjorie Wasserman.

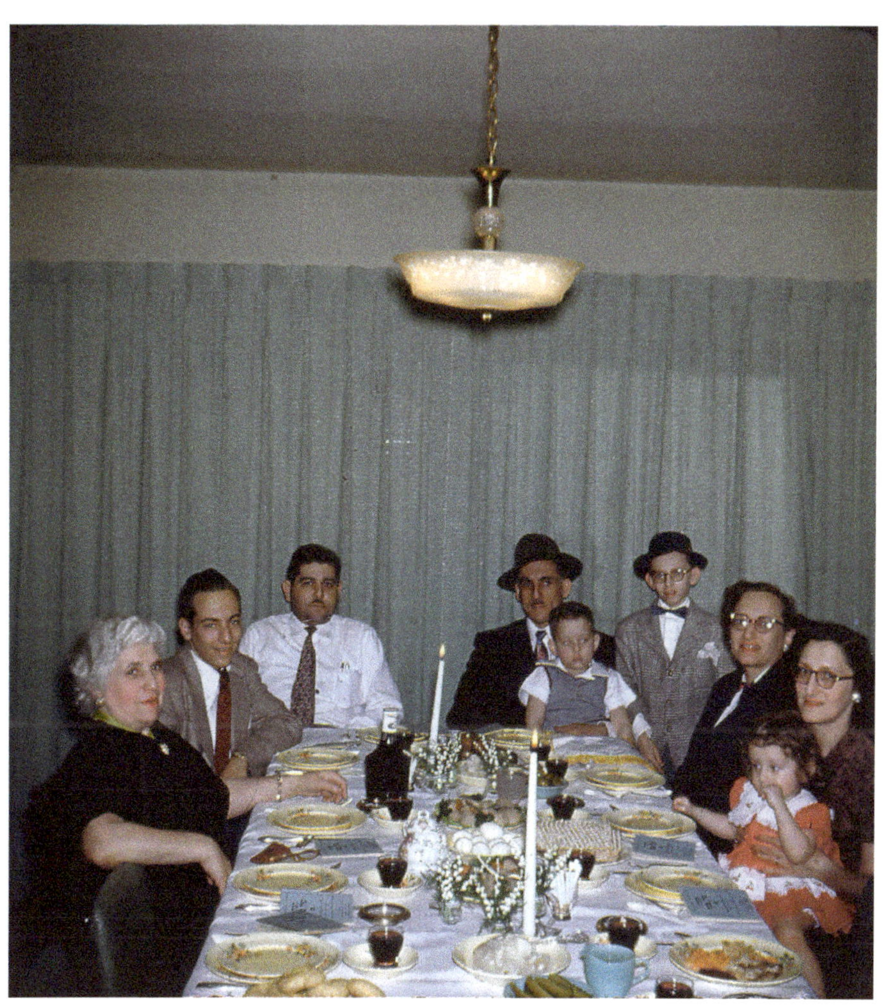

1956 Seder at Anna "Granny" Wasserman's home.

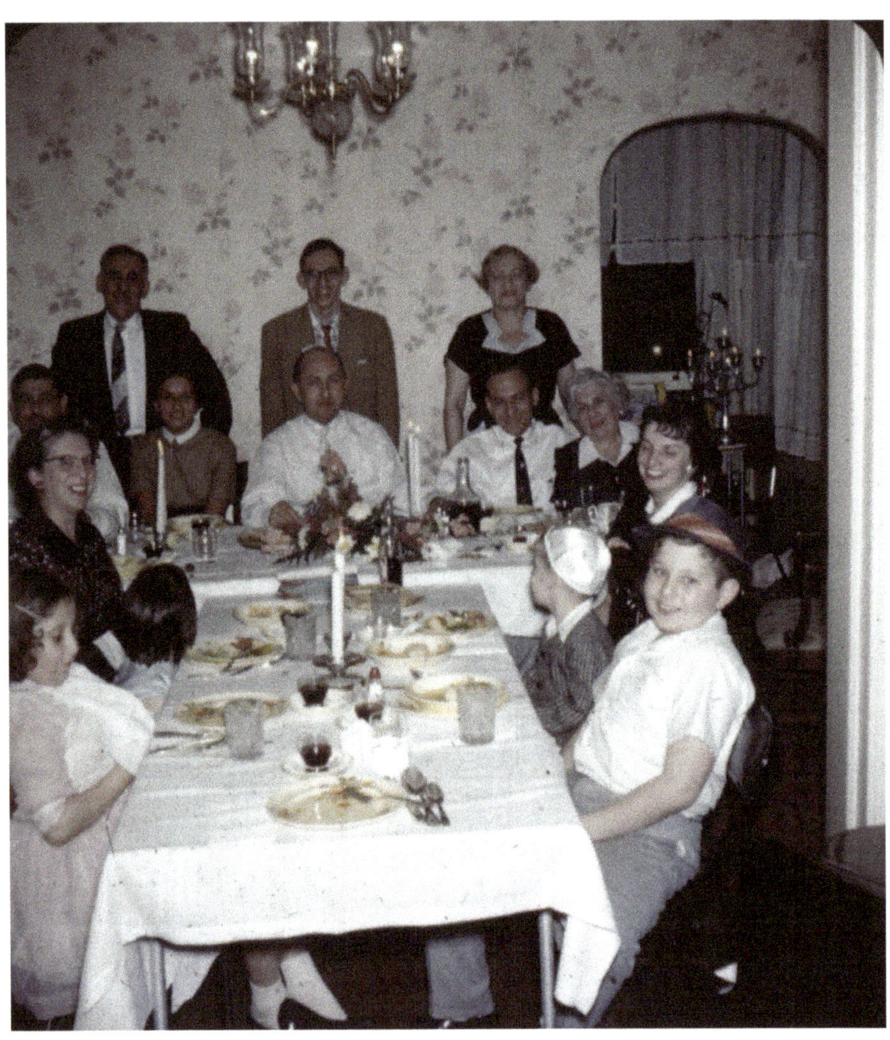

1958 Seder. Standing: Joe Cohen, Mark Cohen, and Hilda Cohen; L-R clockwise: Cookie Aronoff, Margie Wasserman, Trudy Houser, Nate Aronoff, Rocky Wasserman, Jay Wasserman, Sandy Cohen, Anna Wasserman, Renate Wasserman, Steve Wasserman (looking away from the camera) and Michael Aronoff.

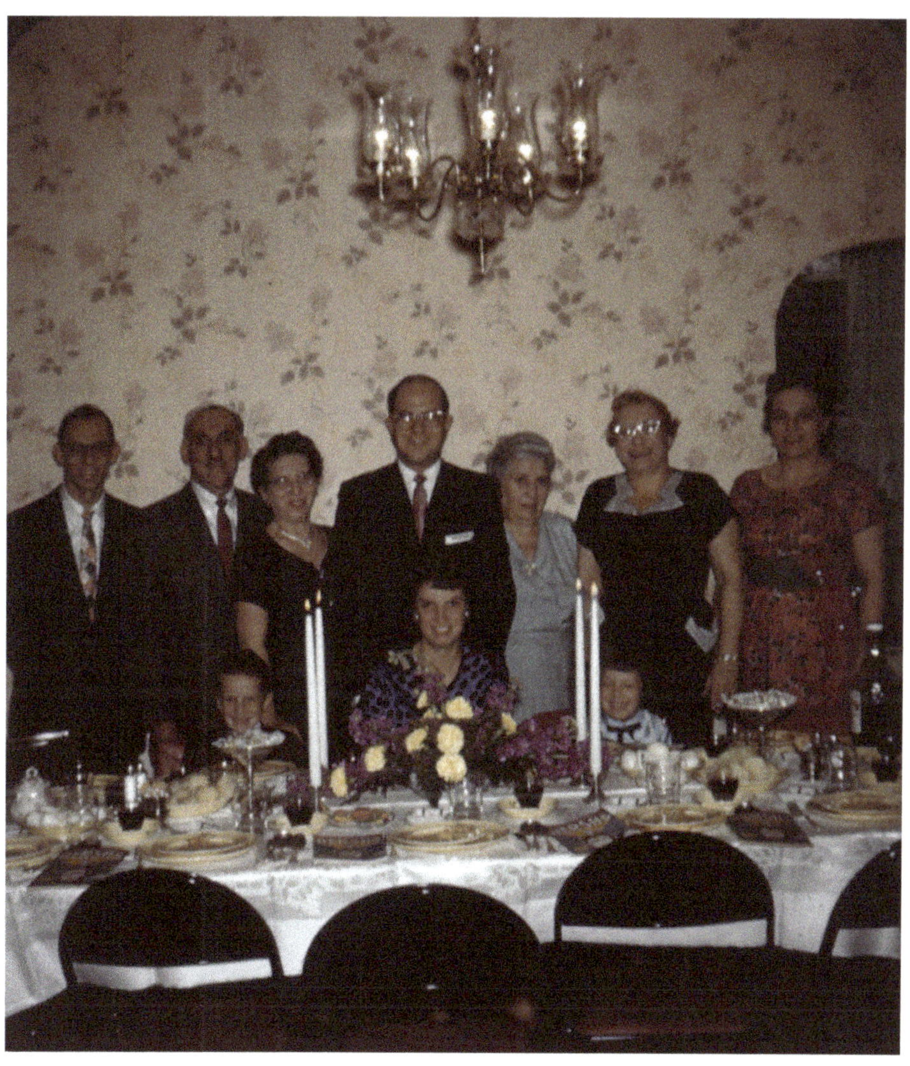

1959 Seder. L-R: Mark and Joe Cohen, Trudy Houser, Allan Wasserman, Anna Wasserman, Hilda Cohen, Joyce; Seated: Steven, Renate, and Margie Wasserman.

JOYCE RENÉE

Supreme talent, and a winning personality, are only two of the many enviable assets of the noted American violinist, Cincinnati born Joyce Renée, who at the age of seventeen, had the musicianship and experience of a seasoned veteran.

A former Paris Artist Student of Georges Enesco, her world famous teachers also included, Kochanski, Arthur Hartmann, Rubin Goldmark, and Dr. Edgar Stillman-Kelley.

The holder of both National and International awards, including the Julliard Graduate School, Schmidlapp, Fleischmann, and Woolley International scholarships, Miss Renée also has the distincion of being the youngest artist ever to have achieved the highest honor diploma in violin, and a Bachelor of Music Degree, from the Cincinnati Conservatory of Music.

Additional honors bestowed on her are a medal presented by the late Wendell Willkie, two medals from the Ohio Society of New York, an Ohio Federation of Music Clubs prize, the Margaret Walters Town Hall award, honor bar emblems from the Stage Door Canteen and Merchant Seaman's Club, as well as citations from the Merchant Marines, U.S.O Camp Shows, and the United Theatrical Wing Hospital Committee.

At the World's Fair, in New York, Miss Renée was chosen to appear for Ohio Day, and the American Music Festival. She was soloist on the occasion of the first personal concert tour of Dr. Frank Simon and his famous Armco Radio Band - and appeared on two tours as soloist with the Conductor, Joseph Cherniavsky, and his orchestra.

Joyce Renée, Draft Biography (page 1 of 6).

-2-

For the past five years Joyce Renée has been re-elected to honorary membership in the International Lyceum Association, for the highest artistic integrity. Among other tributes, are the naming in her honor, of a Recording Club at Pembroke State College, and request performances at West Point, and Annopolis. She was invited to be the guest artist for the Daughters of the American Revolution, at their National Convention and honored by the Phi Delta Gamma, honorary sorority. SHE IS A FOUNDER MEMBER OF THE MUSICIANS CLUB OF AMERICA.

Joyce Renée was chosen by Dr. Stephen Wise to be the first Young woman to perform the Kol Nidrei, for the High Holy Days, at Carnegie Hall. She was chosen also to appear on the Golden Rule Mother's program with Dr. Fosdick, and presented with a medal by Dr. Ralph Sockman, past president of the Ohio Society of New York. At Ursuline College, Sister Elizabeth Marie, says a daily Novena for Miss Renée's Art. After her scheduled concert, at Ursuline, Joyce Renée gave a special program for the Cloistered Nuns, and it was after that, that Sister Elizabeth Marie dedicated the daily Novena to Miss Renée.

Joyce Renée was a great admirer, and friend of the late Pietro Yon, organist of St. Patrick's Cathedral in New York. Pietro Yon invited her to sit with him in the organ loft while he played for the funeral service of the late Paderewski, a lingering and touching tribute to a great artist, which will live long in her memory, and the memory of all those who were privileged to attend. Vierne, the organist of Notre Dame Cathedral, in Paris, gave Joyce Renée his sonata, which she has performed. Many outstanding contemporary compositions have been dedicated to her, and she has given first performances of works by Kubelik, English, Seismit-Dodo, Haufreucht, Gaines, Chernavisky, Sherman, Beautee and others. In all her concerts, she uses a special kind of mute, made for her by a friend, of a substance that looks like glass, and which gives to the soft violin tones a heavenly kind of purity.

Joyce Renée, Draft Biography (page 2 of 6).

-3-

For a goung artist, Miss Renée has covered a lot of territory. She has been heard at Carnegie Hall, Madison Square Garden, Town Hall, and Radio City Music Hall, in New York City, at the great auditorium in Ocean Grove, New Jersey; at West Point and Annapolis, at Colleges, Universities, Concert Halls and as soloist with Symphony orchestras throughout the United States.

During the entire history of Radio City Music Hall, in New York, only a few violinists have been featured. Last year, Joyce Renée was chosen to appear at Radio City Music Hall for an extensive engagement. While there, she performed before a million and a half people.

During the war, when she forgot about her career to entertain the men and women in uniform, Joyce Renée travelled thousands of miles, appearing at hundreds of Camps, Canteens, Hospitals, Convalescent Centers, Service and Officers Clubs, and greeting returning Pacific and E.T. O. veterans. Joyce Renée and Lanny Ross gave the program for the first returned wounded veterans to the United States, and their signatures were written, by request, on the walls of the hospital auditorium of Fort Dix. A popular favorite of the Armed Forces, Joyce Renée worked untireingly. Mrs. Brock Pemberton, wife of the producer, wrote,"To Joyce, with love and thanks - the boys all love you, that you know." Herb Symmons, war correspondent, called her "Bombshell on the Fiddle."

Returning to her concert career, Joyce Renée found bigger and more audiences, and those who hadn't forgotten. Internationally acclaimed, Joyce Renée has toured the length and the breadth of the United States, and has been enthusiastically received in her appearances in Canada and Europe as well.

Joyce Renée, Draft Biography (page 3 of 6).

-4-

In addition, she has appeared repeatedly over the major radio networks, playing as soloist on such programs as "Music at Twilight," "Works of the Masters," "American Festival Series," American Federation of Music Clubs program," "Community Chests Drive," "American Rolling Mills Program" "The Red Cross Series," "Homefront Favorites,", "The Stromberg Carlson Commercials," "Joe Cherniavsky's Orchestra, the Barbara Lee Show, and on several television shows.

When Joyce Renée was just a little girl, Dr. Frank Simon gave her, her first big radio chance. It was at Crosely, in Cincinnati, on New Year's Eve, and she played the "Faust Fantasie" of Sarasate, and the "En Bateau" of Debussy - a chubby curly haired, bright eyed little girl who wanted to have her uncle in Mississippi hear her play the violin. It was an exciting experience - everyone at home was listening, too, and it was her first important appearance, and her radio debut. The success of the evening turned into a lasting friendship with Dr. Simon, and many appearances with him, since then.

In New York, Columbia gave Joyce Renée her first radio break on the Golden Rule Mother's Hour, which featured that grand old lady of song (in her last broadcast), the late Madame Ernestine Schumann-Heink, and Dr. Emerson Fosdick and the Studio Orchestra. From Dr. Vickery, president of the Golden Rule Mother's hour, came a letter saying - "Wish you could see the fan mail across my desk. There are 1018 letters commenting about how much they particularly enjoyed the violin solos." Since then, Joyce Renée has been starred repeatedly over the major Radio networks.

Joyce Renée, Draft Biography (page 4 of 6).

In her climb to prpminence, this gifted artist has played before all kinds of audiences from the Bowery Mission to Carnegie Hall, and has performed every kind of music from the St. Louis Blues to the Brahams violin Concerto. During her studies at the Julliard Graduate School, she earned her way, by doing an early - morning stint over a "milkman's program", on a local radio station.

All violinists cherish the tonal beauty of fine insturments, and Joyce Renée is no exception. She has had the privilege of playing on most of the world's greatest violins, including the fabulous Henry Ford collection, at Dearborn, Michigan, the rare Wurlitzer collection which she demonstrated at the Music Merchandiser's Convention in New York, and some of the great violins from the Hermann Collection, ~~where she played~~ AS WELL AS the famous Aranyi Stradivarius, earliest Strad in existance, the Auer Strad, played by Auer during his lifetime and the Enesco Guernarius.

Miss Renée has received highly favorable criticism from critics everywhere. But the tribute she values most of all was that paid her by Composer-Conductor - Violinist, Georges Enesco, with whom she studied in Paris. Enesco said of her playing, "Her art is of the highest order and her knowledge of the instrument perfect. She has personality and great Fire. The successes she has reaped are the most highly merited, and she deserves a distinguished solo career."

Another tribute typical among the many favorable notices she has received is one that appeared in the Cincinnati Enquirer, "Joyce Renée who is easy to look at, swung into her progrma with verve, ease and a rythmic aplomb that seemed to mark her as one of those rare souls to whom music becomes a passion and which offers those who listen, an intent sensation of a vivid personality at the helm and which makes for musical artistic and personal success upon the artist's rostrum."

Joyce Renée, Draft Biography (page 5 of 6)

-6-

Joyce Renée is one of the most popularly loved violinists now before the public. Wherever she appears, the press and public are unanimous in acclaiming her great gifts, and she wins their ready admiration for her technical abilities, her beautiful rich tone, the fire, the charm, and her penetrative interpretations. There is drama and poetry in her art, that makes for excitment, matched by few artists of the day. She has "That certain something," that appeals to every day folks as well as to the connoiseur.

In a recent southern tour for the Haynes Town Series, the Manager said,"Never have I seen audiences so completely spellbound."

A colorful personality, Joyce Renée is artistically gifted in many ways. She is a composer, author and successful designer.

***************** *********

Joyce Renée, Draft Biography (page 6 of 6).

After her concert at Northrop Memorial Auditorium in Minneapolis Aug. 6th, Joyce Renee will spend a few days with friends in Chicago and return to New York City to give a joint concert with the Russian baritone, Lidor Belarsky, Aug. 15th, for the benefit of the Jewish Educational Fund.

Miss Renee is the daughter of Mrs. Max Wasserman of 765 Greenwood Avenue.

Article in the *American Israelite*, Aug. 7, 1947.

Joyce Renee, noted American violinist, will be a guest of honor soon at the Advertising Club of New York City.

Miss Renee also will appear on the "night of Stars" at Madison Square Garden. In early December she will be heard at Annapolis.

She was elected recently to membership in the International Lyceum association, for the fifth successive season. Election is based on reports of top-notch performances, and the furthering of cultural activities in America.

Miss Renee is the daughter of Mrs. Max Wasserman, 765 Greenwood Avenue.

Article in the *American Israelite*, Nov. 13, 1947.

Miss Joyce Renee, noted American violinist, was a guest at the party given by Mrs. Henry Blums, at the Marguery. Among the distinguished guests were Prince Bernadotte of Sweden, Lee Schubert, Mr. Carlson, the Norwegian Ziegfield, and Russell Markert, associate producer of Radio City Music Hall.

Miss Renee is the daughter of Mrs. Max Wasserman, 765 Greenwood Avenue.

Article in the *American Israelite*, Nov. 27, 1947.

Miss Joyce Renee has been invited to apper at Annapolis. She is the daughter of Mrs. Max Wasserman, Greenwood Avenue. Mrs. Wasserman joined her daughter recently for a birthday celebration in Chicago when Miss Renee was en route to New York after her appearance in Minneapolis.

Article in the *American Israelite*, Oct. 2, 1947.

Miss Joyce Renee, violinist, daughter of Mrs. Max Wasserman, 765 Greenwood Avenue, performed on the Community Chest Drive rally program over W.J.Z. on Monday, Oct. 6th.

Article in the *American Israelite*, Oct. 9, 1947.

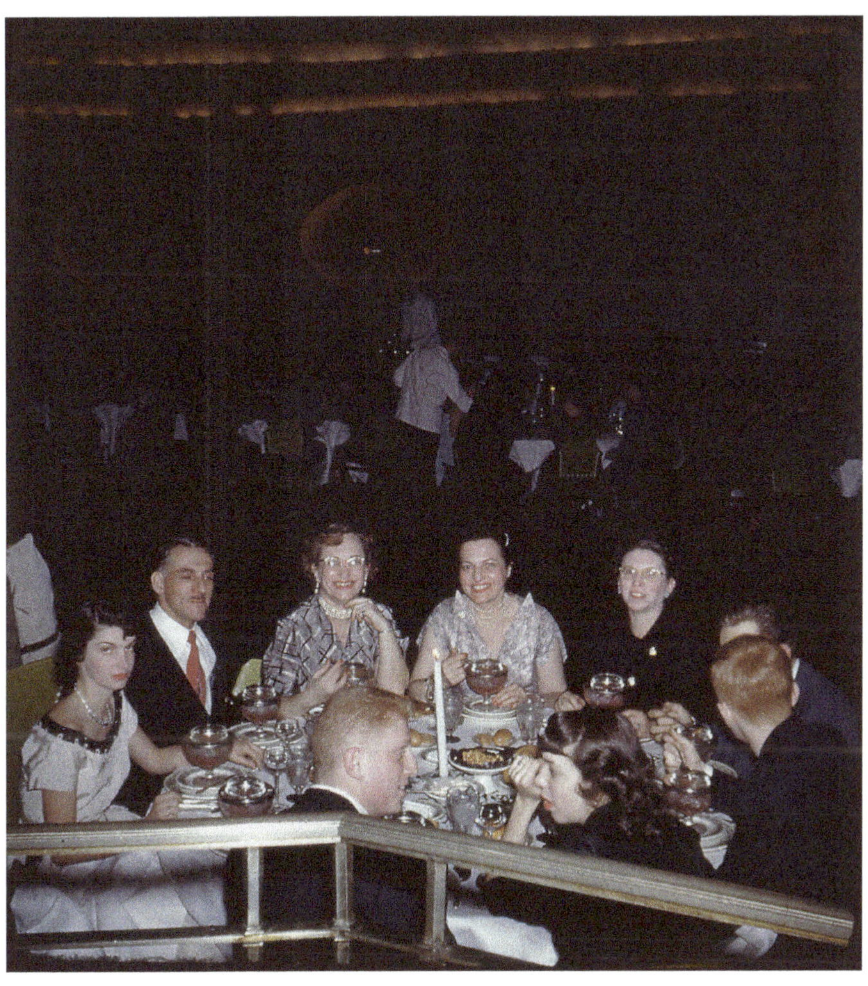

Big night out, 1950. L-R: Renate Wasserman, Joe Cohen,
Hilda Cohen, Joyce, Trudy Houser.

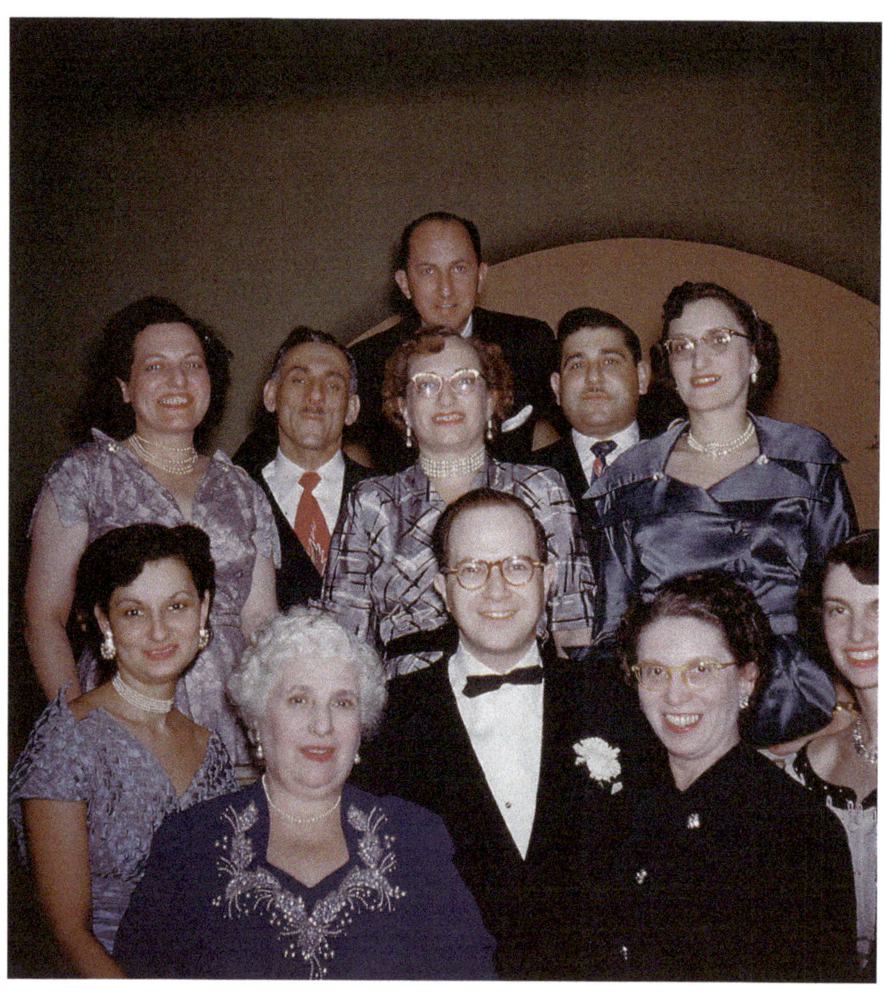

Family Big Night Out, 1950. At top: Jay Wasserman; Second row from left: Joyce, Joe Cohen, Hilda Cohen, Nate and Rose Aronoff; Bottom row: Rocky Wasserman, Anna Wasserman, Allan Wasserman, Trudy Houser, Renate Wasserman.

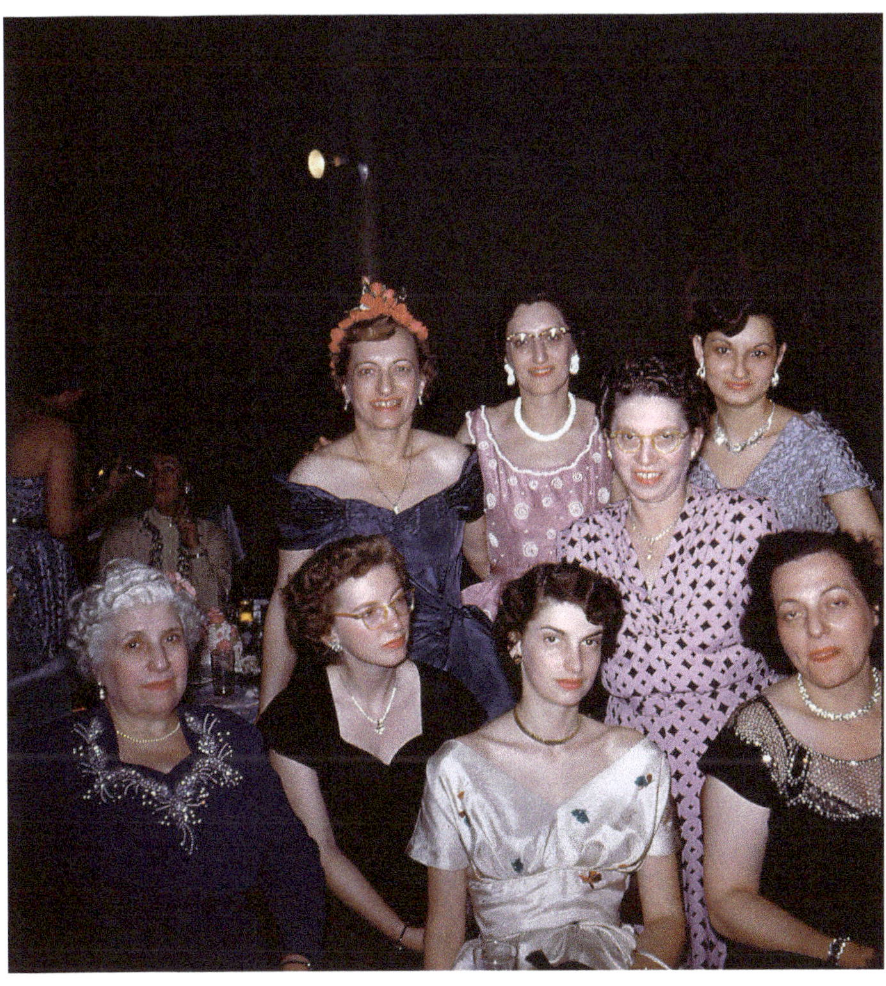

Family gathering, c. 1950. Anna Wasserman, Erica Houser, Renate Wasserman, Trudy Houser, Rocky Wasserman, and Joyce at lower right.

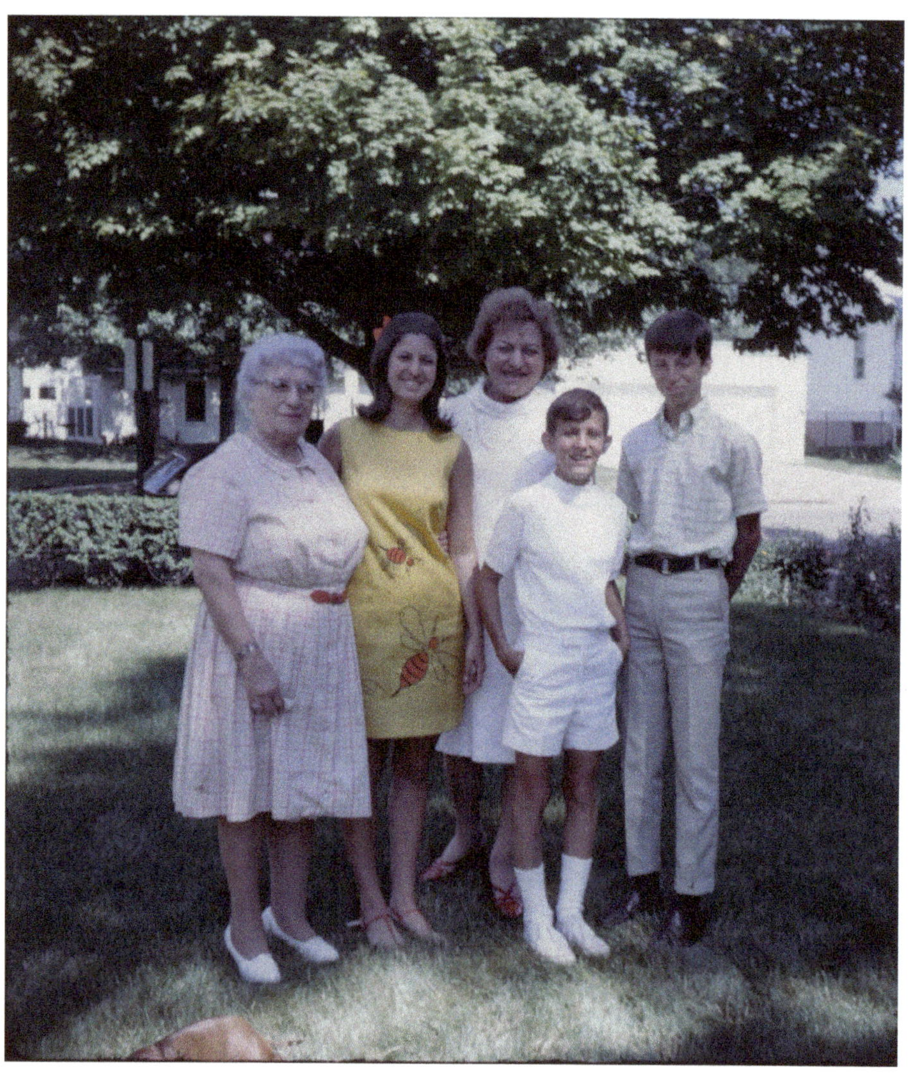

Summer 1967. L-R: Anna Wasserman, Margie Wasserman, Joyce, Jeff Wasserman and Steve Wasserman (the latter at an awkward thirteen years old).

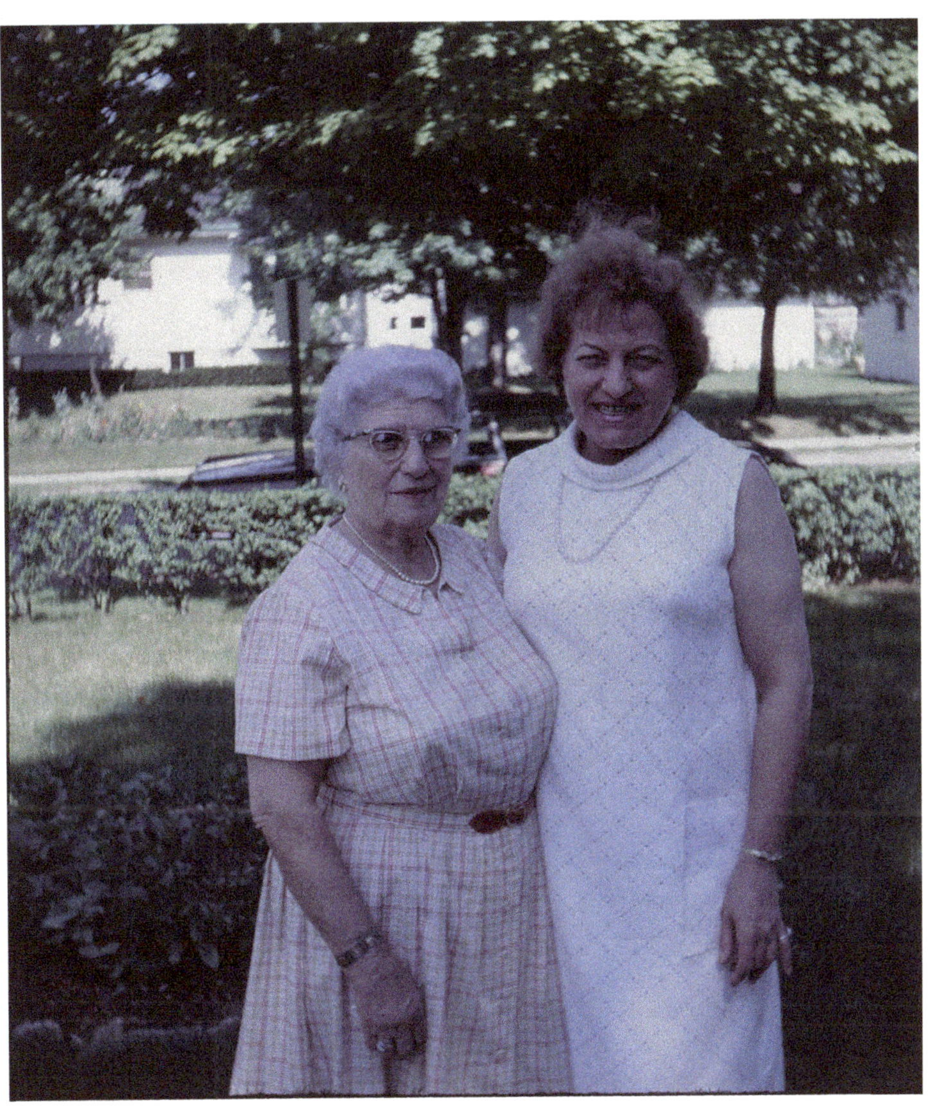

Anna and Joyce, summer 1967, at Trudy Houser's home in Cincinnati.

Obituaries

Esther Wasserman

Esther Wasserman, American violinist known professionally as Joyce Renee, passed away Tuesday, Sept. 2, at Jewish Hospital. She was 64.

A native Cincinnatian, Miss Wasserman made her debut when 9 with Dr. Frank Simon's Armco Band on WLW and the Blue Network.

She was the youngest honor graduate in the history of the Conservatory of Music.

During her musical career Miss Wasserman received numerous awards including the Fleischmann's, Schmidlapp and Juilliard International Fellowships.

While in Paris she was the recipient of the Institute Instrumental award and was holder of the Wooley International Fellowship when studying under Georges Enesco. She was awarded the coveted Walters Townhall Award and three medals from the Ohio Society of New York.

She interrupted her career during the second World War to perform for the armed forces and was recognized with citations from the Stage Door Canteens, Merchant Marine and U.S. Camp Shows.

She appeared on nationwide radio and television and performed at Carnegie Hall, Madison Square Gardens, Town Hall and Radio City Music Hall, New York City.

Miss Wasserman was a member of the Musicians Union, and Phi Beta Epsilon and a life member of Zonta International. She is listed in Who's Who in Music, International Who's Who in Music and recognized by the Distinctive Women of America.

She is survived by her mother, Anna R. Wasserman, and one brother, J. Robert Wasserman.

Services were on Sept. 4 at the Weil Funeral Home. Interment was in Love Brothers Cemetery, Rabbi Fishel J. Goldfeder officiating.

Esther Joyce Wasserman Obituary, September, 1975.

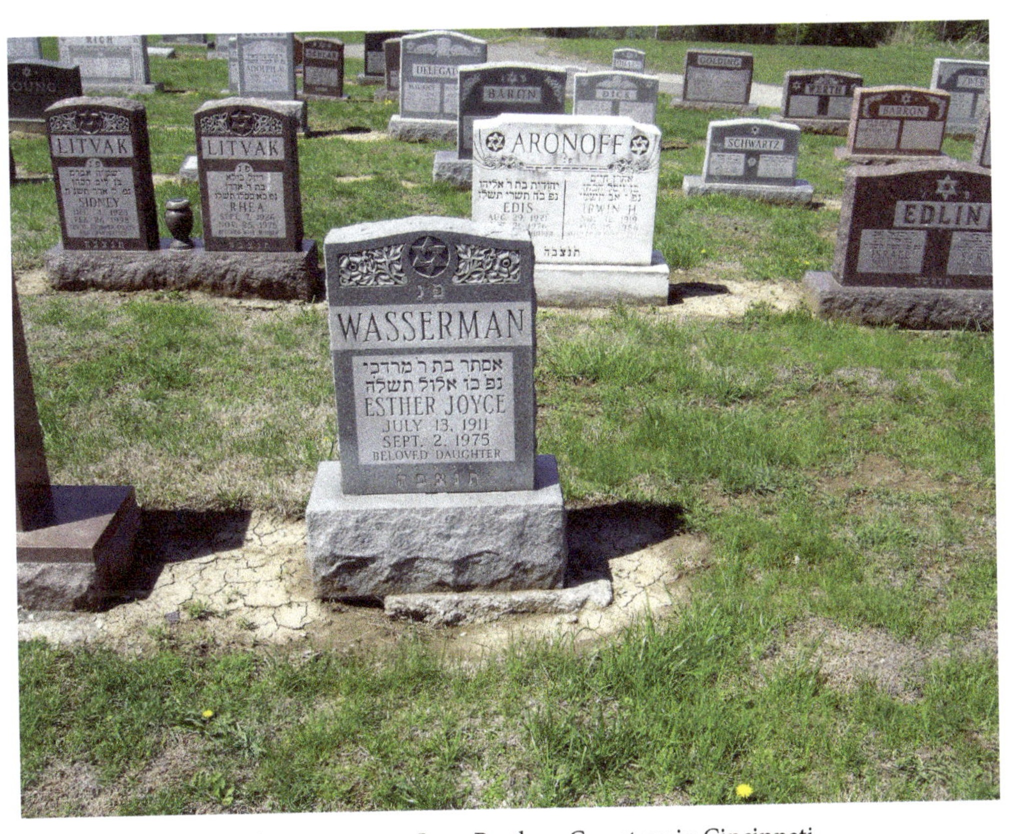

Joyce's gravestone at Love Brothers Cemetery in Cincinnati.

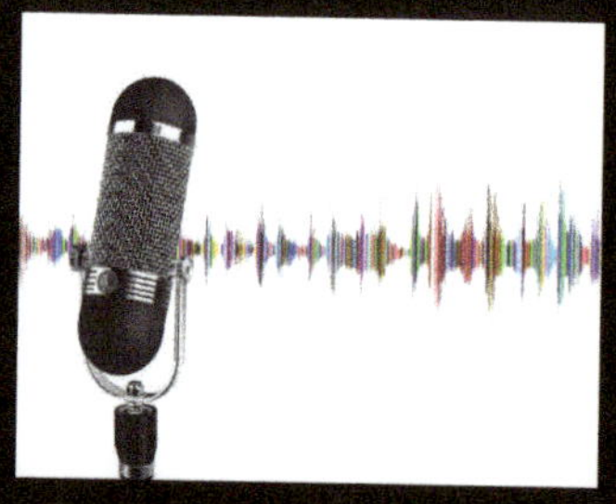

The American Israelite Podcast - Let There Be Light is a weekly podcast that's gives an overview and personal insight into articles of the week from The American Israelite newspaper, in Cincinnati, Ohio. Though published in Cincinnati, and the oldest english language Jewish newspaper in the country, The American Israelite has for nearly 200 years devoted itself to not only local news, but regional, national and global articles of interest to any Jewish community. Hosted by Netanel (Ted) Deutsch, publisher of The American Israelite and a few rotating friends that share funny anecdotes and memories of the community they support and love.

It's not often that the #LetThereBeLight #Podcast comes across a snippet on Page 18, the "From The Pages", in The American Israelite

that makes us take pause. In this week's issue, from 75 years ago, December 20, 1945, we learn about the concert violinist "Joyce Renee" (Esther Wasserman daughter of Mrs. Max (Anna Rabkin) Wasserman of 765 Greenwood Avenue), who had been chosen as the greatest living female violinist by Gordon Curie of the Australian Broadcasting System.

Esther Jovce Renee Wasserman made her debut at 9 years old on WLW in Cincinnati. When she attended college at the University of Cincinnati she was the youngest honor graduate of the University of Cincinnati College-Conservatory of Music – CCM at that time. Joyce Renee continued her musical studies in Paris as a student of Julie Riegg "Georges" Enesco, famous Romanian violinist, conductor, teacher and composer. While in Paris she was hailed as "America's violin sensation" and a recipient of the Institute Instrumental Award and was a holder of the Wooley International Fellowship. She was also awarded the Walters Townhall Award and three medals from the Ohio Society of New York.

Miss Renee was a star of concert, radio, television and stage and the recipient of the Fleischmann's and Schmidlapp Awards and the Juilliard International Fellowships. After a concert at the Tuskegee Institute she was presented with a piece of lace from the George Washington Carver Museum, lace that was made by the late famous scientist George Washington Carver.

At the height of her career she played repeatedly in New York City at Carnegie Hall, Town Hall, the New York Advertising Club, Madison Square Garden and Radio City Music Hall.

Aunt Joyce: Article from the *American Israelite's* Let There be Light Podcast.

During WWII, Miss Renee interrupted her concert tours to entertain the troops making two coast-to-coast tours of camps and hospitals in the US and then spending five weeks greeting Pacific veterans on the West Coast. She was recognized with citations from the Stage Door Canteens, Merchant Marine and U.S. Camp shows.

Joyce Renee was a member of the Musicians Union, and Phi Beta Epsilon, and a life member of Zonta International. She was listed in the Who's Who in Music, International Who's Who in Music and recognized by the Distinctive Women of America.

The American Israelite followed her throughout her career and many articles were written about her, especially when she came to Cincinnati to visit her family.

Unfortunately this all came to a halt when in 1951 Joyce Renee fell on the streets of New York City, injuring her frontal lobe and inevitably ending her concert career.

She came back to Cincinnati to the arms of her mother, Anna Rabin Wasserman and siblings, Dr. Allan and Mrs. Renate "Ronnie" Houser Wasserman, Mr. Joseph and Mrs. Hilda Ruth Wasserman Cohen, and Dr. Nathan and Mrs. Rose Wasserman.

Still today there are many who remember Joyce Renee the concert violinist, one being her niece Margie Kessel (Margie Wasserman Kessel, wife of Charles Kessel of Wyoming, Ohio). Margie tells us that although Joyce Renee could no longer play the violin as she once had, she still practiced, played the piano, composed music and continued her studies.

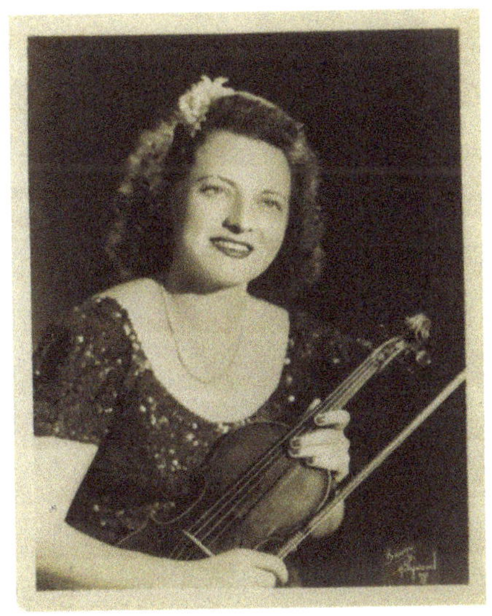

Joyce Renee Esther Wasserman passed away in 1975 at the age of 64. Life can change in a moment... may her memory be for a blessing to all who knew and loved her.

Aunt Joyce: Article from the *American Israelite's* Let There be Light Podcast.

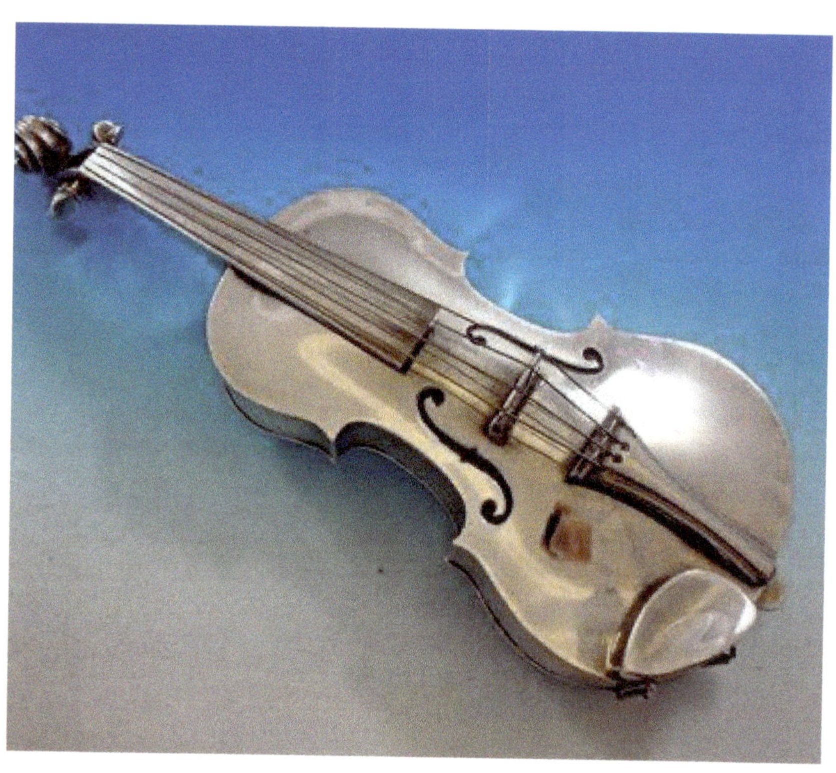

Joyce Wasserman Becomes Joyce Renée

Joyce eventually adopted the stage name Joyce Renée. Based upon news reports, it appears that she adopted her stage name during WWII. While research has not disclosed why Joyce did so, the most likely explanation was the rampant anti-Semitism in the United States in the 1920s and 1930s, including at the highest levels of the State Department. As an example of how widespread anti-Semitism and racism were in the United States, the Ku Klux Klan had four million members by the mid-1920s.

Anti-Semitism was not limited to diplomats or "average" citizens. It was also present in some of the highest reaches of private enterprise. Industrialist and leading auto manufacturer Henry Ford was a strident anti-Semite. Ford published the "Protocols of the Elders of Zion," an infamous Czarist-era forgery purporting to reflect minutes of meetings in which Jews plotted to take over the world. Ford railed against Jews in the *Dearborn Independent*, a newspaper he purchased and whose content he controlled. Ford attributed all evil to Jews and "Jewish capitalists."

Ford fulminated that "the Jews" had caused World War I. He published a series of articles over the course of ninety-one issues of the *Dearborn Independent* claiming a vast Jewish conspiracy was infecting the United States. Ford went so far as to distribute bound volumes of these insidious tracts to Ford dealerships across the country. Ford dealers sometimes "paid the hate forward" by placing copies of Ford's tracts and newspapers on the passenger seats of vehicles they sold.

Famed aviator Charles Lindbergh was an unabashed anti-Semite who became a vocal supporter of the Nazi regime. He went so far as to travel to Germany to receive a medal of honor from Hitler. Lindbergh testified before the House Foreign Affairs Committee and argued that the United States should negotiate a neutrality pact with Hitler. In a speech on September 11, 1941, Lindbergh fulminated that "the three most important groups who have been pressing this country toward war are the British, the Jewish, and the Roosevelt administration for angling to get the United States to enter WWII." His anti-Semitic and pro-Nazi rhetoric became so extreme that President Roosevelt ultimately denounced Lindbergh in 1941.

Perhaps worst of all was Father Charles Coughlin, who eventually became known as the "father of hate radio." Coughlin began broadcasting in 1926 on station WJR in Detroit. While purportedly a man of the cloth, Coughlin spewed virulently anti-Semitic venom on his weekly radio program to an audience of tens of millions of listeners. His influence and reach were so wide that the post office constructed a facility to handle the 80,000 letters he received each week at the height of his popularity.

A Canadian-born Catholic priest, Coughlin was initially posted to a parish in Michigan. He soon began to share his anti-Semitic, anti-Communist, and isolationist views. There was nothing subtle about Coughlin's attacks. His weekly attacks on Jews were outrageous, going so far as to argue that the Nazi pogrom known as Kristallnacht, in which thousands of Jewish homes, businesses, and synagogues in Germany were destroyed and tens of thousands of Jewish men were arrested solely for the crime of being Jewish, was justifiable retaliation by Germans for purported (but, in truth, nonexistent) Jewish persecution of Christians.[70]

Coughlin claimed that in Russia, "the Lenins and Trotskys...atheistic Jews and Gentiles" had murdered twenty million Christians and stolen billions of dollars of Christian property.[71] This, too, was an absurd fiction, but Coughlin, like some broadcasters today, was not one to let truth get in the way of his hateful agenda.

Coughlin helped inspire and foment the creation of a political group known as the "Christian Front." The Front organized "Buy Christian" rallies across the United States. This program was no different from the Nazi-led boycott of Jewish businesses and professionals in Germany. The Front's language and its members became increasingly violent. Coughlin, like Lindbergh, hallucinated that Jews were inciting the war in Europe and were trying their level best to get the United States involved.

After the United States entered the war following the Japanese attack on Pearl Harbor, the FBI raided Coughlin's headquarters. The federal government soon prohibited Coughlin from distributing materials through the mail because the government concluded his Nazi sympathies

---

70 United States Holocaust Museum, "Father James Coughlin."

71 *Id.*

and baseless accusations leant aid and comfort to the enemy. In May 1942, the leaders of the Catholic church in Detroit at long last ordered Coughlin to cease all non-pastoral activities. However, the fact that the church allowed him to spew his vile rhetoric for so long was shameful and a sign of how commonplace anti-Semitism was in the United States.

The existence of high-profile and widespread anti-Semitism may have caused Joyce, and perhaps her agents, to conclude that Esther Joyce Wasserman's name and Jewish background would limit her career. They may have feared that her name Esther too readily marked her as a "Jewess." They may have had the same concern even as she performed as Joyce Wasserman. Research has not revealed why Joyce chose the surname Renée. In any event, Esther Joyce Wasserman the violinist was, at some point during WWII, no more. She was replaced by Joyce Renée who, hopefully, would be able to navigate her musical career without suffering for being Jewish.

Joyce Renée—The Person and the Performer

Lest anyone think music was Joyce's entire life, she had other interests as well. She enjoyed designing clothing, writing, swimming, and horseback riding. Joyce also had a sweet tooth for chocolate sundaes. She no doubt treated her sweet tooth by indulging in Cincinnati's famous Graeter's ice cream. Graeter's was founded in 1870 by owners who initially sold their ice cream at Cincinnati's street-markets. They soon began to open storefront ice cream shops and eventually their rich ice cream became famous throughout the Midwest.

The Redpath Bureau, whose promotional materials described the agency as "serving the cultural life of America for 79 consecutive years," represented Joyce for several years. Redpath's flyers declared that "today, as never before, our speakers and entertainers are 'hand-picked' leaders of their respective fields. From our varied lists we suggest the following for your immediate consideration..." Along with news correspondents, authors, sculptors, actors, and singers, Redpath promoted Joyce in its talent brochures:

Joyce Renee, Young American Violinist: "Great Fire!" says Georges Enesco, composer and conductor, who likens her talent to Menuhin. "Encore," cry the audiences of Carnegie Hall, Madison Square Garden, Town Hall, Radio Music Hall, West Point, and three major networks of the United States. Critics acclaim—"Virtuoso violinist of skill" *Daily News*, N.Y.— "Sensational artist thrilled Ocean Grove audiences the past two seasons." *Ocean Grove Times*, N.J.—Brilliant tone, fluent technique, vibrant style, vivid personality." *Daily News*, Miami, Florida.

As part of her publicity efforts, Joyce posed for elegant promotional photographs. "Bruno of Hollywood" in New York City took one such photograph in which Joyce leaned on a faux Greek column, delicately holding her violin. Joyce wore a long gown with billowing sleeves. The dress featured a scoop neck trimmed with sequins. Joyce, with her thick, dark hair framing her face, gazed off-camera for the publicity shot. Another photograph had Joyce sitting with her violin in one hand and her bow in the other. She wore a floral hair clip on the right side of her head, along with a simple pearl necklace, while wearing a short-sleeved gown covered with sequins. Her lips were slightly parted in a warm smile.

Joyce toured the United States, performing at colleges and universities, including Columbia, Duke, the University of Minnesota, and Dickinson College. She performed five times at the State Teachers College in Bloomsburg, Pennsylvania, as well as at the Teachers' College in Fayetteville, North Carolina. She performed several times at West Point and Annapolis. In her hometown, Joyce played at Xavier University, Hebrew Union College, and her alma mater the University of Cincinnati.

On March 5, 1940, Joyce appeared in recital at the Brantwood Hall School for Girls in Bronxville, New York, where she played an extensive program: "Serenade Capricieuse" by Granville English; William Kroll's "Out of the East"; "Canebreak" by Samuel Gardner; "Subway" by Herbert Haufrecht; "Frolic" by Mana-Zucca; "Praeludium and Allegro" by Paganini and arranged by Kreisler; Bach's "Air on G String"; "Gavotte" by Mozart; Smetana's "Ans der Helmant"; and "Danse Espagnol (La Vida Breve)" composed by Manuel de Falla and arranged by Fritz Kreisler. "La Vida Breve" (Spanish for "Life is Short" or "The Brief Life") was an opera De Falla wrote in 1903-05 that did not premier until 1913. While the opera is infrequently performed, the Dance espagnole is popular as a stand-alone piece due to its rhythm, passion, and pizzicatos.

Joyce played the same program later that month at a concert in Miami, Florida.

Joyce was now performing with symphony orchestras across the country. In 1941, at age thirty, she toured with Frank Simon and the Armco Band, playing solo violin pieces with the band at thirty-three engagements across the Midwest. In 1942, she toured throughout the eastern portion of the country and New England with Joseph Cherniavsky, who commented that Joyce was marvelous and "always brings down the house." Cherniavsky was a Jewish-American cellist, theater and film composer, orchestra director, and recording artist, whose father and grandfather were klezmer musicians.

In 1943, Joyce played for five weeks as a soloist with Cherniavsky's orchestra at the Center Theater in Norfolk, Virginia. The concerts were also broadcast. Joyce's engagements included performing with symphony orchestras in Canada and in Europe. The reviews of her concerts were smashing:

> "Great artist!" (*Atlanta Constitution*)
>
> "Taste...charm...artist of skill...ovation." (*New York Times* and *Daily News*)
>
> "Renée's appearance [was a] high spot of the season... Lalo's Symphony espagnol danced in her hands with all of its Spanish charm and rhythmic fervor...Refreshing rendition...ovation. (*Norfolk* (Va.) *Ledger Dispatch*)[72]
>
> "[Renée] Combined delicacy of a woman with the strength of a man...brilliant interpretations, vibrant style, beautiful tone, vivid personality...sensational artist...ovation." (*Miami Herald and Daily News*, Miami, Florida)
>
> "One of the best concert performers we have ever had...memorable occasion." (*New Orleans Times Picayune*)
>
> "Charm...Great Artist!" "Holiday for Strings and Home on the Range proved special favorites in the America group...and the Boulanger Nocturne was a dream in its so French charm...great artist." (*Montclair* [New Jersey] *Times*)
>
> "A Star to Claim the Attention of the Elect...Packed auditorium...Applauded to the guards [sic] by this sophisticated, very musical lot of listeners! One of those rare souls...beautiful taste...vibrant style...rhythmic aplomb...great fire...vivid personality at the helm...Artistic Revelation...A star to claim the attentions of the Elect!" (*Cincinnati Enquirer* and *Times Star*)
>
> "Exquisite balance between Miss Renée's solo and the Radio City Music Hall Orchestra and Glee Club...lush tones...nifty performance...Brilliant artist." (*Billboard* and *Variety*, New York City)
>
> "Bombshell on the fiddle." (*San Francisco Examiner*)

---

72 Édouard Lalo's Symphonie espagnole in D minor is a work for violin and orchestra that Lalo composed in 1874. The work was premiered in Paris on February 7, 1875. "Although called a 'Spanish Symphony'... it is considered a violin concerto by musicians today. The piece, featuring Spanish motifs, launched a period when Spanish-themed music came into vogue." (Wikipedia.)

> "Charmed [the] audience...Masterful Performance...Bach Chaconne a Revelation...great mistress of her instrument...artist of the highest order." (*Nashville Daily Banner*)
>
> "Scored Hit...Top form...The Mozart Rondo had charm and delicacy...Sheer Translucent Beauty...The Corelli was broad and noble...The kind of art we have come to expect of her... Artistic Triumph!" (*Stamford Advocate*)[73]

Joyce's skill was such that Gordon Curie of the Australian Broadcasting System hailed her as the greatest living female violinist.[74] In recognition of her skill and success, the Ohio Society of New York awarded medals to Joyce in 1941, 1943, and 1946.

Joyce's musical tastes were varied. She played pieces as disparate as the St. Louis Blues and the Brahms Violin Concerto. As the *Cincinnati Enquirer* put it: "Joyce Renée, who is easy to look at, swings into her programs with verve, ease and a rhythmic aplomb that seemed to mark her as one of those rare souls to whom music becomes a passion and which offers those who listen an intent sensation of a vivid personality at the helm, and which makes for musical artistic and personal success upon the artist's rostrum." Joyce Renée was, by every measure, a star.

---

73 Research has not disclosed if Joyce played Mozart's Rondo in C Major or his Rondo in B-flat.

74 the *American Israelite* "Let There be Light Podcast."

Radio City, Carnegie Hall, and Town Hall

Radio City Music Hall engaged Joyce to perform in one of the venue's famous shows. Her performance was so well-received that Radio City held her over and had her play for eight weeks. Radio City Music Hall was the largest concert hall in the United States, capable of seating 6,000 patrons. Today it remains the largest indoor theater in the world. Likewise, the shimmering gold stage curtain is the largest in the world. The Hall's mighty Wurlitzer organ was custom-built for Radio City, with pipes as small as a few inches in length to ones as large as thirty-two feet tall. Radio City not only presented live musical performances, but also served as a venue for film premiers. Since its opening on December 27, 1932, more than 700 films have premiered there.

Joyce also played five concerts at Madison Square Garden. The original Garden, opened in 1879, was located on Madison Square at East 26th and Madison Avenue. A second iteration was constructed at the same location, followed by a third venue at 8th Avenue and 50th Street. The Garden then moved to its current location in Midtown Manhattan between Seventh and Eighth Avenues and extending from 31st to 33rd Street. The Garden has hosted top performers throughout its history. Among the top contemporary acts who have played there are Elvis Presley, the Rolling Stones, Dylan, Madonna, Elton John, Stevie Wonder, The Who, U2, Bruce Springsteen, and Taylor Swift. The Garden has also hosted three Democratic conventions as well as New York Knicks' games and other sporting events. It seemed there was no stage too grand or venue too large for Joyce's talent.

New York's Town Hall was another top-of-the-line concert venue at which Joyce performed. Located at 123 West 43rd Street, between 6th Avenue and Broadway, it had a seating capacity of 1500. Town Hall has a rich history:

Town Hall has played an integral part in the electrifying cultural fabric of New York City for more than 90 years. Disclosing a tale of a vibrant group of suffragists (The League for Political Education) whose fight for the 19th Amendment led them to build a meeting space to educate people on the important issues of the day. The Hall was designed by renowned architects McKim, Mead & White to reflect the democratic principles of the League. Box seats were eliminated, and no seats had an obstructed view, giving birth to the term "Not a bad seat in the house." During completion of the building the 19th Amendment was passed (women's right to vote), and on January 12, 1921, The Town Hall opened its doors and took on a double meaning: as a symbol of the victory sought by its founders, and as a spark for a new, more optimistic climate."[75]

As evidence of its political origins, the Hall's website explains that Margaret Sanger was arrested on Town Hall's stage "during a public meeting on birth control. She was an avid supporter of women's sexual rights and founded the American Birth Control League, now known as Planned Parenthood." Sanger felt that for women to have equal status in society and to be able to lead healthier lives, they had to be able to decide whether and when to have children. To that end, in 1916, she opened the first birth control clinic in the United States. The Hall's "Legendary Ladies" series was initiated with a program featuring Bette Davis.

Town Hall boasted an incredible list of guest performers that included Marian Anderson, Billie Holliday, and Langston Hughes. Emma Goldman returned from fourteen years of self-exile to speak at Town Hall. Classical musicians who performed at Town Hall include composers Richard Strauss and Sergei Rachmaninoff, and world-class musicians Pablo Casals, Andres Segovia, and violinist Isaac Stern who made his debut at Town Hall at age seventeen. Joyce joined this esteemed roster to play in the Hall's rarified atmosphere.

Carnegie Hall opened in the spring of 1891 at 881 7th Avenue between 56th and 57th Streets. Carnegie Hall was the product of a drive to construct a world-class concert hall in New York City. Walter Damrosch, conductor and musical director of the Symphony Society of New York, introduced the idea of such a project to industrialist Andrew Carnegie.

Walter Damrosch, a German American composer and conductor, was the brother of Frank Damrosch who founded the predecessor institution to The Juilliard School. He is perhaps best known for serving as the

75 Town Hall website.

musical director of the New York Symphony Orchestra. He conducted the world premiere of George Gershwin's Piano Concerto in F in 1925, as well as the premier of "An American in Paris." He also conducted the first performance of Rachmaninoff's Third Piano Concerto with Rachmaninoff himself as the soloist.

Walter pioneered the performance of music on radio and helped popularize classical music in the United States. He was the music director of the National Broadcasting Company and, for fourteen years from 1928 to 1942, hosted the network's Music Appreciation Hour, which was a series of lectures about classical music geared towards students. Walter and his brother Frank were such leading figures in American classical music that Damrosch Park at Lincoln Center was named in honor of their family.

Damrosch met Carnegie on a cruise from New York to Carnegie's native Scotland and introduced Carnegie to Damrosch's desire to build a superb concert facility in New York. Carnegie, famous for construction of public libraries across the United States, was enthused with the idea. The result of their collaboration was construction of the then state-of-the-art building renowned for its striking Italian Renaissance-style façade composed of terra cotta and iron-spotted brick.

The stunning facility, widely regarded as one of the best, if not the best, concert venue in the world, had three performance spaces. The Main Auditorium (now known as the "Isaac Stern Auditorium and Ronald O. Perelman Stage") seated 2,800 concert goers. The Carnegie Recital Hall (now known as the "Joan and Sanford I. Weill Recital Hall") seated 1,200. Adjacent to the Main Auditorium was a 250 seat Chamber Music Hall. Research has not revealed in which of the halls Joyce performed nor has research found recordings of her performances.

Joyce also played many dates at the massive Ocean Grove Theater in New Jersey. The Grove Theater was in Ocean Grove Township, just a few blocks from the Jersey shore in Asbury Park. A group of Methodist ministers founded Ocean Grove in 1869 as a place where people could escape hectic city life and enjoy time in a reflective, pastoral setting. The ministers laid out what became one of the first planned communities in the United States.

Ocean Grove's Great Auditorium, built in 1894 of wooden siding with iron trusses on stone foundations, had spectacular acoustics, due in large measure to the barrel vault ceiling. Leonard Bernstein reportedly commented that its acoustics rivaled those of Carnegie Hall. The auditorium could seat up to 10,000 attendees, so Joyce played to thousands of concertgoers during her engagements there.

Joyce had reached the peak of her art. She was playing on the world's largest stages and in its finest venues to tens of thousands of concert goers. Her reputation continued to grow, her reviews were wonderful, and she continued her ascent to the highest heights.

Playing for the Troops

During and after WWII, Joyce made coast-to-coast tours, performing as a soloist, entertaining troops at camps, bases, and hospitals.[76] Her three tours over the course of 1944-1946, had her appear at U.S.O. camp shows and veterans' hospitals across the country.

Miss Joyce Renée returned recently to New York City after four months of appearances on the west coast, which included greeting returning Pacific veterans, appearances at [military] installations and hospitals, and club and radio engagements.

After engagements in the east, Miss Renée hopes to join her family and many Cincinnati friends for a long-awaited reunion before returning to the west coast to fulfill engagements.

She is the daughter of Mrs. Max Wasserman, 765 Greenwood Avenue.[77]

The military asked Joyce to perform in San Francisco and Seattle for troops returning from the Pacific theater of war. She also played for outgoing and returning servicemen in New York and New Jersey at camps and bases, hospitals, servicemen's and officers' clubs, as well as aboard naval ships, including destroyers and troop transports. Mrs. Brock Pemberton, wife of the producer of many shows for the armed forces, wrote: "To Joyce, with love and thanks—the boys all love you, that you know." Herb Symmons, a war correspondent, caller her a "Bombshell on the Fiddle." In 1944, she toured coast to coast performing at hospitals and U.S.O. camp shows. In 1945 and 1946, she toured the northwest and west coast performing at U.S.O. shows.

Joyce played numerous dates at the Stage Door and Merchant Marine Canteens as well as the Merchant Seaman's Club, which led to her being awarded Honor Bar Emblems and citations by the Stage Door Canteen,

76 The *American Israelite* "Let There Be Light Podcast."

77 The *American Israelite*, June 6, 1946.

the Merchant Marine, U.S.O. Camp Shows, the United Theatre Wing Hospital Committee, and the Merchant Seaman's Club.[78] Her concert tours included repeat performances at West Point and Annapolis. With Lanny Ross (an American singer, songwriter, and pianist), Joyce gave the first program at Tilton General Hospital at Fort Dix in New Jersey for wounded servicemen returning from combat in North Africa.[79]

A popular favorite with the Armed Forces, Miss Renee has appeared at hundreds of camps, hospitals, and canteens, and has just returned from 18 weeks of coast-to-coast appearances at the Army, Navy and Marine hospitals and convalescent centers. She has been elected to membership of the U.S.O. Camp Shows, in recognition of her patriotic participation in the task of entertaining men and women of the Armed Forces and is the recipient of a citation from the Merchant Marine and Honor Bar pin from the Stage Door Canteen.[80]

Joyce also tried her hand at designing clothing. During the war she produced a series of sweater designs for the armed forces: "Your Heart's in the Navy," "Your Heart's in the Army," "Your Heart's in the Air-Corps," and "Your Heart's in the Marines." Unfortunately, research has not discovered any images of her designs.

Joyce also played concerts for charitable organizations, including Allied Relief Organizations, the Community Chest, the Red Cross, and more.

On September 12, 1946, with her concerts for the armed forces winding down, Joyce returned for an engagement at Radio City Music Hall. The program began with a piece played on the Music Hall's Grand Organ, followed by the Hall's Symphony Orchestra, led by Charles Previn, and then Colorama, in which Joyce played "Laura" by David Raksin, from his film score for the movie of the same name, as part of the presentation of "Painting the Town." The last portion of the program featured the movie "Notorious" starring Cary Grant and Ingrid Bergman.

---

78 The *American Israelite*, Dec. 20, 1945.

79 Lanny Ross was a classically trained tenor who gained fame during the early years of radio. He starred in a short-lived eponymous television program and was one of the most widely known and played American vocalists in the late 1930's and 1940s. While an undergraduate at Yale, he earned money singing in order to pay for law school. By the time he obtained his law degree, NBC offered him more money to perform than he could make as a lawyer, and his professional die was cast. Ross studied at Juilliard, which may be where he met Joyce.

80 The *American Israelite*, Nov. 16, 1944.

For individual bookings after WWII, including engagements with symphony orchestras and radio broadcasts, Joyce was represented by Redpath, the Alkahest Celebrity Bureau, Willard Mathews, and Am. Can. Concerts, Inc. Management. One Redpath brochure proclaimed: "Joyce Renee, Young American Violinist. 'Great Fire' says George Enesco, composer and conductor, who likens her talent to Menuhin. 'Encore', cry the audiences of Carnegie Hall, Madison Square Garden, Town Hall, Radio City Music Hall, West Point, and three major networks of the United States."

Joyce Renée, the daughter of an immigrant bricklayer and an immigrant saleslady, was an international star.

Loving Paris, Love in Paris

Joyce was a lifetime member of the International Institute of Arts and Letters based in Switzerland. She was also a member of the American Concert Artists Guild and the British American Club in Paris. Most likely Joyce became familiar with and joined the British-American Club while she was studying in Paris with Enescu.

Joyce fell madly in love with a British serviceman. She likely met him at a function sponsored by the British American Club. Investigation has not revealed in which branch of the British armed services he served.

Many of Joyce's compositions were in the style of the day in the 1940s and 1950s. Some of her love songs might be taken as expressions of her feelings for her British love. For example, the lyrics of "When We're together" declare:

My heart starts in dancing and I want to sing,
The world is mine when we're together.
It's not just romancing, for love is the thing
That claims my heart when we're together.
The moment that you leave me,
Old gloom comes walking in,
And you're the only one I know that can get rid of him.
So, let's call the preacher
and tell him that we
were always meant to be together.

In "Just Like a Dream," Joyce wrote about when she first met her love:

Just like a dream you came to me
From out of nowhere, sweetheart of my dreams.

Just like a dream, fate chanced a way
For great romance, for love of my dreams.
For dreams are a way to say things,
A way to let me dream this day.
Just like a dream, you are divine,
You came to bless this heart of mine.

In "When I Think of You," (Robert Russell Bennett collaborated with Joyce on the words and music for this song) Joyce reveled in the joy of being in love:

When I think of you and all your lovely charms,
I long to hold you in my arms.
And when I think of you and all you are to me,
I know that Cupid found true love for me.
The plans we plan, the dreams we dream,
The fun we have with ev'ry scheme.
When I think of you I long to hear your voice
And dream along with you forever, dear.

In her song "As Long as There's a You," Joyce contemplated how fortunate she was to have met her love:

You are the angel Heaven has sent me.
My heart is brimming with ecstasy.
I'll be seeing you,
I'll be wanting you,
I'll be loving you,
As long as there's a you.

There are few cities more romantic than Paris and few more likely to cause visitors to fall in love. And why should not the same be true for Joyce. Joyce was twenty-eight years old when she studied in Paris in 1939. She was young, beautiful, and supremely talented. She was fêted in Paris as an American violin sensation. With Europe on the brink of war (Germany invaded Poland on September 1, 1939, igniting WWII), a longing, even compulsion, to wring as much from life as possible before the apocalypse may have ignited passions that otherwise might not have arisen.

The fear of what might happen if Britain and Germany went to war hung over them. "Don't Forget" addressed emotions that no doubt percolated beneath the surface for them, as the storm clouds over Europe darkened. They knew their time together might be short and that her love might be at risk if war broke out.[81]

Don't forget my lips when this night is old.
Don't forget my kiss, don't let its touch grow cold.
Don't forget my arms that held you, held you near.
Don't forget the words that only you will hear.
Now that I've found you fate takes you away.
My arms will stay empty till you're back to stay.
But please don't leave me yet while my cheeks are wet,
Kiss my tears and say you won't forget.

If Joyce met her love in Paris, it is easy to understand how she would have been inspired to write songs expressing her feelings for him. They may have strolled arm in arm past the bouquinistes along the banks of the Seine, sat on benches in the Jardin Luxembourg admiring the flowers and watched children sail toy boats on the fountain ponds. Sipping Beaujolais in cafes in the Saint Germain district or on the slopes of Montmartre, Paris was such a romantic setting that mere introductions could evolve quickly into deeper feelings. And so, Joyce, amid her meteoric rise as a musician and while studying with one of the world's leading violinists and composers, found herself enthralled with another passion.

Unfortunately, Joyce's beloved was not Jewish. Joyce's mother Anna disapproved of the interfaith relationship and refused to countenance marriage. Unable to win her mother's approval and unwilling to continue in the face of her mother's opposition, Joyce ended the relationship. Joyce's songs reflect her heartache. In "Love of my Heart, she wrote:

I can't forget you, tho' we're apart.
I can't forget you, love of my heart.
I can't forget you, tho' I must try.

81 Joyce wrote the melody for "Don't Forget," while James Beni wrote the lyrics.

I can't forget you, I pray and cry.
So please remember dear, tho' you're not near
I think of you always, wish you were here,
I can't forget you, tho' we're apart,
I'll love you always, love of my heart.

Joyce's lyrics in "When My Fiddle Dreams" provide further evidence of her loss:

Some words are never spoken,
Somehow, they're hard to say,
But I can reveal to you what I feel,
when you hear my fiddle play.
When my fiddle dreams, dreams of long ago,
memories it brings of love we used to know.
When my fiddle sighs,
Tenderly and low,
I can see your eyes,
Dark eyes that haunt me so;
Gazing in mine as they used to do,
Swearing that we'd be together, forever,
I'm in heaven then,
You are mine again,
But only when my fiddle dreams.

And so, as war loomed, Joyce had already fought one battle and lost.

Butterflies for the Most Seasoned Performer

Even as a seasoned and accomplished performer, Joyce still sometimes had nerves before performing:

> "Before every performance, when I am feeling the usual apprehension until I see my audience, I pick up the medal [given to her by Wendall Willkie] and remember Mr. Willkie's words, and I tell the medal to bring me luck, and then I walk out on to the stage with a prayer in my heart for all the beauty I want to give."
>
> And here is an amusing story. She says, "One evening, just before curtain time, an old friend came backstage to see me," and she said, "I can't understand it, an artist who can give people goose flesh and carry them off into another world, like you do, and the hundreds of wonderful performances that you've given, and you still get nervous?" And I said, "Well, if I never play like I really want to in this world, I hope I will play like I want to, at least once, after I am dead." And then came the curtain, and then when the concert was over, many people came backstage, and along came my old friend, and to the consternation of everyone there, my friend shouted, "Joyce, you played like you were dead." Nobody knew our secret, and I think some people are still wondering." (Unattributed article about Joyce.)

Joyce loved her audiences because she felt they helped her produce great music that she could never have achieved simply playing in an empty rehearsal hall or studio. "I always have an indescribable feeling of gratitude to people, and I always wish I could tell them, if I played beautifully, it was because they inspired me to do so."

When Joyce was living and performing in New York, air travel was not commonplace. She typically took the train between Cincinnati and New York. While Cincinnati's Art Deco Union Station, situated just west of downtown, was the city's grand, main train station, Joyce usually boarded at the more convenient Winton Place Depot on Spring Grove Avenue, near the Procter & Gamble plant roughly two miles from Joyce's mother's home. The one room Winton station had a peaked roof and wood-sided exterior. Behind the depot was a huge water tank with "Chester" emblazoned on it for the Chester Park neighborhood in which the Depot was located.

Joyce took the "Ohio State Limited" to New York on a route operated by the New York Central Railroad. The Central ran trains from New York to St. Louis, with stops in Pittsburgh and Cincinnati. The Central advised would-be riders that "Speed-Safety-Comfort, the three essentials to enjoyment of travel, are yours on the Water Level Route." Most of the Central's routes were situated alongside rivers. That meant the trains did not have to climb or descend significant grades, allowing them to go faster and with less need for massive engines on the relatively flat topography. The Ohio State Limited routes headed northeast from Cincinnati through Columbus to Cleveland and on to Buffalo. From Buffalo, the route headed east to Albany before making a sharp turn south to New York City.

Train service from Cincinnati to New York City was initially provided by the Cleveland, Cincinnati, Chicago, and St. Louis Railway, known as the "Big Four," before the New York Central acquired the line. The Central was able to use locomotives that were built for speed, as opposed to locomotives built for raw power that were needed to haul massive tonnage over mountain passes. The famous locomotives the New York Central used on its passenger lines included "4-6-4" Hudson engines, so named because they had four leading wheels, six powered and coupled driving wheels, and four trailing wheels that were well-suited for hauling cars over flat terrain at high speeds. Joyce rode on speedy, well-appointed trains when she traveled between Cincinnati and New York.

The Ohio State Limited's route ended at Grand Central Terminal at 42nd Street and Park Avenue in Midtown Manhattan. Architects at the Reed & Stem firm designed Grand Central, now a National Historic Landmark, in a Beaux Arts style. The New York Central Railroad built the station, which opened in 1913. The huge facility covers forty-eight acres and has forty-four train platforms, more than any other train station. The main concourse, with its information booth in the center of the vast space, sat below a massive blue ceiling dotted with gold stars and outlines of the zodiac constellations. Grand Central was good to its name in providing a grand, in fact, awe-inspiring, entrance to travelers visiting New York City. Not to mention the possibility of popping into the famous Grand Central Oyster bar, with its fire station brick décor and red-checked tablecloths, for a dozen oysters, bowl of clam chowder, or fried calamari.

The Tuskegee Institute, Pembroke College, and Immanuel Baptist Church

During one of her tours of the southern United States, Joyce gave a concert at the Tuskegee Institute in Tuskegee, Alabama, roughly forty miles east of Montgomery. Booker T. Washington founded the Institute in 1881. Famed agriculturalist and scientist George Washington Carver joined the Institute's staff as its Director of Agriculture in 1896:

Born a slave, George Washington Carver (1864-1943) is one of the most historically prominent African American scientists. Carver was a pioneer as an agriculturalist and botanist by introducing methods of soil conservation for farmers, inventing hundreds of by-products from peanuts, pecans, sweet potatoes, and soybeans, and practicing "zero waste" sustainability.[82]

What is not well-known is that Carver was also an artisan proficient in textile techniques such as embroidery, weaving, crocheting, knitting, and basketry.[83] As a token of appreciation for her performance, the Tuskegee Institute presented Joyce with a piece of lace Carver made that had been in the George Washington Carver Museum collection.[84]

Joyce also played at Pembroke College in North Carolina, originally established as the Croatan Normal School in March 1887.[85] Its mission was to train Native American teachers. The school began in a two-story clapboard building, but in 1909 moved to its present location in Pembroke, which was the center of the native American community

82 *George Washington Carver: Textile Artist*, Eulanda Sanders, Chanmi Hwang, DigitalCommons@University of Nebraska Lincoln, Textile Society of America Symposium Proceedings at 895.

83 *Id.*

84 The *American Israelite* "Let There Be Light Podcast."

85 The Croatan were a native American people of limited numbers. They lived primarily along the North Carolina coast, including Roanoke and Ocracoke islands and portions of the Outer Banks.

in North Carolina. In 1941, the North Carolina General Assembly changed the school's name to Pembroke State College for Indians and later changed the name yet again, this time to Pembroke State College. The school was so enthusiastic about Joyce's performance that it named a recording club in her honor.

Although Joyce had already established an extraordinary career performing across the United States, in April 1947 Georges Enescu wrote a note in support of her career:

Miss Joyce Renée has studied with me and is a young artist of real talent, who has already demonstrated her ability in successful public appearances. I feel that she is worthy of being helped in any way, so that she may establish herself in a distinguished solo career. I am willing to suggest her on European appearances.[86]

One of Joyce's engagements in 1947 was on April 12 at the Immanuel Methodist Church at 422 Dean Street near Fifth Avenue in Brooklyn. Immanuel Methodist was a bilingual church attended by many congregants from the Caribbean. The Immanuel Choir, under the direction of Birger E. Ambrose, invited the community to attend its annual concerts, at one of which Joyce was to be the star performer.

In addition to Joyce, the concert was to feature the church's choir with Irene Strong Huntley as the choir's vocal soloist. In addition to listing the many awards Joyce had received, the program noted she had performed before more than 1.5 million people during her eight weeks of concerts at Radio City. The program also notified attendees that a "traditional social and fellowship will follow the Concert in the Vestry. Refreshments will be served by our ever faithful ladies of the Womens [sic] Society of Christian Service at a nominal charge." Tickets to the concert were available for one dollar.

86 Note from Georges Enescu, April 1947.

Debut Works

Joyce was a friend and admirer of Pietro Yon, the organist at St. Patrick's Cathedral in New York City. Yon, a native of Italy's Piedmont region, served for a time as an organist at the Vatican and Royal Church in Rome. He came to the United States in 1907 and in 1914 opened a studio at Carnegie Hall for liturgical musicians. In 1926, he became the assistant organist at St. Patrick's and in 1928 was appointed its music director. Mr. Yon invited Joyce to sit with him in the organ loft while he played during the funeral service for Ignacy Paderewski, the famed Polish pianist and composer.

Louis Vierne, the famed French organist, and composer at Notre Dame Cathedral in Paris, composed a sonata for Joyce to perform. Vierne composed six symphonies for organ and a mass for choir and two organs. Joyce also performed debut performances of works composed by Rafael Kubelík (a Czech conductor and composer), Granville English (an American composer), Albano Seismit-Doda (an Italian composer), Herbert Haufrecht (an American composer and pianist), Shelby Gaines (an American composer), Joseph Cherniavsky (an American cellist, film and theater composer, and orchestra director), and others.[87]

Joyce did not care whether she performed on a grand stage, at a small church, or for a tiny college; Joyce simply wanted to share her music.

87 This information is from an unattributed biography of Joyce.

A Busy Career in 1947

During the summer of 1947, Joyce, by now thirty-six, was living in New York City at the Hotel Lincoln, the self-designated "House of Hospitality," on Eighth Avenue between 44th and 45th Streets. The Lincoln advertised itself as offering "1400 rooms with bath and shower, radio and servidor." Servidors were full-length, two-way cabinet doors that allowed items like shined shoes and pressed clothes to be left for guests without disturbing them. The massive hotel, which opened in 1928, was twenty-seven stories tall and hosted salesmen, tourists, and people associated with the theater district. The Lincoln Hotel is now the Row Hotel and was also the Milford for a while.

Joyce found time to write to Renate Houser (who went by "Ronnie"), who was engaged to marry Joyce's younger brother Allan:

> Dear Ronnie,
>
> You were such an angel to fix me that lovely box of cookies, and I am still enjoying them. Thank you very, very much, Ronnie dear. It was certainly an unexpected and delightful surprise, and you were very sweet and thoughtful to send them to me.
>
> I have always adored Al, and I couldn't have wished for him to have picked a lovelier girl, and I'm happy that you have him too, 'cause he's pretty "special," absent-mindedness and all.
>
> When I can get around to it, I'll mail you something I bought—seems quite the vogue in new fall showings of costume jewelry, and when you can get around to it, please send me your address, 'cause Al hasn't yet.
>
> Lots of love to both of you and your charming mother and sister, too.

Joyce (July 4, 1947, letter to Renate Houser)[88]

Lacking Renate's home address, Joyce addressed the letter to Allan and Ronnie at the Wasserman family home at 765 Greenwood Avenue in Cincinnati's Avondale neighborhood.

That same month, Joyce's mother Anna took the train to Chicago to meet Joyce and celebrate Joyce's birthday on July 13. Joyce was on her way from Minneapolis to New York; Chicago was a convenient midpoint where she and her mother could connect. Joyce's schedule in 1947 was hectic. She performed not only in Minnesota, but also in Virginia, North Carolina, Pennsylvania, New Hampshire, and New York.

On August 6, 1947, Joyce returned to Minnesota to perform at the Northrop Memorial Auditorium on the campus of the University of Minnesota in Minneapolis. Joyce was accompanied on piano by Laura Forde Giere. Joyce opened her program with Handel's Violin Sonata in E Major, HWV 373. Joyce next played the Praeludium and Allegro by Fritz Kreisler, a work in the style of Gaetano Pugnani. The Praeludium, first published in 1905, was an extremely popular work in the violin repertoire. Joyce followed that with Bach's Chaconne, the latter written for violin without accompaniment. The chaconne is a continuous variation, usually in triple meter and a major key, with a short repeating bass line. It is from Partita No. 2 for Solo Violin in D Minor, BWV 1004.

The program continued with "Songs of Home" by Smetana. Smetana is generally considered to be one of Czechoslovakia's (now "Czechia") greatest composers. He wrote a great deal of music celebrating Czech history and folk music. His symphonic poem "The Moldau" is perhaps the most famous of all Czech classical music.

Joyce's program included a Gavotte by Mozart and a Nocturne by Lili Boulanger. Boulanger, a French musical prodigy, composed her Nocturne for violin and piano in 1911 when she was only eighteen. The gavotte is a dance that originated in southeastern France; it is a type of folk-dance set to a moderate tempo. Next on Joyce's program was the Ghost Dance, Opus 16 in D Minor, published by Ellis Levy in 1920.

The last portion of Joyce's program consisted of: "Jota" by De Falla, arranged by Kochanski; "Old Refrain" by Kreisler; "Subway" (which its American composer, Herbert Haufreucht, dedicated to Joyce); and De Falla-Kreisler's "Dance espagnole" from "La Vida Breve."

---

88 Renate Houser is the author's mother.

After her concert in Minneapolis, Joyce returned to New York to perform with the Russian baritone Sidor Belarsky on August 15th at a benefit for the Jewish Educational Foundation.[89] Belarsky was a Ukrainian-born basso known for singing Yiddish and Hebrew songs.[90] He was a graduate of the State Conservatory in Leningrad and had been a star of the Leningrad State Opera Company.

Belarsky came to the United States in 1930 with his wife and daughter. They settled in Los Angeles where Belarsky embarked on a career with the Los Angeles Symphony. Belarsky devoted much of his career to teaching music at the Jewish Teachers' Seminary in New York City, which may be where he met Joyce. He became known as a leading interpreter and performer of classic cantorial music, Chassidic nigunim (a type of Jewish religious songs or tunes sung by groups, such as "Bim Bam" or "Lai, Lai, Lai"), Yiddish folk songs, and Hebrew songs from Israel.[91]

Joyce continued to perform at fundraising events. the *American Israelite* reported that in October 1947 Joyce performed as part of the Community Chest Drive conducted on WJZ television in Baltimore. The *Israelite* also reported that in November 1947 Joyce was to be a guest of honor at an event sponsored by The Advertising Club of New York City.[92] Joyce was also scheduled to appear on the "Night of Stars" at Madison Square Garden, while in early December she was engaged to perform at Annapolis.[93] The *Israelite* reported that the International Lyceum Association had elected Joyce to membership for the fifth year in a row, with membership being based upon top-notch musical performances and the furthering of cultural activities in the United States.[94]

Joyce's career was white hot. She was recognized across the United States, as well as internationally, as a stellar performer. She was in demand for performances of all kinds, in concert halls with symphony orchestras, at colleges and universities, and in smaller venues such as churches and synagogues. The auburn-haired violin prodigy from Ohio had come a long way.

---

89 The *American Israelite*, Aug. 7, 1947.

90 The *New York Times*, June 8, 1975.

91 Recorded Sound Archives, www.library.fau.edu/depts/spc/special.htm.

92 The *American Israelite*, Nov. 13, 1947.

93 *Id.*

94 *Id.*

The Crowds Go Wild

Joyce's agents prepared a promotional brochure featuring a photograph of Joyce standing with her violin while leaning on a fluted column. She wore a floor-length gown with flowing sleeves and sequins stitched around the scalloped neckline. The flyer noted that Joyce had been a featured artist at Carnegie Hall, had an extensive engagement at Radio City Music Hall, and was signed to five return engagements at the famed Ocean Grove auditorium. The flyer quoted one of Joyce's hometown newspapers: "Your being with us added prestige and your playing was sublime. The many tributes paid [by] your musical critics were echoed."

Additional glowing tributes lauded Joyce:

> "One of those rare souls...success from every viewpoint... verve... ease... rhythmic aplomb... vivid personality... packed auditorium... applauded to the guards!" (*Cincinnati Enquirer*)
>
> "Virtuoso violinist of skill." (*New York Daily News*)
>
> "Astonishing." (*Cincinnati Times Star*)

Joyce's concert tours included guest performances with symphony orchestras across the United States. She performed frequently on major radio networks, including "Music at Twilight," "Works of the Masters," "American Festival Series," and many television shows. She appeared on programs with artists and personalities as diverse as Eleanor Roosevelt, Lowell Thomas, Madame Chiang Kai-shek, Wendell Willkie, Edward G. Robinson, and Kate Smith.

Joyce mailed one of her promotional flyers to Renate and Allan, as well as an autographed 8x11 promotional photograph taken by Bruno of Hollywood on which she wrote: "To Al and Ronnie, may the Gods and Angels smile down on you always, with a heart full of love, Joyce, Dec. '47."

Mark Barron, a Broadway columnist for the *New York Herald Tribune*, devoted an entire column to Joyce:

> From her name and from her voice, you would think that Joyce Renee [sic] is the most French Mademoiselle you could meet anywhere removed from the Champs Elysée or removed from Avenue D'Orleans or the Louvre.
>
> It is true that she has a great deal of French background, but Mlle. Renee is truly American. She was the youngest honor graduate in the history of the Cincinnati Conservatory of Music. But, in Paris, she studied with Georges Enesco, one of the masters, and she also studied with such famous teachers as Kochanski, Arthur Hartmann, Rubin Goldmark and Dr. Eggar Stillman-Kelley.
>
> Mlle. Renee has also been acclaimed for her violin solos in Carnegie Hall, Madison Square Garden, Radio City Music Hall and at West Point and Annapolis.
>
> During the war, she did what many other musical artists did. She gave up her professional career while she performed for soldiers and hospitalized veterans. For her shows, she received citations from the Stage Door Canteen, the Merchant Marine, USO Camp Shows, the United States Theater Wing Hospital Committee and the Merchant Seaman's Club.
>
> Mlle. Renee is an artist of the violin, but this Cincinnati girl uses her talent to benefit the underprivileged. In her native Cincinnati, for instance, the proceeds from her concerts are given to children who may not get all the nourishment they need.[95]
>
> Other than being a brilliant violinist, Miss Renee's talents have won her reknown [sic] as a musical composer. The first of her compositions happened at an early age, when she was a mere nine years old. At that time she was looking out the window at a snowfall and wrote a symphony called "Snowflakes," being a quiet interpretation of snowflakes falling gently to the ground. She was only nine years old at the time, but her sensitive mind

---

95 This concert was held at Cincinnati's Taft Auditorium on April 2, 1950. Sponsored by the Zonta International Club of Cincinnati, the event generated sufficient proceeds to provide underprivileged children in Cincinnati with a healthy breakfast for an entire school year. Joyce played many concerts to raise funds for charity, including performances for Allied Relief organizations, The Community Chest (which eventually became The United Way), the Red Cross, and others.

> reflected the feeling of this happenchance of nature and the one way she could express it was in gentle music.
>
> Since then she has written many other songs, and improvises on her violin chords of musical numbers which are suggested, apparently, from her mind as a composer. Mlle. Renee is a gifted composer, an artist of rare skill and effervescent personality.[96]

One thing that stands out is that notwithstanding Joyce's renown and skill, she did not perform as a soloist with the largest symphony orchestras in the United States, such as those in New York, Philadelphia, and Chicago. The reason for this had nothing to do with her skill. Rather, the fact of the matter is that during the 1940s and 1950s, there simply were no women soloists playing with such institutions. All soloists at that time and on those stages were men.

Joyce's brother Allan married Renate in June 1948. Joyce interrupted an extended tour through Virginia, North Carolina, Pennsylvania, New Hampshire, New York, and Minnesota to head home for Allan's wedding. Her touring schedule had been so hectic that returning to Cincinnati for the wedding was her first visit in three years.

Joyce continued to perform around the country to great acclaim. Her career was so extraordinary that, in 1950, Cincinnati presented the key to the city to her.

96 Mark Barron, the *New York Herald Tribune*, date unknown.

Joyce Speaks

Earl Wilson was a nationally syndicated newspaper columnist who spent four decades chronicling New York's night life. He wrote a column titled "It Happened Last Night" which he filled with news about performers and other members of New York's artistic and social scene. Wilson wrote a column about Joyce entitled "Cincinnati Violinist at Work on Memoirs":

> Her next concert tour won't get under way for a while, so Joyce Renee, the talented Cincinnati violinist, is fiddling the time away on a typewriter.
>
> She's writing a book she'll call "On the Way Up," a series of anecdotes collected since she came out of the Cincinnati Conservatory of Music at 17, the youngest honor graduate in the school's history.
>
> One of her favorites is the story of how she met Georges Enesco, the famous French violin virtuoso, and became his student in Paris.
>
> "I wanted so much to meet him," Joyce said, "But didn't know how to go about it. I thought If I wrote to him, someone else would see the letter first and into the waste basket it would go.
>
> "One evening I went into a little restaurant near Carnegie Hall. There were some musicians talking at the next table," she continued.
>
> "One of them asked, 'Where is Enesco stopping now?' Another musician answered, saying he was at a certain hotel here. The next morning," she said, "I phoned the hotel and spoke to Enesco himself and he agreed to hear me play.
>
> "Eventually I went to Paris to be his pupil," she said. "I had to sell my fiddle to pay for the trip."
>
> At nine she was playing violin solos on Dr. Frank Simon's Armco programs on WLW and the Blue Network. Since that

> time she's appeared in some of the biggest concert halls here and in Europe.
>
> In Cincinnati she has given many concerts in Taft Auditorium, the Cincinnati Woman's Club Auditorium, and South Hall, Xavier [University]. She's appeared in New York at Carnegie Hall, Town Hall, and Radio City Music Hall, and at a Madison Square Garden benefit on the same stage with Mrs. Eleanor Roosevelt and Edward G. Robinson.
>
> Part of Joyce's book will be devoted to her experiences at the Conservatory.
>
> "There were about 50 other students waiting to play for the final examinations ahead of me," she told me. "I didn't want to sit indoors until my turn came, so I put my violin and music down on my seat and took a walk in Burnet Woods. It was such a beautiful day," she said.
>
> "But the others got through faster than I thought they would. A searching student," she said, "found me and rushed me back to the examination hall.
>
> "When I got there, I found my violin but not my music," she said. "So, I played without music."
>
> Joyce collects violins as a hobby, and prizes a little silver Strad given to her by the late Mrs. John Withrow, wife of the man whose name was given to Withrow High School.
>
> She's had plenty of trouble with violins. A string once snapped in the middle of a performance at Radio City. While she was playing on the radio program "Music at Twilight," the fiddle came apart in her hands.
>
> "There isn't much you can do standing there with your hands full of violin parts," she said. "I walked off."
>
> "Before I'm through playing I suppose there'll be more to write about. "That's why I'm planning two sequels," she said. "The next book I'll write will be 'On Top' and the second—'On the Way Down'."[97]

Joyce had the privilege of playing many superb instruments, including violins from the famous Henry Ford collection in Dearborn, Michigan, the Wurlitzer rare instrument collection, and the Emil Herrmann collection of rare violins, violas, and violoncellos. Her most extraordinary

97 Earl Wilson, Broadway columnist, the *New York Post,* June 23, 1951. Unfortunately, research has not revealed whether Joyce completed these books, nor have any drafts of them been found.

such experience was when she had the opportunity to play the famous Aranyi Stradivarius, crafted in 1667, which was the earliest Stradivarius then in existence. She also played the Auer Stradivarius and the Enescu Guernarius violins. It is ironic that Joyce, being Jewish, played some of the most prized possessions owned by the rabid antisemite Henry Ford. If Ford rolled in his grave at the news of a Jewish performer making music with his prized violins (Ford died on April 7, 1947), perhaps he at least rolled in time to Joyce's music.

Another article, this one in the *Daily Record*, noted that Gordon Currie of the Australian Broadcasting System, in his book "World Famous Personalities," listed Joyce as the world's greatest female violist. The article also reported that Joyce was listed in *Who's Who in Music*, *Who's Who in America*, *Who's Who in the East*, the *International Who's Who*, and *Distinctive Women of America*. The *Daily Record* reported that Joyce was to perform a program including Handel's "Sonata No. 6 in E Major," Mozart's "Gavotte," and "Old Refrain" by Fritz Kreisler.

The *New York Journal-American* reported that Joyce was going to perform "a long-forgotten composition by the 18th century Italian musician Vivaldi." The *Journal-American* noted that "Miss Renee" had performed to critical acclaim in major concert halls in the United States and abroad. Joyce obtained the Vivaldi piece from Giuseppe Adami, a conductor and arranger who found it in the archives of the Naples Conservatory of Music. "This music has not been heard in our time," says the dark-haired, handsome Miss Renee. "I am looking forward to introducing it to music lovers of the present and consider it a privilege to do so."[98]

The *New York Journal* noted that Miss Renee had appeared, among other places, as a soloist on "the huge Radio City Music Hall stage" for eight weeks. The *Journal* commented that if "Miss Renee were not so good to look at, one could forget that there was a young woman at the helm of this magnificent performance—few men have such power." Joyce played a tour of southern states for the Haynes Town Series, leading the program manager to comment that "Never have I seen audiences so completely spellbound."

Joyce also performed at the College of New Rochelle under the auspices of the Ursuline Guild. Mildred Gould, President of the Guild, enthused over Joyce's performance: "The Ursuline Guild wishes to thank you for a most memorable evening of music. Not only is your

98 *New York Journal-American*, July 29, 1951.

musicianship perfection itself, but your magnetic charm completely captivated us…Those of us who were lucky enough to hear you will always remember with a thrill of pleasure your superb artistry and how very gracious you and your splendid accompanist, Miss Adele Bay, were to us."[99]

Joyce also played a concert at Ursuline College in New Orleans. She was sufficiently impressive that "Mother Elizabeth Marie dedicated a daily novena to Miss Renee, for her art, health and protection during her many travels, with the promise that this daily group of prayers will be said for her, at Ursuline College, as long as she lives."[100]

Joyce's performances at religious institutions ran the gamut from churches and synagogues to religiously affiliated colleges and universities. Rabbi Dr. Stephen Wise, the highly regarded leader of Reform Judaism in the United States, asked Joyce to perform the Kol Nidre service for the High Holyday services at Carnegie Hall. Kol Nidre, a haunting melody played at services on erev Yom Kippur (the evening that marks the beginning of Yom Kippur), releases Jews from vows they may have made before they seek to atone for their sins. The music for the service is beautiful, albeit mournful. Cellists often perform the melody because the cello provides the low, rich tone appropriate for the liturgy, but violins can produce the same rich, emotional timbre the service calls for. Playing Kol Nidre for Rabbi Wise at Carnegie Hall was one of the most significant performances that a Jewish musician could be asked to undertake.

Joyce participated in many organizations devoted to music. She was a member, honorary member, or patron of the Phi Delta Alpha Medical Honorary Fraternity, The Three Arts Club, Phi Delta Gamma, the Studio Club, The International Platform Association, Phi Beta Fraternity, the American Musicological Society, the Musicians' Club of America, the Cincinnati Conservatory of Music, and Juilliard Alumni Associations. Her fellowships included the Fleishmann, Schmidlapp, Juilliard Musical Advisory Council, Enescu, and Woolley International Fellowships.

Joyce Renée was on top of the world.

---

99 October 8, 1951, letter from Mildred Gould to Joyce Renée.

100 Cincinnati newspaper, July 19, 1951. (The newspaper's name is not on the copy of the article available to the author). Ursuline College is a private Roman Catholic liberal arts institution in Pepper Pike, Ohio. The Ursuline Sisters of Cleveland founded the college in 1871. It was one of the oldest institutions of higher education for women in the United States and was the first Catholic women's college in Ohio.

DISASTER

In 1951, Joyce was at the height of her powers. At age forty, she was a major violin soloist paying concerts across the United States for tens of thousands of admirers. She was engaged to play at the most important venues in the country, as well as including many charitable programs in her concert schedule. Joyce not only played incredibly well, but she did good too. Joyce still made New York her home.

And then, on October 17, 1951, disaster struck. Joyce was in Manhattan walking on the northeast corner of 76th and Broadway. Crews were performing roadwork; they had placed soft asphalt in the street. While Joyce was crossing the street, one of her shoes stuck in the soft tar, causing her to fall and hit her head on the pavement.

The impact caused a cerebral concussion, post-concussion syndrome, headaches, blurred vision, loss of memory, and inability to concentrate. Joyce never fully recovered. Given the nature of her injuries, Joyce was unable to return to performing. With her career over, she eventually left New York to return to Cincinnati. While Joyce could no longer perform, she continued to play piano occasionally in the apartment she shared with her mother. She also composed songs and continued to study music, even though she was unable to return to the stage.

Joyce hired an attorney to file suit against the Edenwald Contracting Company, the New York Telephone Company, and Empire City Subway Co. Unfortunately, her attorneys did not file her claim within the statutory period, and she was unable to pursue the lawsuit. She then filed a malpractice claim against her attorneys. However, to compound the tragedy of her injury, the New York court dismissed Joyce's malpractice claim when she was medically unable to appear in New York for her deposition.

Her career over and her lawsuit mishandled, New York, which had for so long been the center of her life, now had nothing for Joyce but memories. She was left to try to find peace and a future at home.

Life in Cincinnati

Joyce spent the rest of her life living with her mother in the apartment at 7333 Brookcrest Drive, just a few blocks off Section Road, in Cincinnati's Roselawn neighborhood. The two-bedroom apartment was on the second floor of a two-unit building. The sides and lower level of the building were clad in red brick, while the front façade of the second floor was finished in white paneling with gray shutters on the windows.

The second-floor apartment had a spacious living room in which Joyce had a baby grand piano. Notwithstanding her accident, Joyce could still play piano, which she sometimes did after family functions. She kept a small sterling silver violin on the piano, letting it occupy pride of place as a reminder of her true musical love.

As to her ill-fated love affair, several of Joyce's songs reflect her sense of loss. For example, Joyce wrote one song with alternative titles—"When I Think of You" and "Not Only in my Dreams":

Since you're gone, I can't smile,
can't be gay for a while,
Dreams are all I have now,
I'll keep dreaming somehow.
When I think of you
I long to hear your voice
To see your smile
and feel my heart rejoice.
But then I know that this can never be,
You can't belong to me.
But I will always hold you near me.
I have my dreams you are with me

in my heart eternally.
Yet I know that someday you and I will find each other's arms,
will know each other's charms,
Not only in my dreams…

And in "Strange," Joyce wrote:

Being hurt by love must come to everyone.
But when you've been hurt you feel you're the only one.
Strange, when love has gone how the world goes on,
Night still follows day and life keeps on its way.
Strange, your heart can break, what difference does it make.
People pass by not asking why you cry.
Only the heavens can feel your pain.
You cry together alone in the rain.
Time, they say, can heal sorrows that you feel.
Strange, and somehow not so strange.[101]

There were times when Joyce flashed anger at her mother. Whether it was due to frustration over the loss of her career, irritation about going from a global stage to a two-bedroom apartment in Ohio shared with her mother, or resentment at her mother having insisted that Joyce end her love affair, only Joyce could say. But, given the life Joyce once had and lost, it is easy to understand why she might be angry. Joyce had lost her career and the love of her life. Now, she could only sit, compose songs in her mother's apartment, remember when she was on top of the world, and look back on the time when love and the highest level of performing art were hers.

101 James Beni wrote the lyrics; Joyce composed the music.

WASSERMAN FAMILY GATHERINGS

Every spring, the Wasserman family celebrated Passover at Granny's (Anna Wasserman) and Joyce's apartment. Granny broke out her "Pesadic" plates with orange flowers around the edges and prepared a full Ashkenazi spread for the Seder meal, the enticing aromas of which permeated the apartment. The seder meal typically included brisket, chicken soup with matzo balls (medium sized "floaters" as opposed to dense matzo balls known as "sinkers" that fell to the bottom of the soup bowl), a hard-boiled egg and boiled potato for the saltwater portion of the Seder (the boiled potato being a culinary artifact from Anna's Lithuanian/ Belarussian homeland), sweet carrot tzimmes, and, sometimes, myena (a chopped liver type of pâté or pudding).

Granny also made gribenes, bits of chicken skin fried in schmaltz (chicken fat) until crisp (don't tell your cardiologist you ate these fat-soaked bits of deliciousness.) Cousin Cookie Aronoff always brought the brightly colored, sugary fruit-flavored jelly slices that are frequently served at Seders. Dessert was typically a sponge cake served with strawberries or other fruit. Fruit compote made of stewed prunes, pears, and apricots was part of the dessert menu, along with Barton's Kosher for Pesach candies.

Joyce always made tomato aspic for Seder. Aspic is a savory gelatin made with meat stock or broth. While many people may consider it delicious, it was not to the taste of Allan Wasserman's children Margie and Steven. Occasionally, Joyce forgot to serve the aspic. Since the dish had to stay in the refrigerator until it was time for it to be eaten, it suffered from being out of sight and, therefore, out of mind. On those occasions when the aspic failed to make its way to the table, Margie and Steven considered the Seder a success.

Another challenge the Wasserman and Aronoff children faced at Seder was courtesy of Uncle Joe Cohen, husband of Hilda Wasserman, one of Joyce's sisters. Uncle Joe led the Seder, and he was not one to skip any part of the service. He typically read the entire Manischewitz Haggadah in Hebrew. Trudy Houser, mother of Allan's wife Renate, was not an observant Jew and knew only one part of the Haggadah—the page at which the participants could have dinner.

After the Seder, Uncle Joe, exhausted by his efforts, retired to the living room for a nap. When it came time to leave, he gave each child a double whammy: a big kiss on the check with his bristly mustache inflicting a brief derma-abrasion on the children's faces, followed by a firm thumb and forefinger cheek-pinch on top of that.

On rare occasions after the Seder, Joyce seated herself at the baby grand piano in the apartment and played for a few minutes. The family fell into a hush as she played with precision and passion, a cigarette stained with her bright red lipstick smoking in an ashtray on the piano next to her sterling silver violin. While it was wonderful to hear Joyce play, the music and violin were painful reminders of the sterling career that had been but was no more.

Joyce Passes Away

On September 2, 1975, twenty-four years after her accident, Joyce passed away at the age of sixty-four.[102] She had spent twenty-four years in the apartment on Brookcrest Avenue, from the date of her accident until her death. Her extraordinary career had gone from the greatest heights to a lonely, constricted world delimited by the apartment she shared with her mother. the *American Israelite* printed her obituary:

> Esther Wasserman, American violinist known professionally as Joyce Renée, passed away Tuesday, Sept. 2, at Jewish Hospital. She was 64.
>
> A native Cincinnatian, Miss Wasserman made her debut when 9 with Dr. Frank Simon's Armco Band on WLW and the Blue Network.
>
> She was the youngest honor graduate in the history of the [Cincinnati] Conservatory of Music.
>
> During her musical career Miss Wasserman received numerous awards, including the Fleishmann's, Schmidlapp, and Juilliard International Fellowships.
>
> While in Paris she was the recipient of the Institute Instrumental Award and was holder of the Wooley International Fellowship when studying under Georges Enesco. She was awarded the coveted Walters Town Hall Award and three medals from the Ohio Society of New York.
>
> She interrupted her career during the second World War to perform for the armed forces and was recognized with citations

102 Joyce's grave can be found in Cincinnati's Love Brothers' Cemetery at Section Four, Row Three, Grave No. 24. The Hebrew portion of Joyce's headstone reads "Esther daughter of Rav Mordechai died on 26 Elul 5735." The word "rav" is a term of respect; Mordechai was a common Hebrew name for Max. The English portion of Joyce's gravestone reads:" "Esther Joyce, July 13, 1911 – Sept. 2, 1975, Beloved Daughter."

from the Stage Door Canteens, Merchant Marine and U.S. Camp Shows.

She appeared on nationwide radio and television and performed at Carnegie Hall, Madison Square Garden, Town Hall and Radio City Music Hall, New York City.

Miss Wasserman was a member of the Musicians Union, Phi Beta Epsilon, and a life member of Zonta International.[103] She is listed in Who's Who in Music, International Who's Who in Music and is recognized by the Distinctive Women of America.

She is survived by her mother, Anna R. Wasserman, and one brother, J. Robert Wasserman.

Services for Joyce were held on Sept. 4 at the Weil Funeral Home in Cincinnati. Rabbi Fishel J. Goldfeder of Cincinnati's Adath Israel synagogue officiated at the internment.

So ended the triumphant, artistic, and ultimately tragic life of Esther Joyce Renée Wasserman. This daughter of immigrants was a musical prodigy whose career soared to the highest heights. She played to audiences in some of the world's most famous concert venues. Commentators regarded her as one of the finest musicians of her generation.

Joyce continued to be a dutiful daughter after her accident, living with and caring for her mother until Joyce's death. Unable to return to the stage and perform after her injury, her extraordinary career had been cut short. Nevertheless, her life was extraordinary, and her warmth and generosity so manifest, that Joyce Renée, as a daughter, performer, sister, and aunt, deserves to be honored and remembered.

Some words are never spoken,
Somehow, they're hard to say.
I can reveal to you what I feel,
When you hear my fiddle play.[104]

103 Zonta International is an organization dedicated to the empowerment of women worldwide through service and advocacy. Founded in 1919, Zonta "believes in making the world a better place by empowering women." (www.Zonta.org.) "Zonta stands for women's rights. We advocate for equality, education and an end to child marriage and gender-based violence." (*Id.*)

104 From Joyce's composition "When My Fiddle Dreams."

Postscript

I have vivid memories of my Aunt Joyce. She strode through the apartment she shared with Granny Wasserman in high heels, sporting bright red lipstick, with a cigarette dangling from her lips. Joyce was a loving and generous aunt, always sending birthday and Hanukah cards to my sister and me with a cash gift enclosed. I was impressed by Joyce's skill on those rare occasions when the family persuaded her to sit at the piano and play for us after Seder.

However, and perhaps understandably since I only knew her when I was a child, I never appreciated what had transpired in her life. From this late vantage point in my life, I can better understand my Aunt Joyce. I certainly have a far greater appreciation for what a generational talent she was. I wish I had known her better when I was an adult and could better appreciate her.

As described above, Aunt Joyce never married, nor did she have children. But someone so talented, generous, and kind deserves to be honored and remembered. And so, Aunt Joyce, I offer this biography to you in recognition of and appreciation for all you accomplished and everything that made you so special. As put by Joseph Maddy, founder of the Interlochen Center for the Arts, you are loved and in the minds of the living, and, therefore, you will never die.

Appendix: Notes on Joyce's Compositions[105]

Joyce composed music throughout her life. However, most of the music she wrote (at least the music the author has found) were piano pieces and songs she composed after her accident, as opposed to orchestral, instrumental pieces. One might wonder why this violin virtuoso, who performed all manner of complex classical music, composed songs and solo piano pieces instead of orchestral pieces or compositions specifically for violin. One reason may be that Joyce simply enjoyed composing in the musical vernacular of her day. She grew up and performed during the time of big band jazz and crooned love songs. She may have found those genres approachable and enjoyable vehicles through which she could express her feelings.

When assessing her compositions, it is important to keep in mind the effect her accident may have had on her. The extent of residual cognitive problems or limitations Joyce may have suffered, beyond her inability to return to performing and the medical issues raised in her lawsuit, is not known. However, the music she played in concert was often complex and comprised much of the violin concert canon of the time.

It may be that the injuries Joyce suffered limited what she could do creatively. If she could no longer play the violin or play up to her previous capabilities as a virtuoso, perhaps she simply could not bring herself to compose for an instrument she could no longer play to her satisfaction.

105 Much of the analysis of Joyce's compositions is courtesy of Scott Foglesong. Since the author, to his great regret, is not a musician and possesses very limited (read this as almost zero) musical knowledge, Mr. Foglesong assisted as a consultant. He contributed most of the analysis of Joyce's compositions and recorded on piano several of her compositions so that, however briefly and for however limited an audience, some of Joyce's music would live again. Mr. Foglesong is Chair of the Department of Musicianship and Music Theory at the San Francisco Conservatory of Music, a Lecturer at The Fromm Institute of the University of San Francisco, and a Contributing Writer and Lecturer for the San Francisco Symphony,

Her violin, instead of being a source of pride and comfort, may have become a silent and painful reminder of what she had once been but was no longer.

It also may be that if Joyce had residual limitations, they interfered with the extent and clarity of her recollection. To the extent a few of her songs resembled songs that were popular at the time, it may be that Joyce had limited recollection of the other pieces. She may not have been able to recall certain turns of musical phrase as being someone else's and not having sprung from her own imagination. Or, she may simply have decided to adapt other tunes for her lyrics.

The pieces Joyce composed include:

Come and Dance with Me

Little Bouquet,

When We're Together (words and music)

When I Think of You (words and music)

Coronet,

Just Like a Dream (words and music)

In My Heart (words and music)

As Long as There's a You (words and music)

Love of My Heart (words and music)

Match

Cause You Are Mine (words and music)

The Songs of My Homeland I Carry with Me

When My Fiddle Dreams – Just a Melody (words and music)

When I Think of You or Not Only in My Dreams (words and music)

You're So Dear to Me or *As Long as there's a You* (words and music)

Don't Forget [melody "Strange")] (words and music)

When My Fiddle Dreams (words and music), and

Clapping Hands.

Joyce wrote two kinds of compositions: piano pieces and songs. Her piano pieces include: "Come and Dance with Me"; "Little Bouquet"; "Coronets"; "Clapping Hands"; and "March." Her piano compositions are short character pieces, typically thirty-two some-odd measures long.

Two of them are much like songs without a vocal part ("Come and Dance with Me" and "Little Bouquet"), while two are more dance-like ("Coronets" and "March"). None would be out of place in a collection of short pieces for beginning-level pianists. They are written in an easily accessible musical idiom, using traditional harmony, singable melodies, and standard phrase lengths.

For the most part, Joyce wrote as a non-pianist; that is to say, she knows how the piano works, but she is not an actual pianist who can "feel" her way through the idiomatic style that is characteristic of experienced pianists. However, several pieces stand out for being noticeably more idiomatic to the piano: "Come and Dance with Me" and the piano part to "When My Fiddle Dreams" in either of its two versions. "Clapping Hands," "Little Bouquet," and "Coronets" are all at a basic piano level, "Come and Dance with Me" is more advanced, while "March" is more of a sketch than a finished piece.

SONGS

When We're Together
Just Like a Dream
In My Heart
When I Think of You/Not Only in My Dreams (two versions)
As Long as There's a You
Love of My Heart
'Cause You Are Mine
The Songs of My Homeland I Carry with Me
God Love My Country
You're So Dear to Me, or As Long as There's a You
Strange/Don't Forget (four versions)
When My Fiddle Dreams (two versions)

Like songwriters from all eras, Joyce took her inspiration and models from the music of her

era. In her case, that meant popular ballads of the 1940s and early 1950s, during a period that was a golden age for the American popular song. The pervasiveness of radio, records, and movies resulted in a flood of songs from songwriters whose efforts ranged from masterful to merely competent, aided by a post-War surge in Broadway musicals by such brilliant writers as Rodgers and Hammerstein, Lerner and Loewe, Harold Rome, Frank Loesser, and others. Almost all of Joyce's songs are love ballads, much like the material covered by singers such as Bing Crosby, Frank Sinatra, Jo Stafford, and Jane Froman. Joyce composed songs that you might hear on the radio, on records, in movies, or in clubs.

Joyce wrote the lyrics for most, but not all, of her songs. Her lyrics are typical of the era in that they are filled with metaphor. Some lyrics might strike today's listeners as trite: examples are phrasing such as the angels were whispering love, feel my heart rejoice, like a dream you came to me, you are the angel heaven has sent me, heaven's smile on true love, and the like. However, such metaphors were common during Joyce's time as a performer, and few lyricists shunned them.

Joyce was partial to single-syllable end rhymes, such as charms/arms, or dream/scheme. She occasionally indulged in an inner rhyme, such as clear to me, dear to me, and near to me. But she did not indulge in the intricate wordplay of such lyricists as Lorenz Hart, or the sophisticated writing of Ira Gershwin. Overall, she used a clear vocabulary of mostly one- and two-syllable words. Occasionally, she employed parallelism such as "come to ev'ryone/you're the only one, or I'll be seeing you/I'll be wanting you/I'll be loving you."

It may be that Joyce wrote her melodies first, possibly along with the words, but worked out the harmonies later. That can be seen in the more sketch-like songs such as "'Cause You Are Mine", "You Are So Dear To Me", and "The Songs of My Homeland I Carry With Me." In these compositions, she did not include chord symbols. This can also be seen in "God Love My Country" and "When I Think of You" as their chord symbols were clearly added later in pencil.

Joyce employed a professional copyist for some of her work, including most of the piano pieces and about half of the songs. Joyce's handwriting can readily be discerned. She tended to be lax about stemming—the direction, up or down, that the stem goes on a note. The first version of "When My Fiddle Dreams" is not in her handwriting, but it is not quite in a professional copyist's hand, either. The corrections, however, look like Joyce's handwriting.

Since Joyce was clearly influenced by her era's pop ballads, it should not be surprising to find that, occasionally she edged close to imitation. Two of her songs—"When I Think of You" and "Love of My Heart"—bear striking resemblances to well-known songs of the day. "When I Think of You" resembles the 1938 hit, "I'll Be Seeing You" which was on just about every crooner's lips in the 1940s, and the chorus of "Love of My Heart" is almost a note-for-note copy of "You Wonderful You", a song best known from its use in the 1950 MGM musical film *Summer Stock*, starring Judy Garland and Gene Kelly (who sings the song.) Again, these similarities may have been due to Joyce's injury and the impact it had on her memory, or she decided to borrow the melodies for her own purposes.

Songs and their Structure

Most pop songs are written in a standardized form to ensure listeners, dancers, and singers are not taxed by having to traverse unfamiliar territory. The typical layout for such songs is:

Introduction: this is optional, and typically is in the accompaniment alone.

Verse: also optional, typically an 8 or 16-bar passage that leads directly into; the

Chorus: the 'main' tune, typically sung twice, with some lyric and chord changes. Then,

Bridge: a contrasting section, followed by the

Chorus: a final statement of the main tune, typically sung once, after which comes the

Release: which is optional, typically in the accompaniment alone, but can also be sung.

The chorus is typically written in what is called incipient three-part song form, which consists of three parts with the third part a truncated repeat of the first part. If letters are used to identify musical phrases, the usual incipient three-part song form looks like this:

Part 1: a a'

Part 2: b

Part 3: a'

Note that a' indicates a modified repeat of a. Although incipient three-part song form is not the only way to structure a song, it was Joyce's preferred form not only for her songs, but for her piano pieces as well.

"Come and Dance with Me"

This composition is a solo piano piece and is written in a professionally copied manuscript. It is written in F Major and ¾ time. No tempo is given, but 'allegretto' seems right, since it is a waltz. Although it contains abundant phrase marks, there is only one dynamic indication—a hairpin +-crescendo in measure 34. The piece is rather like a 1940s popular ballad without a separate vocal part. The first eight bars are an introduction, while the chorus is repeated.

"Little Bouquet"

"Little Bouquet" is another solo piano piece in a professionally copied manuscript, written in F Major and ¾ time. It is a "bare" score in that it does not have phrase marks, dynamics, or other performance indications. However, it makes sense to assume a waltz tempo, much like "Come and Dance with Me" and an overall legato style of playing. It also resembles a pop ballad of the 1940s. It does not have an introduction; the main body is in incipient three-part song form.

"Coronets"

This is a solo piano piece reflected in a professionally copied manuscript. It was written in G major and ¾ time. Like "Little Bouquet," this is a "bare" score in that it contains only notes, without any other performance indications. However, "Coronets" seems to call out for a robust, quickstep rendition. The piece is in a three-part song form with the structure A-B-C, i.e., three contrasting sections.

"When We're Together"

This piece is a song chart (vocal line, words, and chords) in a professionally copied manuscript.

Joyce wrote the words and music. She wrote it in F Major, cut time, in incipient three-part song form. This is a love song written very much in the idiom of mid-century popular music.

"Just Like a Dream"

This song chart (vocal line, words, and chords) is in a professionally copied manuscript. Joyce wrote the words and music and composed the song in F Major and 4/4 time. Although she did not give a tempo, it may be that this should be sung more slowly than "When We're Together." The reason for this is there are more chord changes, many of which are on single beats, and the 4/4-time signature implies a somewhat slower tempo than the cut time of "When We're Together." This song has relatively sophisticated chord progressions in comparison to the solo piano pieces of "When We're Together." Like "When We're Together," "Just Like a Dream" is in incipient three-part song form.

In My Heart

The song chart has a vocal line, words, and chords with an accompaniment pattern established at the beginning. Joyce wrote the words and music, and they appear in a professionally copied manuscript. Joyce wrote it in E Minor and 2/4 time. "In My Heart" has a tango like feel due to its minor key and the rhythmic pattern. It was written in standard incipient three-part song form, with no verse, but the chorus has unorthodox phrase lengths after the initial 4-bar introduction:

Chorus
- a: 5 – 8 (4 bars)
- b: 9 – 11 (3 bars)
- c: 12 – 16 (5 bars)
- a: 17 – 20 (4 bars)
- b: 21 – 23 (3 bars)
- c: 24 – 28 (5 bars)

Bridge
- d: 29 – 32 (4 bars)
- d': 33 – 36
- d": 37 – 40

Chorus
- a: 41 – 44 (4 bars)
- b': 45 – 52 (8 bars)

"When I Think of You" (first version)

This piece has a song chart (vocal line, words, and chords), appears in a professionally copied manuscript, and has words and music by Joyce Renée. Joyce composed it in F Major using cut time. This composition is very similar to "I'll Be Seeing You," a 1938 song with music by Sammy Fain with lyrics by Irving Kahal that was popular in the 1940s; it is even the name of a 1944 film. "I'll Be seeing You" has been covered by singers such as Bing Crosby, Frank Sinatra, Billie Holiday, and Brenda Lee. It was written in F Major, cut time, with an incipient three-part song form, repeated, with an 8-bar release.

"When I Think of You, or Not Only in My Dreams," second version

This piece has a song chart (vocal line, words, and chords). This composition appears in a handwritten manuscript, likely in Joyce's hand. It was written in cut time, F major, and is dated 1953. The song has an eight-measure verse—unique to this version—followed by a chorus in incipient three-part song form, first and second endings. It should be noted that the verse contains chord symbols, but the chorus does not.

"As Long As There's You"

This piece has a song chart (vocal line, words, and chords). The song appears in a professionally copied manuscript with words and music by Joyce Renée and Robert Russell Bennet. It was written in F Major, ¾ time. This composition has a waltz like feel to it, sort of a slow ballad, with an 8-bar verse that leads into a 36-bar chorus/bridge/chorus.

"Love Of My Heart"

This piece has a song chart (vocal line, words, and chords) and is in a professionally copied manuscript with words and music by Joyce Renée written in F Major, cut time. While it is an attractive song, it is very similar to "You Wonderful You," by Jack Brooks, Saul Chaplin, and Harry Warren, which is best known from being featured in the 1950 movie "Summer Stock."

"March"

This is a solo piano piece appearing in a hand-written manuscript with melody and chord symbols. It was written in F Major with 4/4 time. It clearly would be best performed in march tempo, in incipient three-part song form with no repeats.

"'Cause You Are Mine"

This composition, appearing in a hand-written manuscript, is represented by a melody line with words, but no chord symbols or piano accompaniment. It should be in either common or cut time (this is not specified in the manuscript; cut time is more likely.) The introductory verse starts in G Minor; the repeat of the first phrase (starting measure 9) is in the parallel key of G Major. (The effect of this is to 'brighten' the overall feel of the music.)

The chorus (beginning line 5) is in C major. The chorus is in incipient three-part song form: a a' b a'. On a separate page is a sketch for a "release", that is, a melodic figure to be played to end the song. The release employs some chromaticism (i.e., notes and chords not part of the C Major key.)

"The Songs of My Homeland I Carry with Me"

This song, appearing in a hand manuscript, has a melody line only with no text or chord symbols. It might be a sketch. Either common or cut time (not specified; cut time more likely.) E-flat Major throughout; in incipient song form (a a' b a') after a four-measure introduction. The chorus is repeated with a different ending.

"God Love My Country"

The song chart (vocal line, words, and chords) is written in a hand manuscript, most likely in Joyce's hand. It apparently was a work in progress as it has corrections in the margins, including changes to the lyrics. Joyce wrote it in F Major and cut time. It is in three-part song form (a a' b a a") and is marked to be performed Marcato (emphatic).

“You’re So Dear to Me, or “As Long As There’s a You”

This composition appears in a song chart, but without chord symbols. It is a hand manuscript, likely in Joyce’s own hand, but the verse is without words. Joyce wrote it in ¾ time, in G-flat Major, which is a highly unusual key for a popular song. This composition seems more like a sketch than a finished song. The chorus consists only of two phrases (a a’). Joyce indicated that it is to be repeated, and then “bottom line is the 1st ending; top line is 2nd ending, after it repeats.

“Strange – Don’t Forget” (four songs)

Joyce used this melody for two songs, each time with lyrics by James Beni. “Strange,” first version, has a Song chart (vocal line, words, and chord symbols), is in hand manuscript probably in Joyce’s hand, written in ¾ time, and in F Major. This is the second setting of the tune “Don’t Forget,” this time with a verse. The verse is an inverted (i.e., upside down) version of the chorus. It is written in incipient three-part song form (a a’ b a”) and shows a copyright in 1952.

“Strange” (second version)

The song chart (vocal line, words, and chord symbols) appears in hand manuscript, probably in Joyce’s hand. The lyrics are by James Beni. It apparently is a hand copy of the entry above.

“Don’t Forget” (first version)

This song chart (vocal line, words, and chord symbols) appears in a hand manuscript, probably in Joyce’s hand, with lyrics by James Beni. It was written in ¾ time, F Major. This is the same melody as Joyce’s song “Strange,” but with different words. It is the chorus only, no verse. It is written in incipient three-part song form (a a’ b a’) and is marked “Copyright 1953.”

"Don't Forget" (second version)

Song chart (vocal line, words, and chord symbols). It is in a hand manuscript, probably in Joyce's hand. James Beni wrote the lyrics. This appears to be a hand copy of "Don't Forget," first version, using the same melody as "Strange."

"Clapping Hands"

This piano solo appears in a professionally copied manuscript. Joyce wrote it in 4/4 time in G Major. No dynamics, tempo, or markings of any sort are given, but it is clearly in a bright, march-like tempo. It was cast in full three-part song form (a a' b b a a').

"When My Fiddle Dreams" or "Just a Melody" (first version

This is the first version of two for this piece. Joyce wrote it in D major verse, D minor chorus. It appears in a hand manuscript, but probably not in Joyce's hand. The score contains numerous handwritten corrections (which likely are in Joyce's hand), possibly in pencil (as opposed to ink for the main copy.) It was written as a piano score (two staves) with the words above.

The piano writing is noticeably more sophisticated than in Joyce's other compositions, which suggests she had a consultant for the piano part. She then applied some corrections to that piano part that show up in the second, professionally copied version. This piece is in ¾ time and is marked valse moderato. The Italian musical command moderato is an indication to play in a reasonable, moderate tempo.

An 8-bar introduction leads to the verse, a parallel period (a a') that leads into the chorus, which is in the usual incipient three-part song form (a a' b a'), with a first ending that 'turns back' to repeat the chorus, and a second ending that brings the song to a conclusion. A notation on the bottom of the second page gives copyright by Joyce Renée and Marion Rosette. Perhaps Rosette wrote the lyrics, but nothing indicates what her participation was.)

"When My Fiddle Dreams" (second version)

This piece is for voice and piano and appears in a professionally copied manuscript showing vocal line, chord symbols, words, and a completely written-out piano part. The words and music are by Joyce Renée and Marion Rosette. It was written in ¾ time, with the verse in D major, and the chorus in D minor. This is a fully fleshed-out version with a full piano part and professional-quality notation. The piano part has been modified since it is no longer called on to carry the melody.

This version may have been intended to submit for professional publication. In both this and the alternate, hand-copy version, the piano writing is noticeably more idiomatic than in Joyce's piano pieces, again suggesting she may have had a pianist consultant help her with the piano part.

Sheet Music

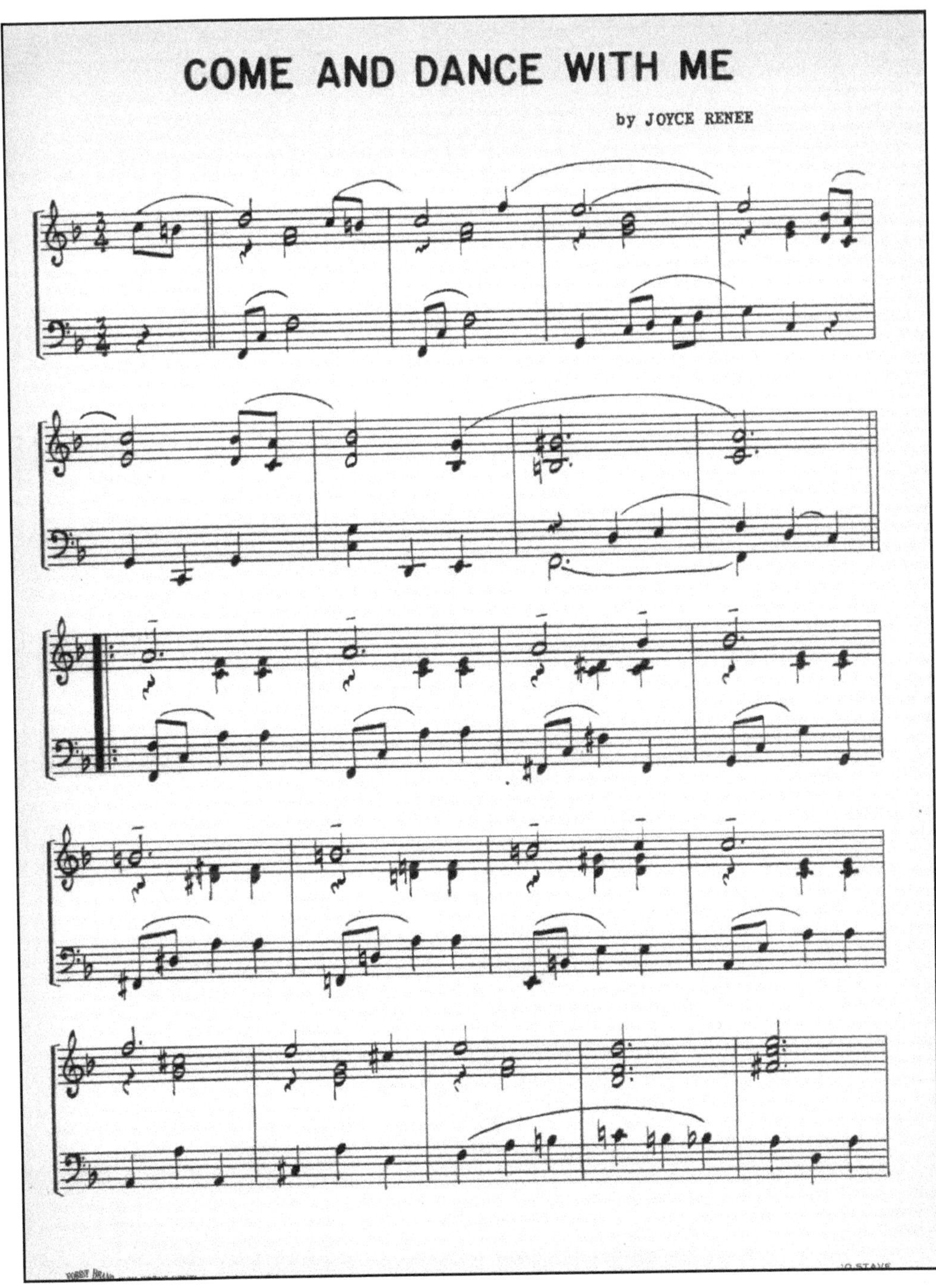
COME AND DANCE WITH ME
by JOYCE RENEE

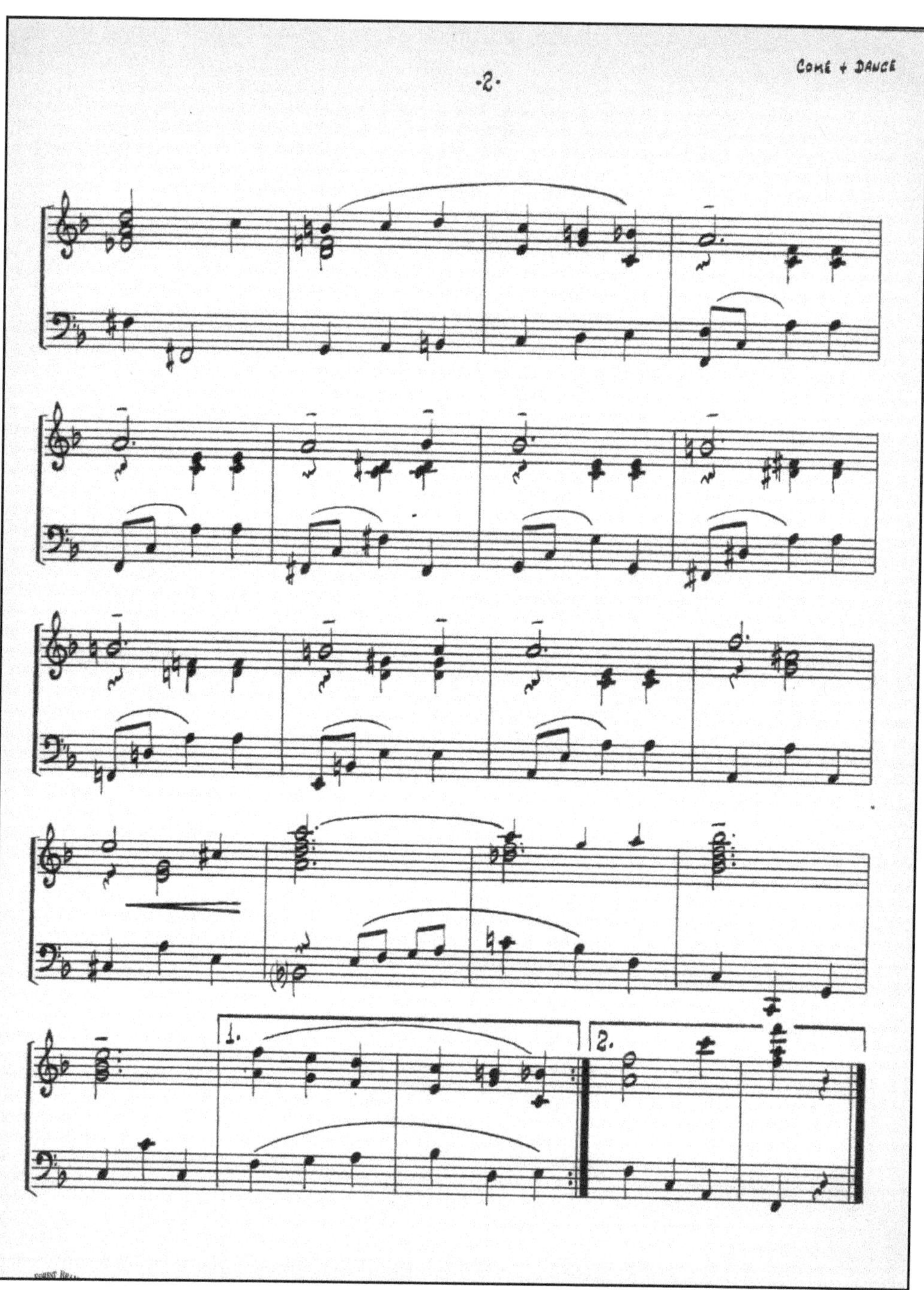
-2-
COME + DANCE
1.
2.

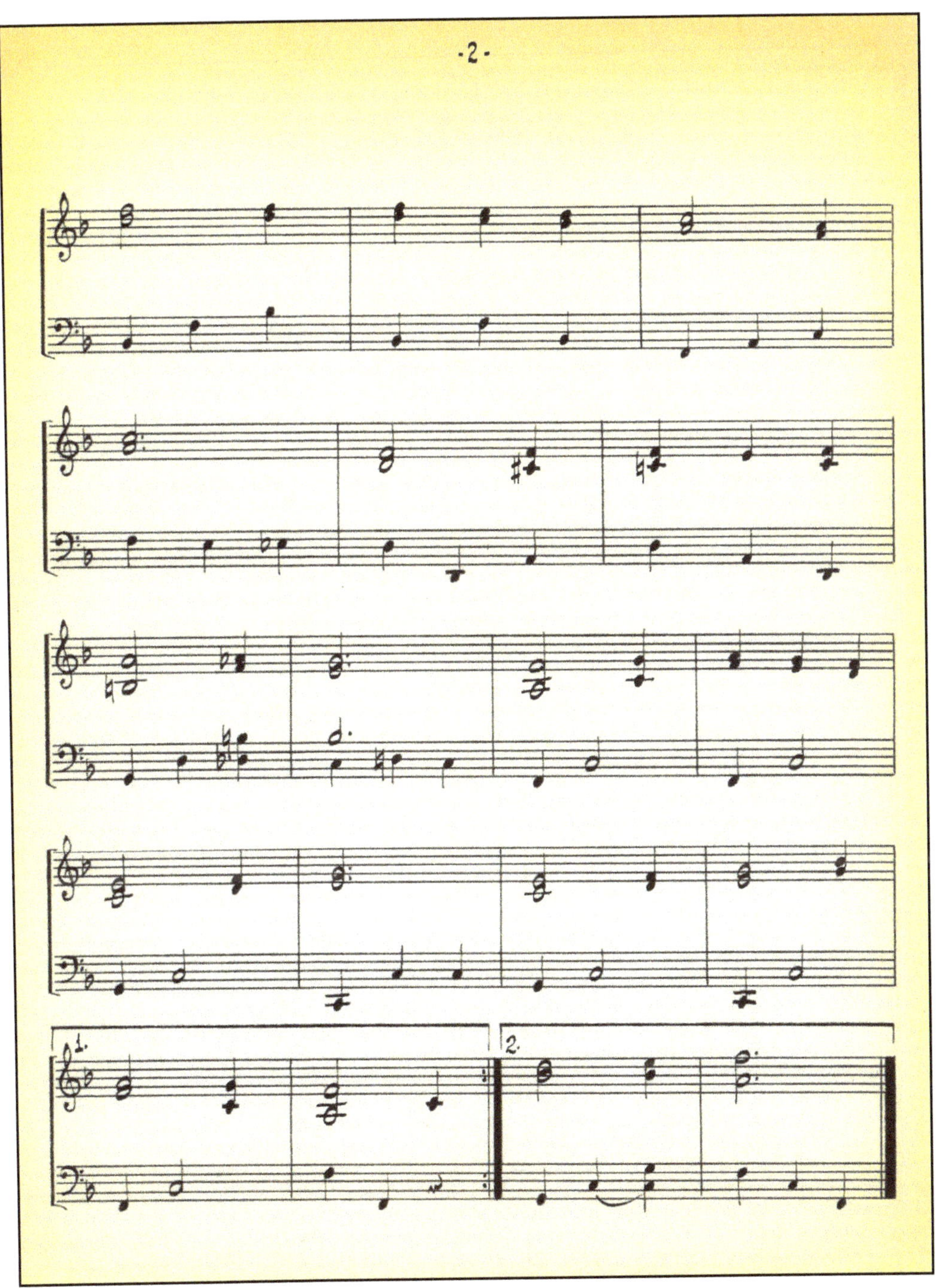

-2-
1.
2.

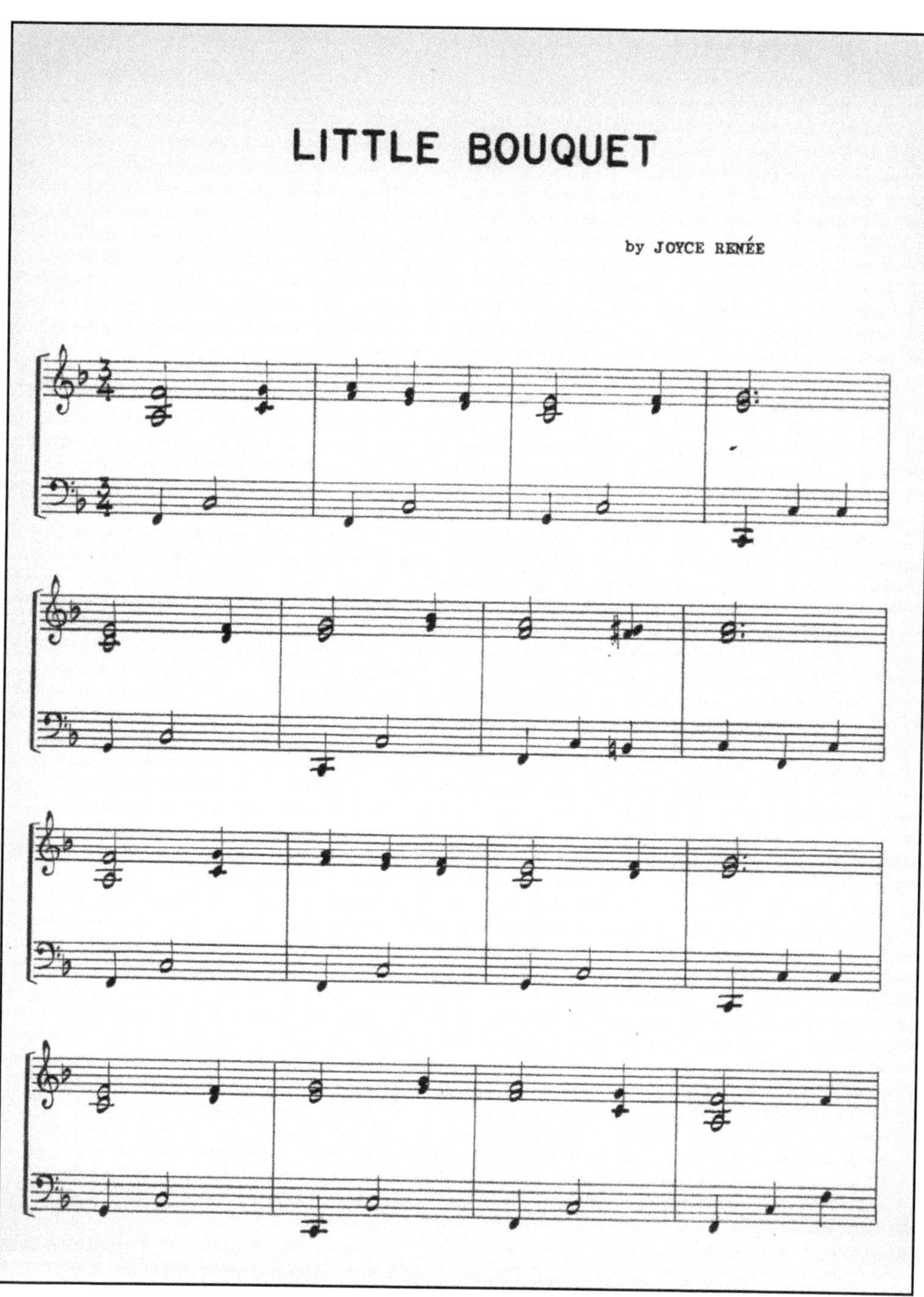
LITTLE BOUQUET
by JOYCE RENÉE

WHEN WE'RE TOGETHER

Words and Music by
JOYCE RENÉE

Not too slow

My heart starts in danc - ing and I want to

sing, The world is mine WHEN WE'RE TO - GETH- ER. It's

not just ro - manc - ing for love is the thing That

claims my heart WHEN WE'RE TO - GETH - ER. The

mo - ment that you leave me, old gloom comes walk- ing

in; And you're the on - ly one I know that

can get rid of him. So let's call the

preach - er and tell him that we Were

al - ways meant to be to - geth - er.

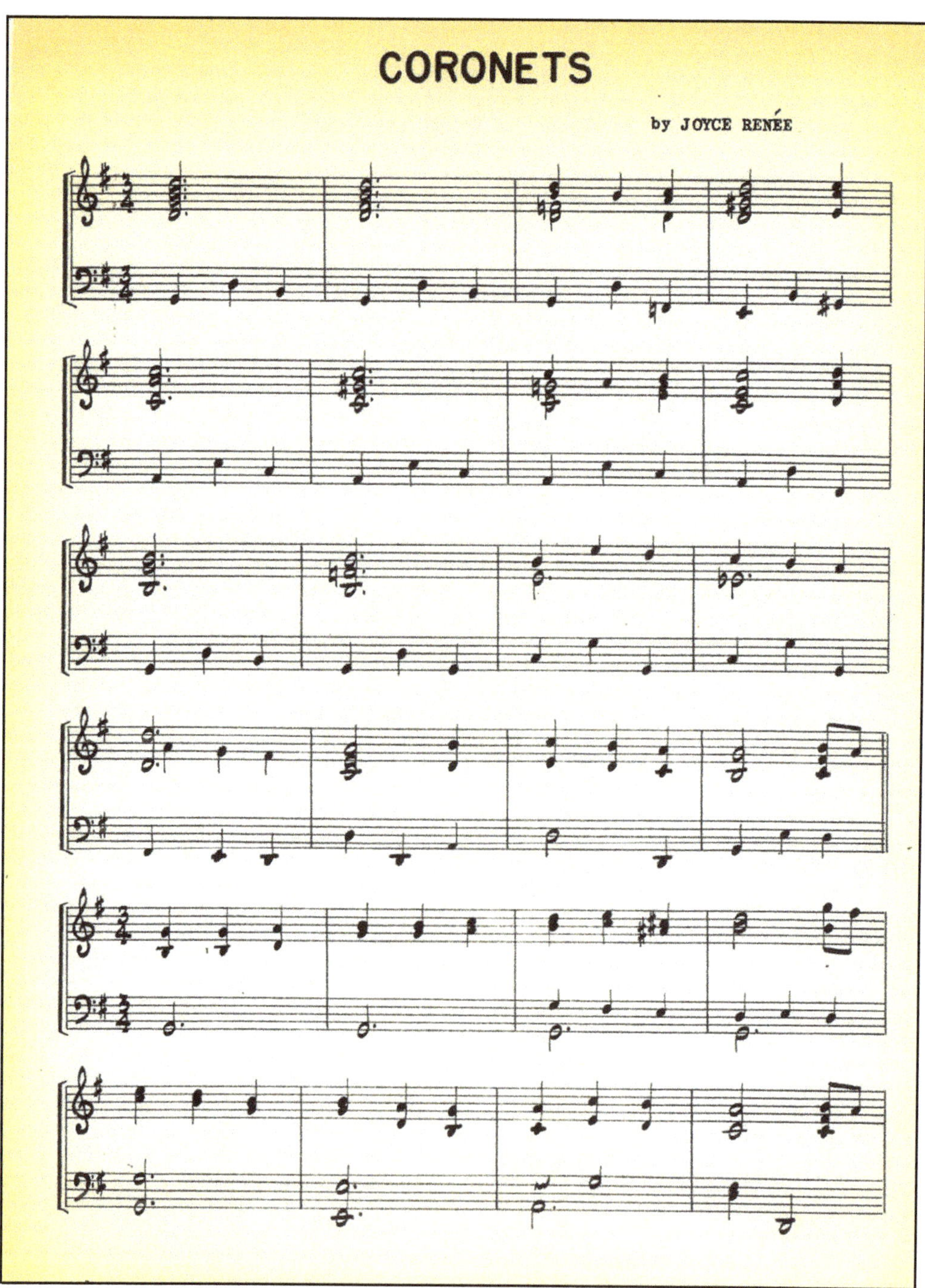
CORONETS
by JOYCE RENÉE

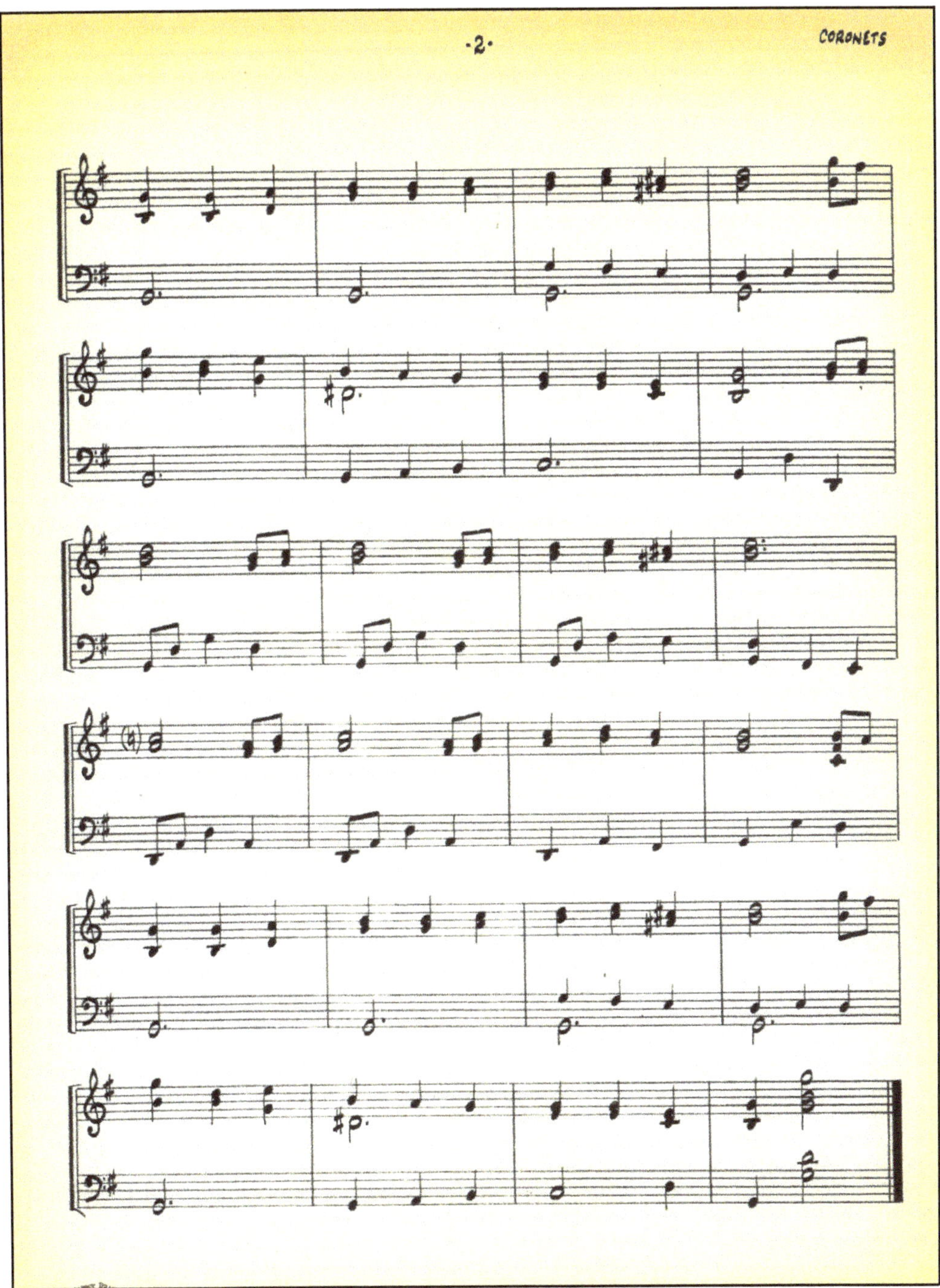
-2-
CORONETS

JUST LIKE A DREAM

Words and Music by
JOYCE RENÉE

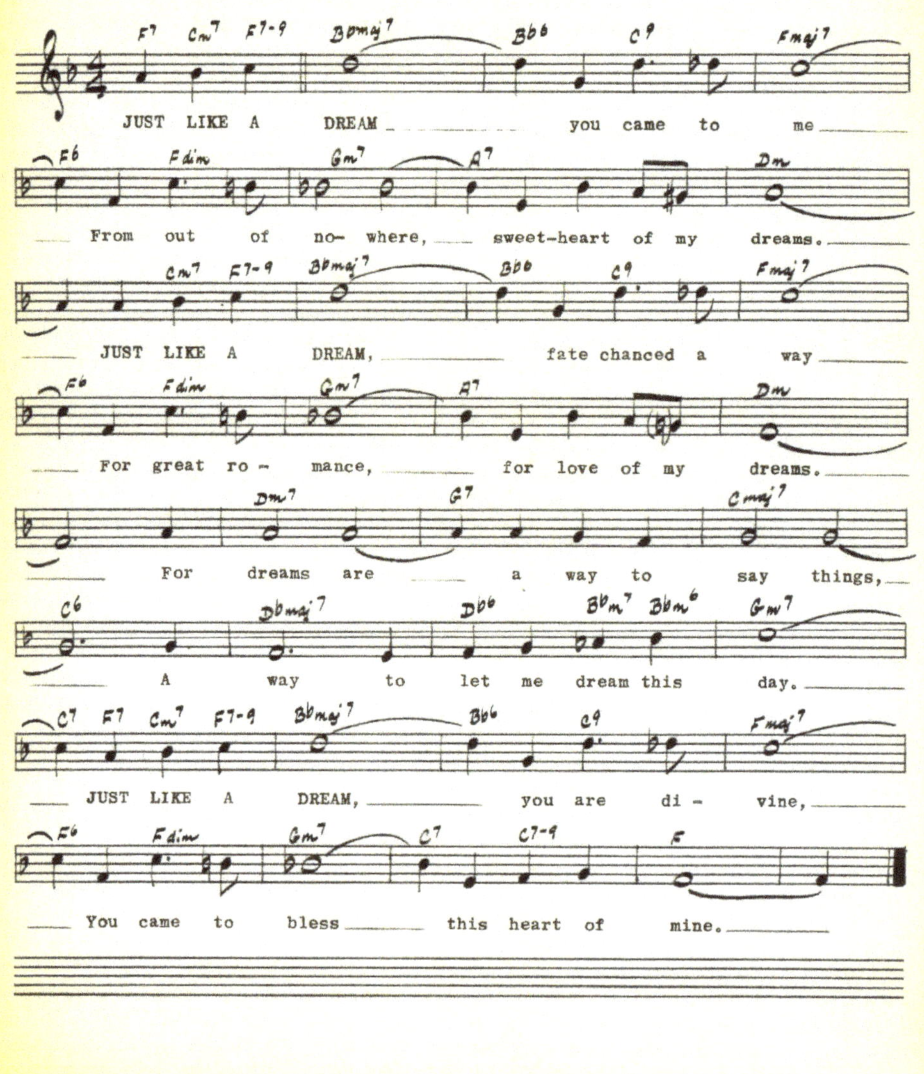

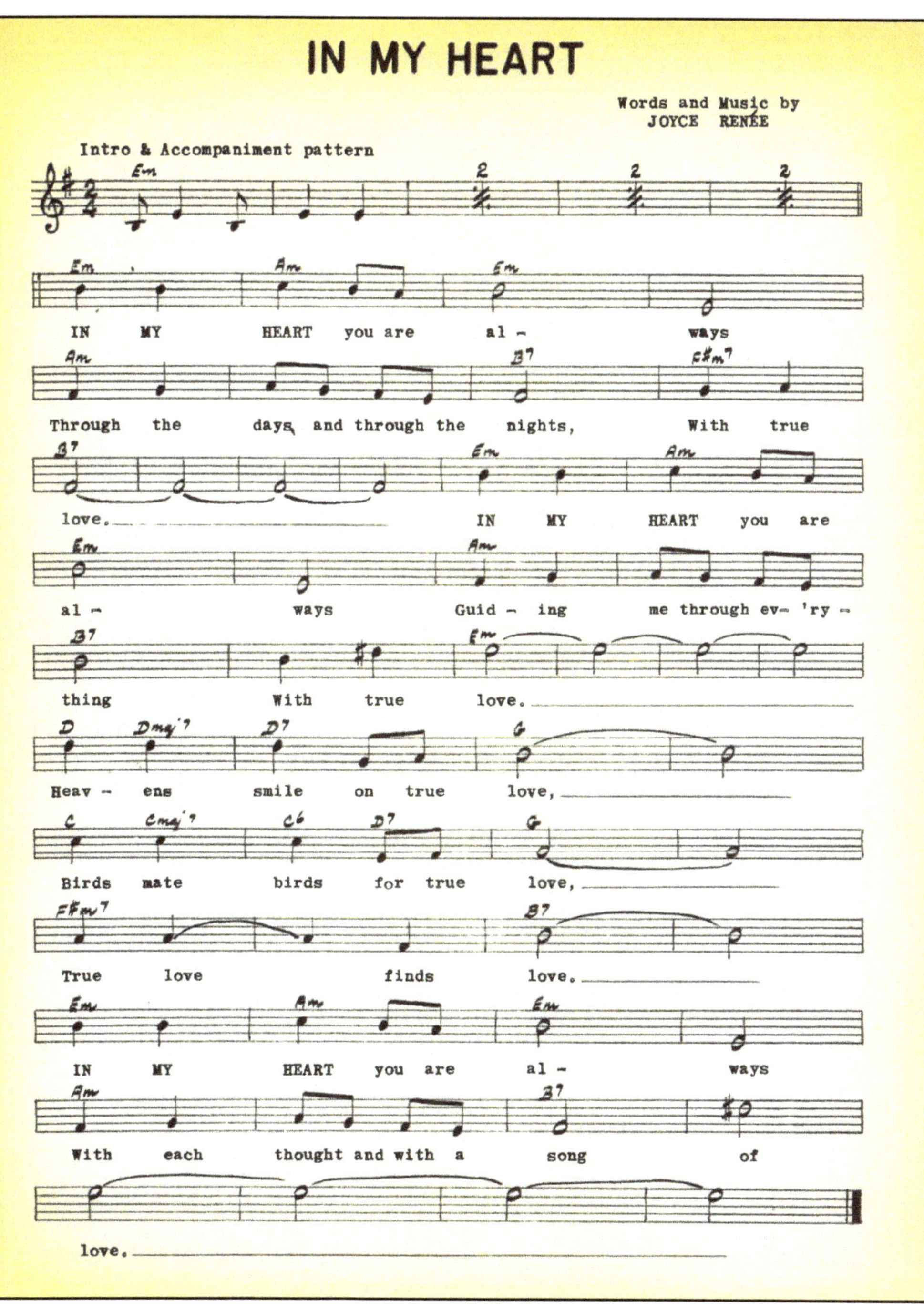
IN MY HEART
Words and Music by
JOYCE RENÉE
Intro & Accompaniment pattern
Em
IN MY HEART you are al - ways
Through the days and through the nights, With true
love.
IN MY HEART you are
al - ways Guid - ing me through ev- 'ry -
thing With true love.
Heav - ens smile on true love,
Birds mate birds for true love,
True love finds love.
IN MY HEART you are al - ways
With each thought and with a song of
love.

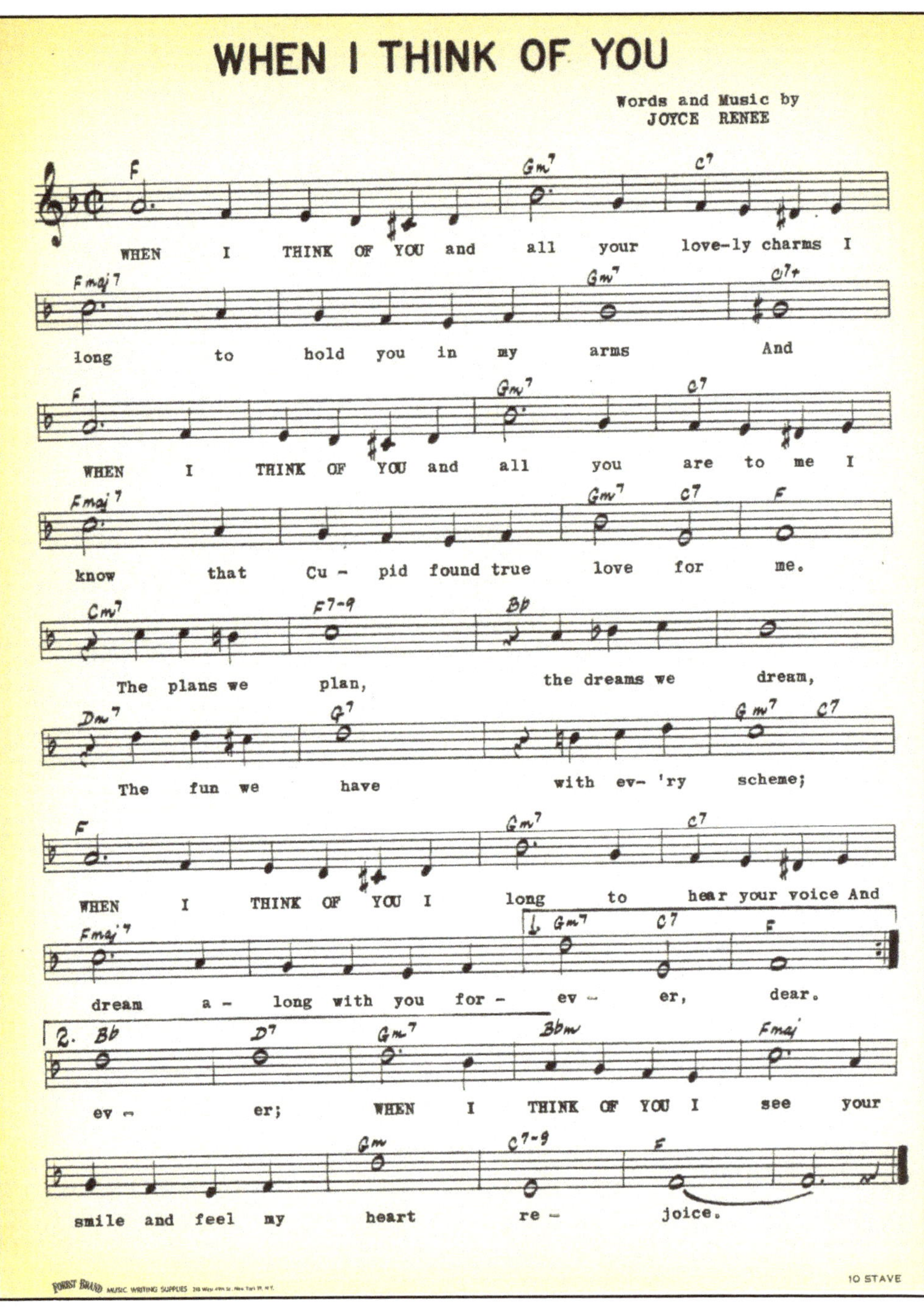
WHEN I THINK OF YOU
Words and Music by
JOYCE RENEE
F
Gm7
C7
WHEN I THINK OF YOU and all your love-ly charms I
Fmaj7
Gm7
C7+
long to hold you in my arms And
F
Gm7
C7
WHEN I THINK OF YOU and all you are to me I
Fmaj7
Gm7
C7
F
know that Cu - pid found true love for me.
Cm7
F7-9
Bb
The plans we plan, the dreams we dream,
Dm7
G7
Gm7
C7
The fun we have with ev- 'ry scheme;
F
Gm7
C7
WHEN I THINK OF YOU I long to hear your voice And
Fmaj7
1. Gm7
C7
F
dream a - long with you for - ev - er, dear.
2. Bb
D7
Gm7
Bbm
Fmaj
ev - er; WHEN I THINK OF YOU I see your
Gm
C7-9
F
smile and feel my heart re - joice.
FOREST BRAND MUSIC WRITING SUPPLIES
10 STAVE

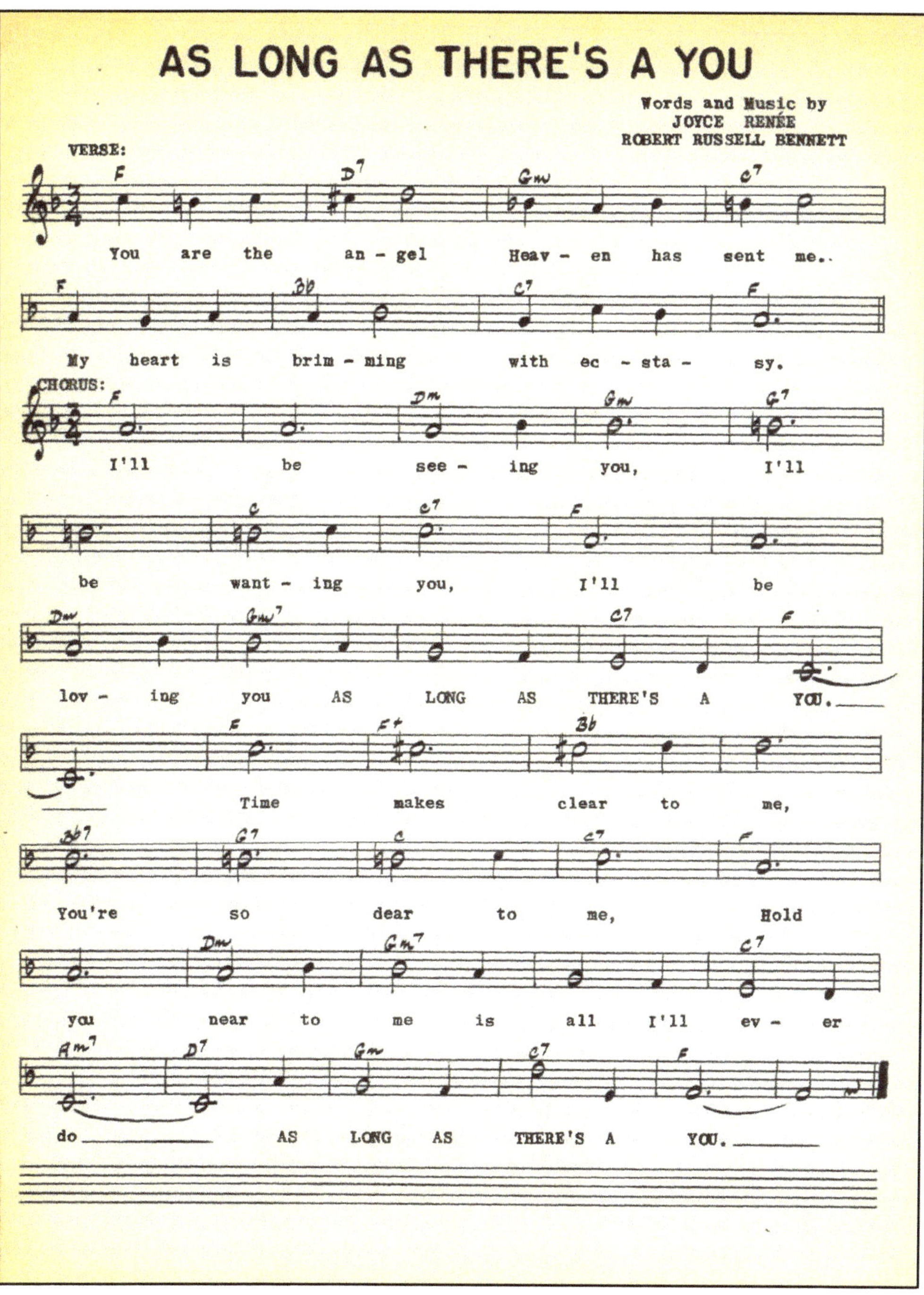
AS LONG AS THERE'S A YOU
Words and Music by
JOYCE RENÉE
ROBERT RUSSELL BENNETT
VERSE:
You are the an - gel Heav - en has sent me..
My heart is brim - ming with ec - sta - sy.
CHORUS:
I'll be see - ing you, I'll
be want - ing you, I'll be
lov - ing you AS LONG AS THERE'S A YOU.
Time makes clear to me,
You're so dear to me, Hold
you near to me is all I'll ev - er
do AS LONG AS THERE'S A YOU.

LOVE OF MY HEART

Words and Music by
JOYCE RENÉE

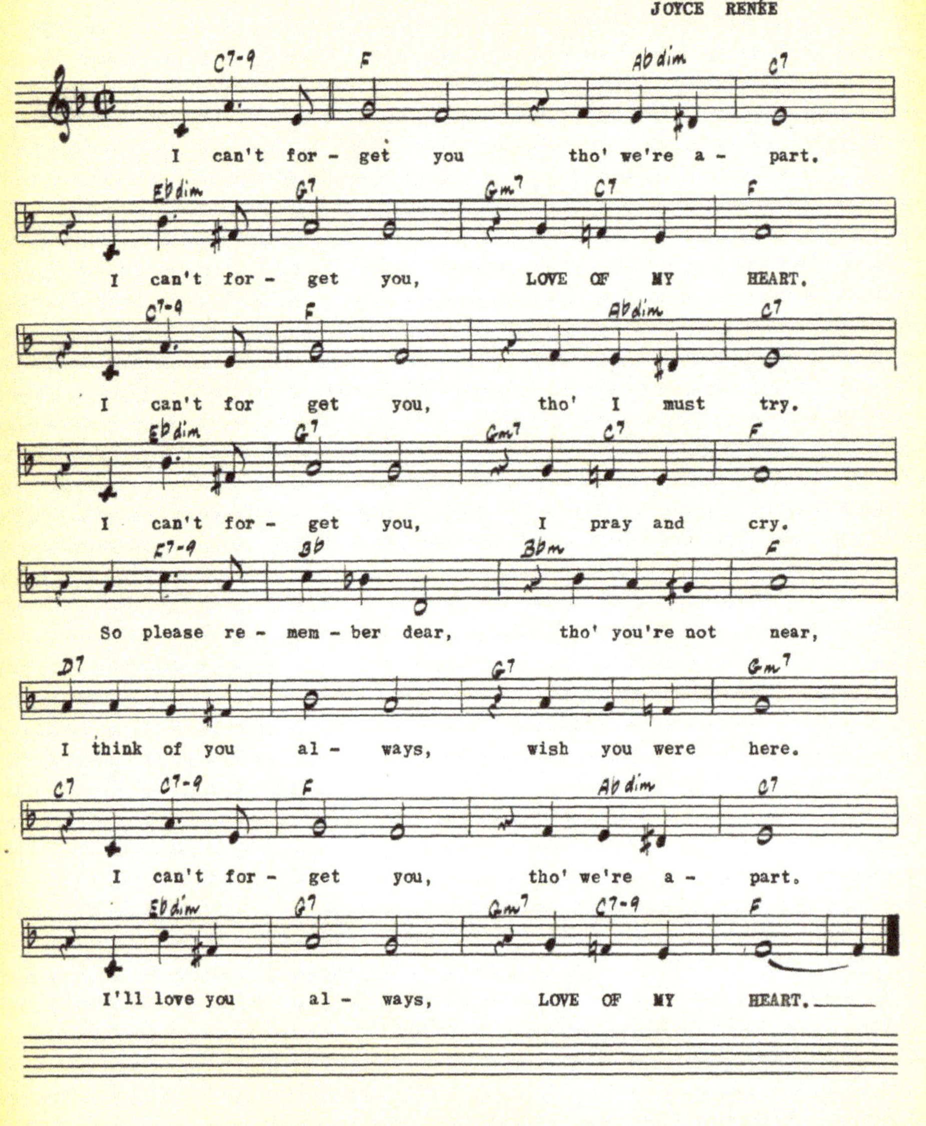

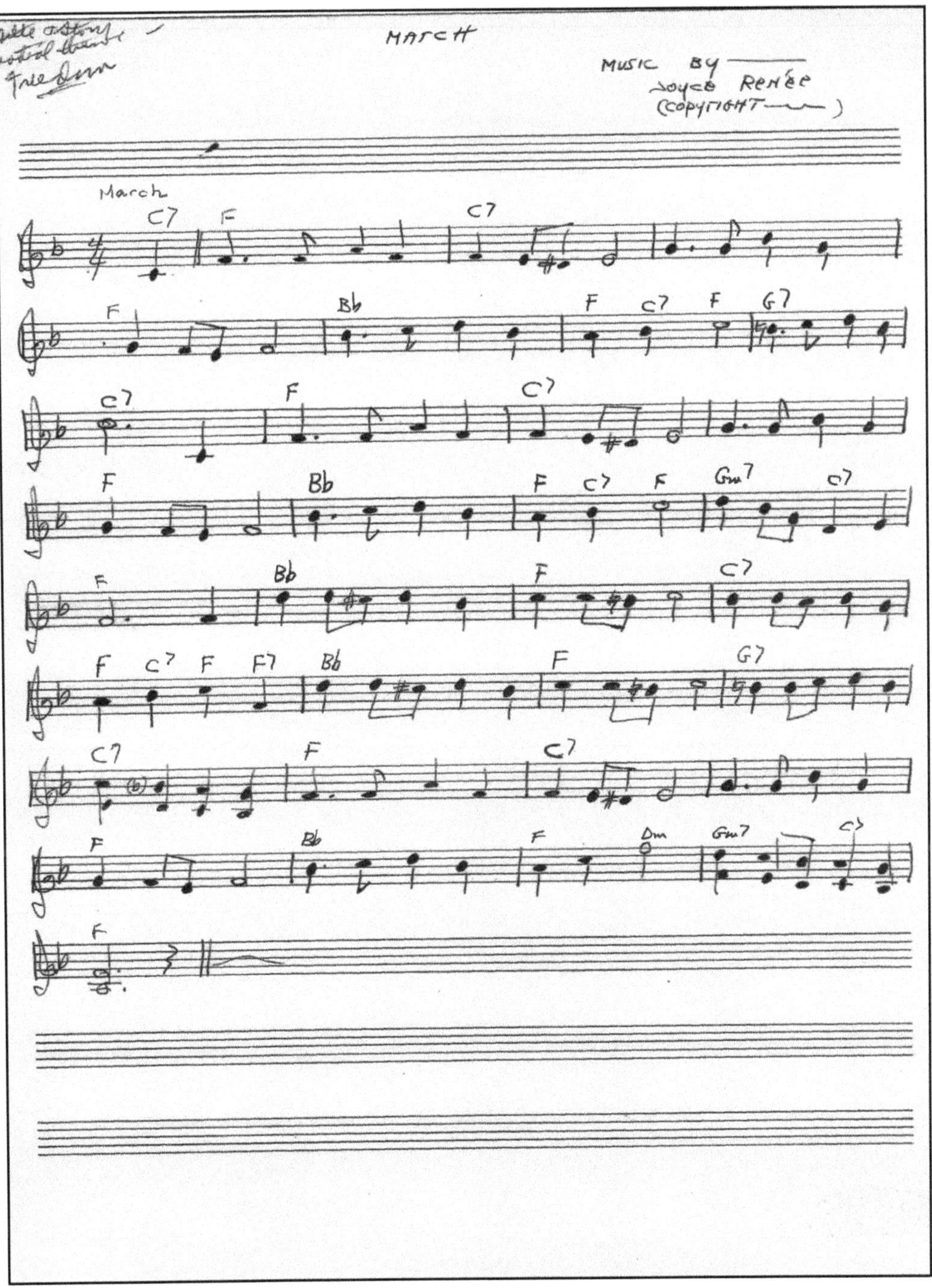
MARCH
MUSIC BY
Joyce Renée
(COPYRIGHT)
March

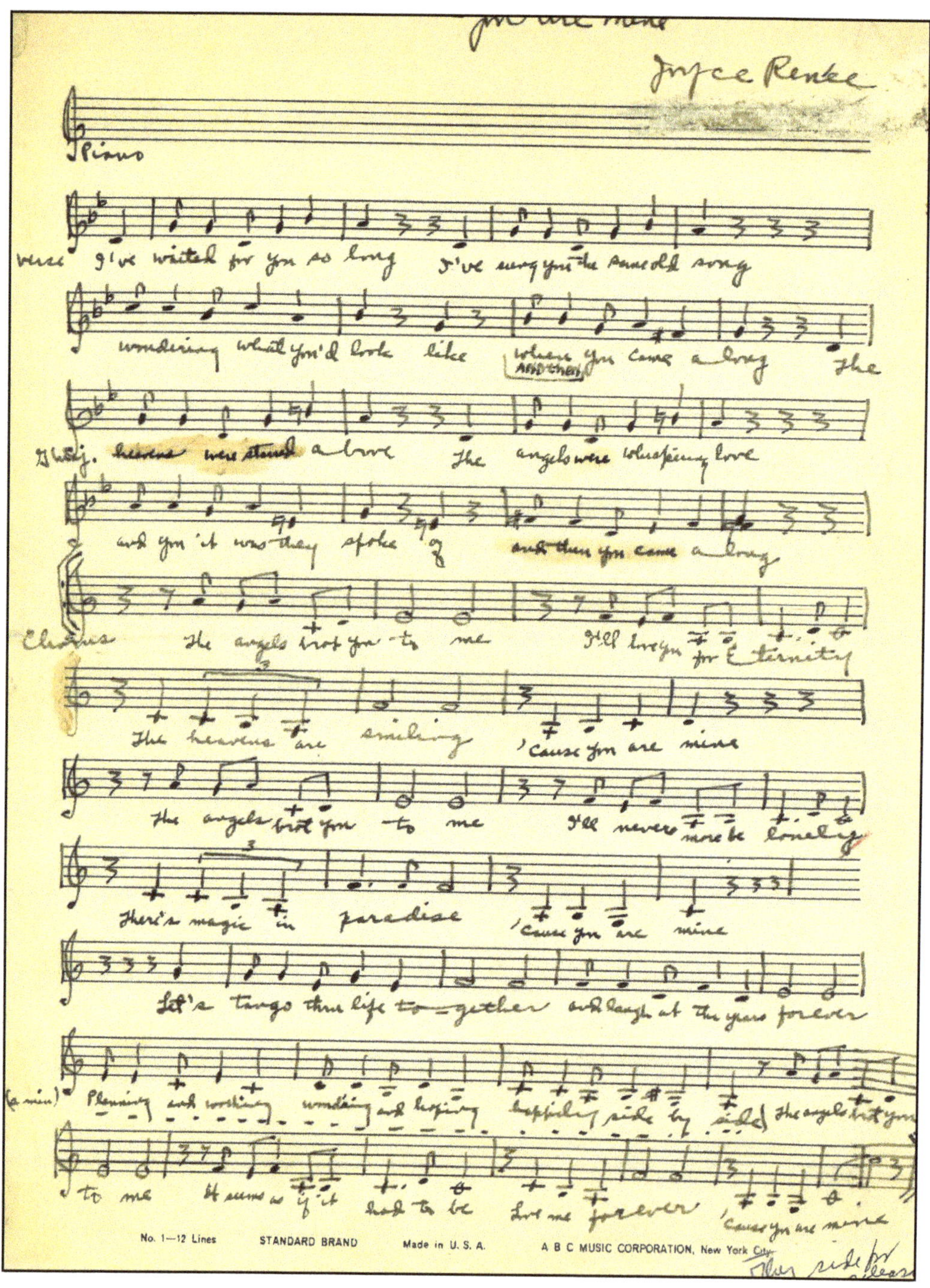
Joyce Renke
Piano
Verse I've waited for you so long I've sung you the same old song
wondering what you'd look like when you came along The
AND THEN
heavens were stirred above The angels were whispering love
and you it was they spoke of and then you came along
Chorus The angels brought you to me I'll love you for Eternity
The heavens are smiling 'Cause you are mine
The angels brought you to me I'll never more be lonely
There's magic in paradise 'Cause you are mine
Let's tango thru life together and laugh at the years forever
Planning and working wondering and hoping happily side by side The angels brought you
to me It seems as if it had to be Love me forever 'Cause you are mine
No. 1—12 Lines STANDARD BRAND Made in U. S. A. A B C MUSIC CORPORATION, New York City

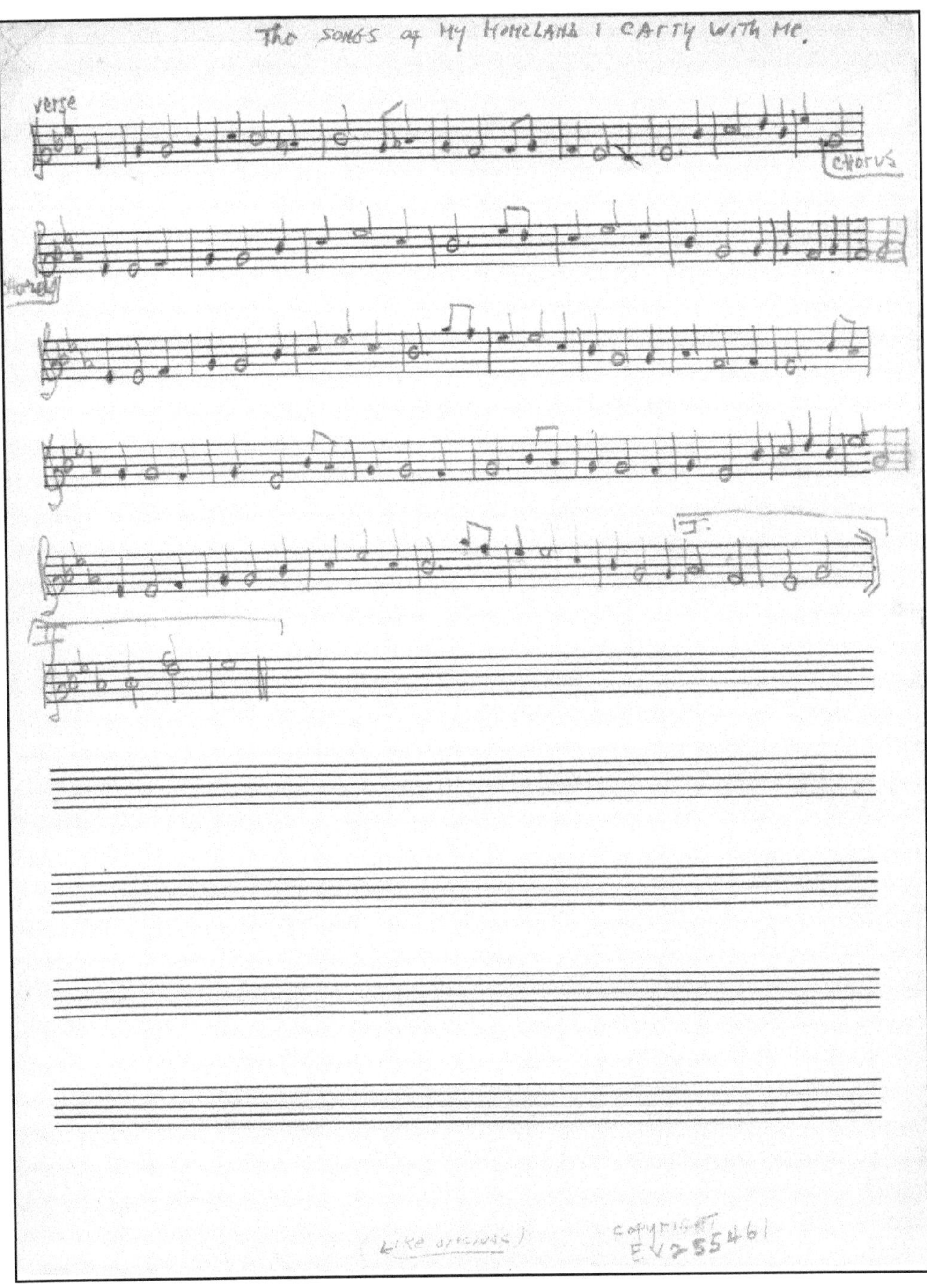
The SONGS of MY HOMELAND I CARRY WITH ME.
verse
CHORUS
copyright
EU255461

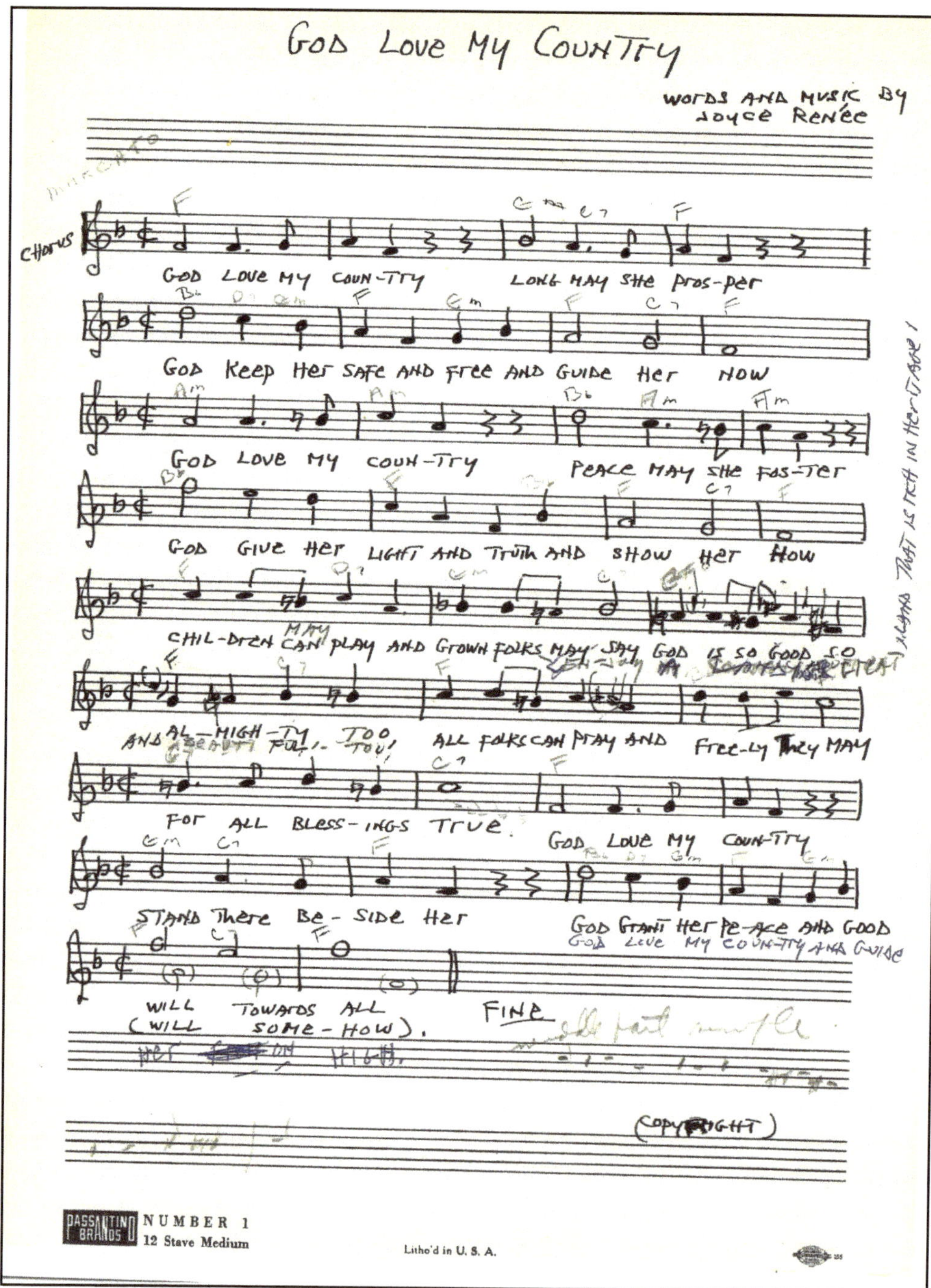
GOD LOVE MY COUNTRY
WORDS AND MUSIC BY
JOYCE RENÉE
Chorus
GOD LOVE MY COUN-TRY LONG MAY SHE PROS-PER
GOD KEEP HER SAFE AND FREE AND GUIDE HER NOW
GOD LOVE MY COUN-TRY PEACE MAY SHE FOS-TER
GOD GIVE HER LIGHT AND TRUTH AND SHOW HER HOW
CHIL-DREN CAN PLAY AND GROWN FOLKS MAY SAY GOD IS SO GOOD SO
AND AL-MIGH-TY TOO, ALL FOLKS CAN PRAY AND FREE-LY THEY MAY
FOR ALL BLESS-INGS TRUE. GOD LOVE MY COUN-TRY
STAND THERE BE-SIDE HER GOD GRANT HER PE-ACE AND GOOD
GOD LOVE MY COUN-TRY AND GUIDE
WILL TOWARDS ALL
(WILL SOME-HOW).
FINE
(COPYRIGHT)
PASSANTINO BRANDS NUMBER 1
12 Stave Medium
Litho'd in U.S.A.

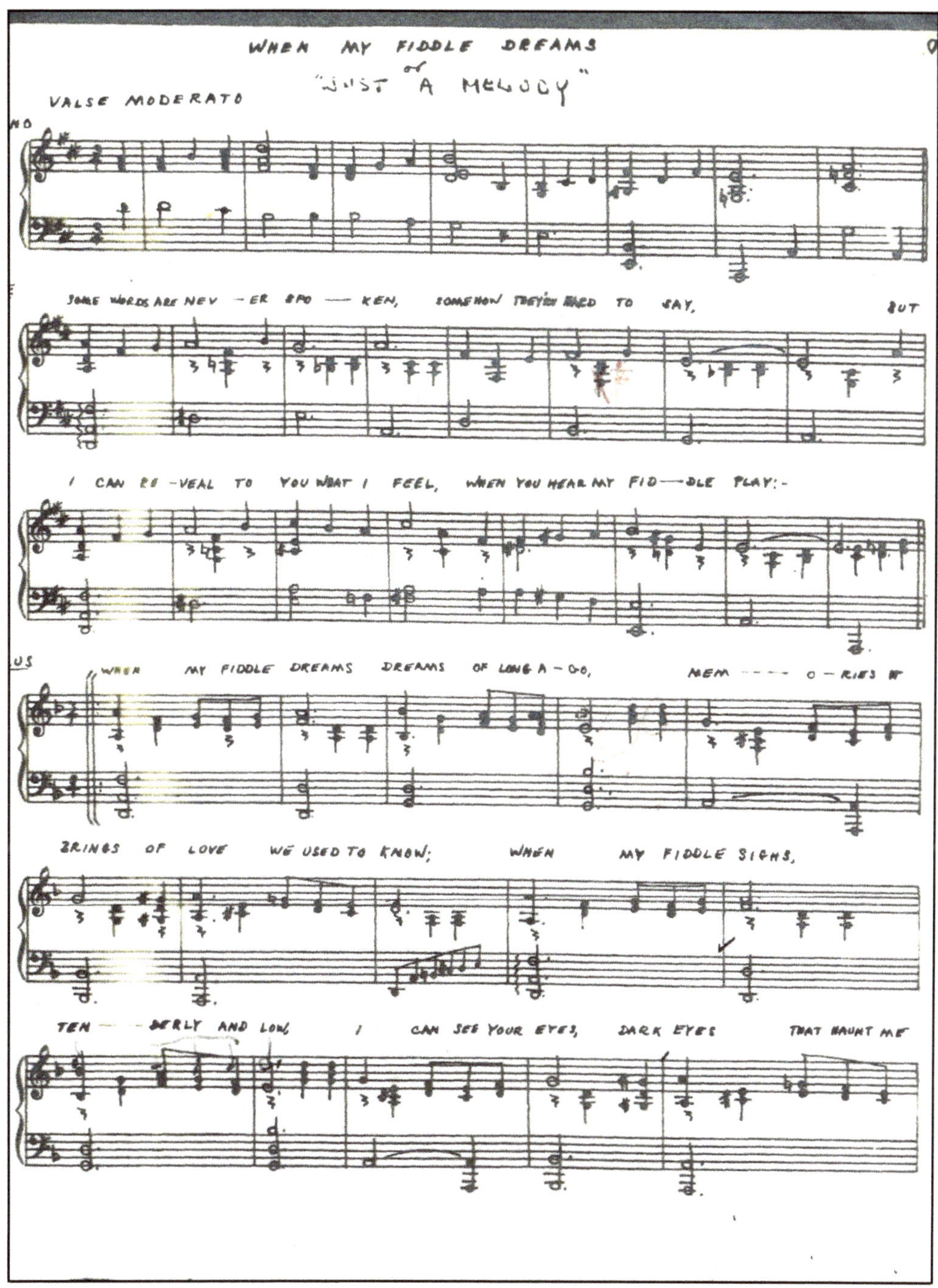
WHEN MY FIDDLE DREAMS
or
"JUST A MELODY"
VALSE MODERATO
SOME WORDS ARE NEV - ER SPO — KEN, SOMEHOW THEY'RE HARD TO SAY, BUT
I CAN RE - VEAL TO YOU WHAT I FEEL, WHEN YOU HEAR MY FID—DLE PLAY:-
WHEN MY FIDDLE DREAMS DREAMS OF LONG A - GO, MEM - - - O - RIES OF
BRINGS OF LOVE WE USED TO KNOW; WHEN MY FIDDLE SIGHS,
TEN - - DERLY AND LOW, I CAN SEE YOUR EYES, DARK EYES THAT HAUNT ME

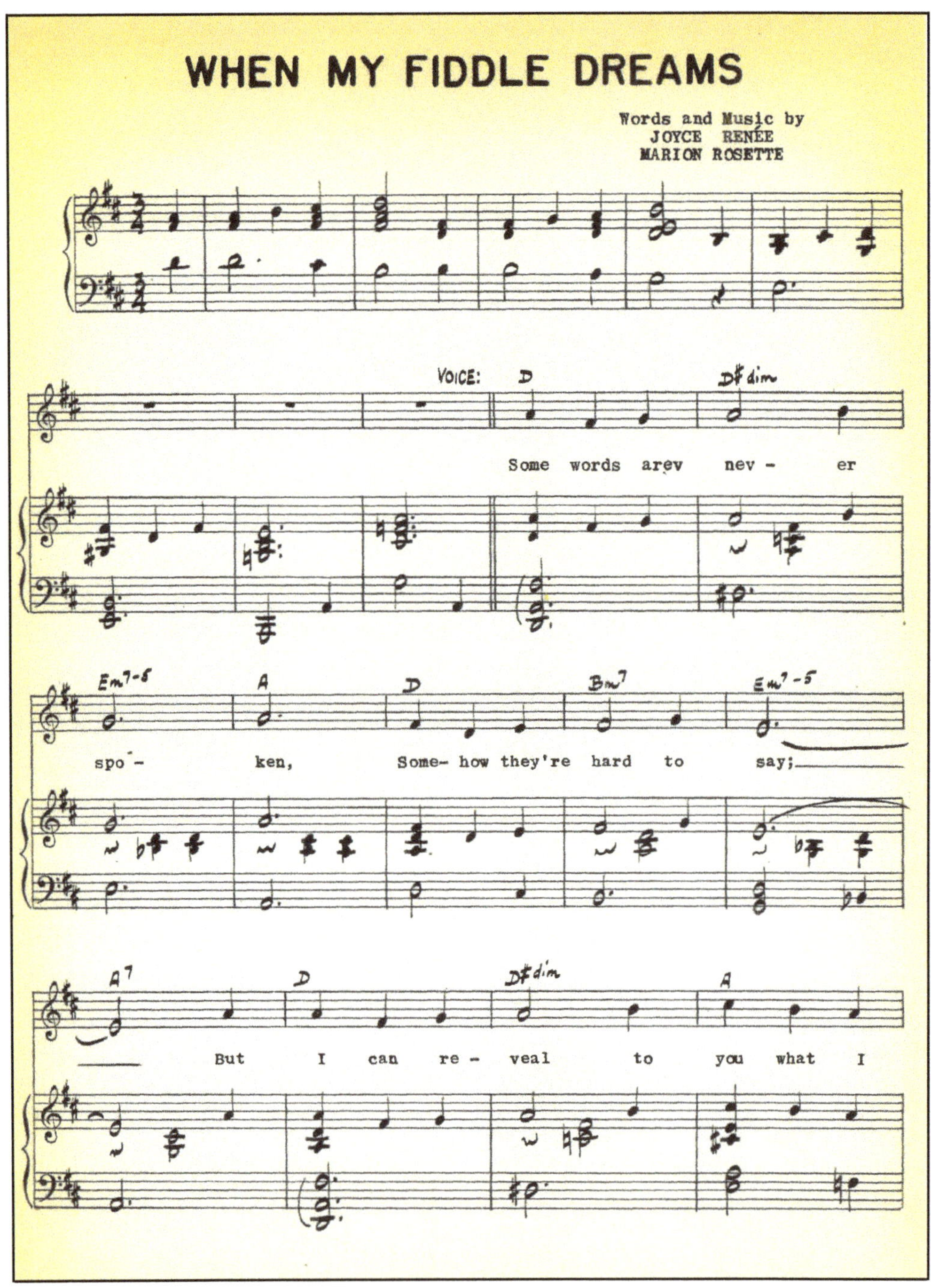
WHEN MY FIDDLE DREAMS
Words and Music by
JOYCE RENÉE
MARION ROSETTE
VOICE:
D
D♯dim
Some words arev nev - er
Em7-5
A
D
Bm7
Em7-5
spo - ken, Some- how they're hard to say;
A7
D
D♯dim
A
But I can re - veal to you what I

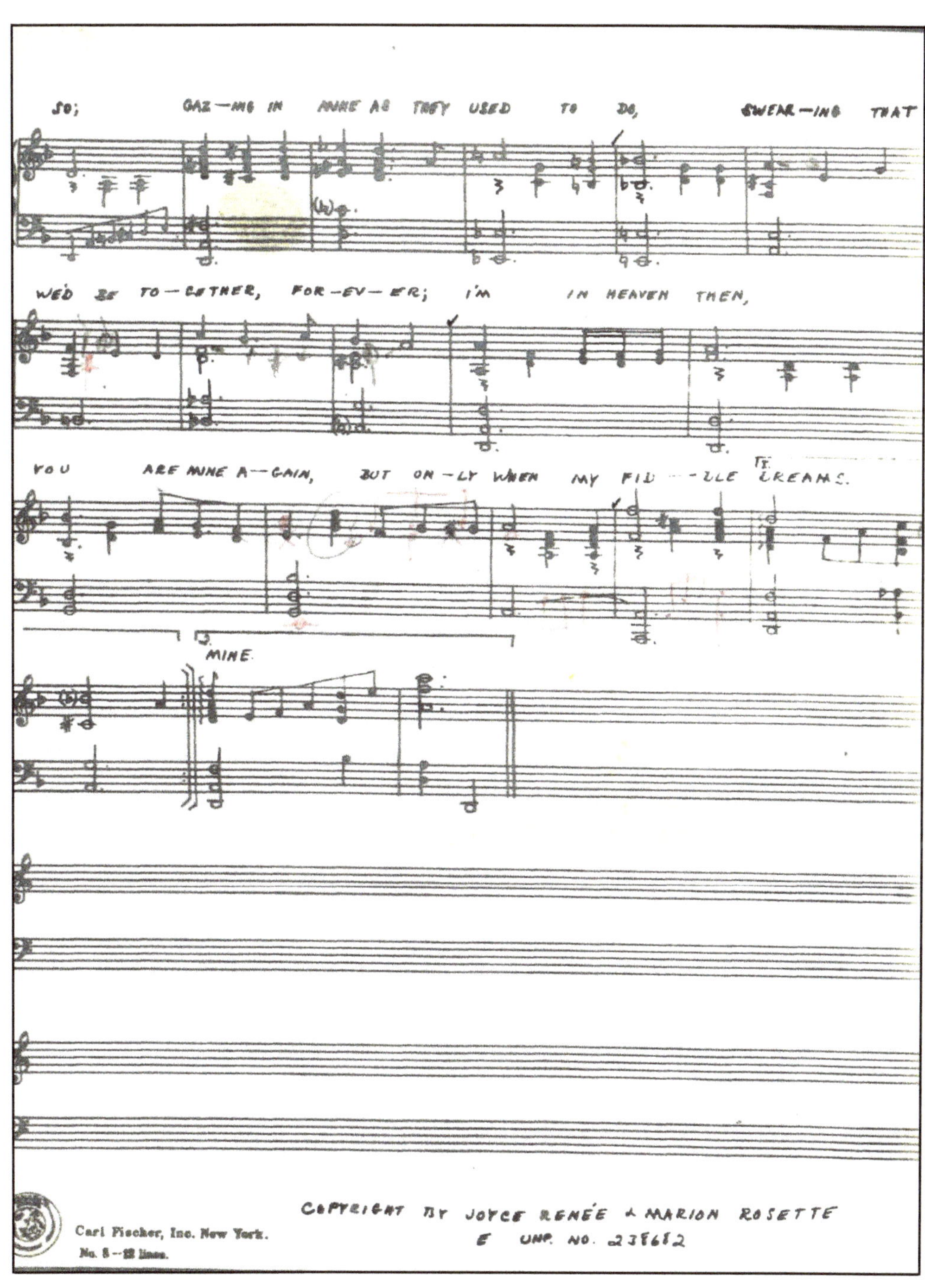
SO; GAZ-ING IN MINE AS THEY USED TO DO, SWEAR-ING THAT
WE'D BE TO-GETHER, FOR-EV-ER; I'M IN HEAVEN THEN,
YOU ARE MINE A-GAIN, BUT ON-LY WHEN MY FID--DLE DREAMS.
MINE
Carl Fischer, Inc. New York.
No. 5 -- 12 lines.
COPYRIGHT BY JOYCE RENÉE & MARION ROSETTE
E UNP. NO. 238682

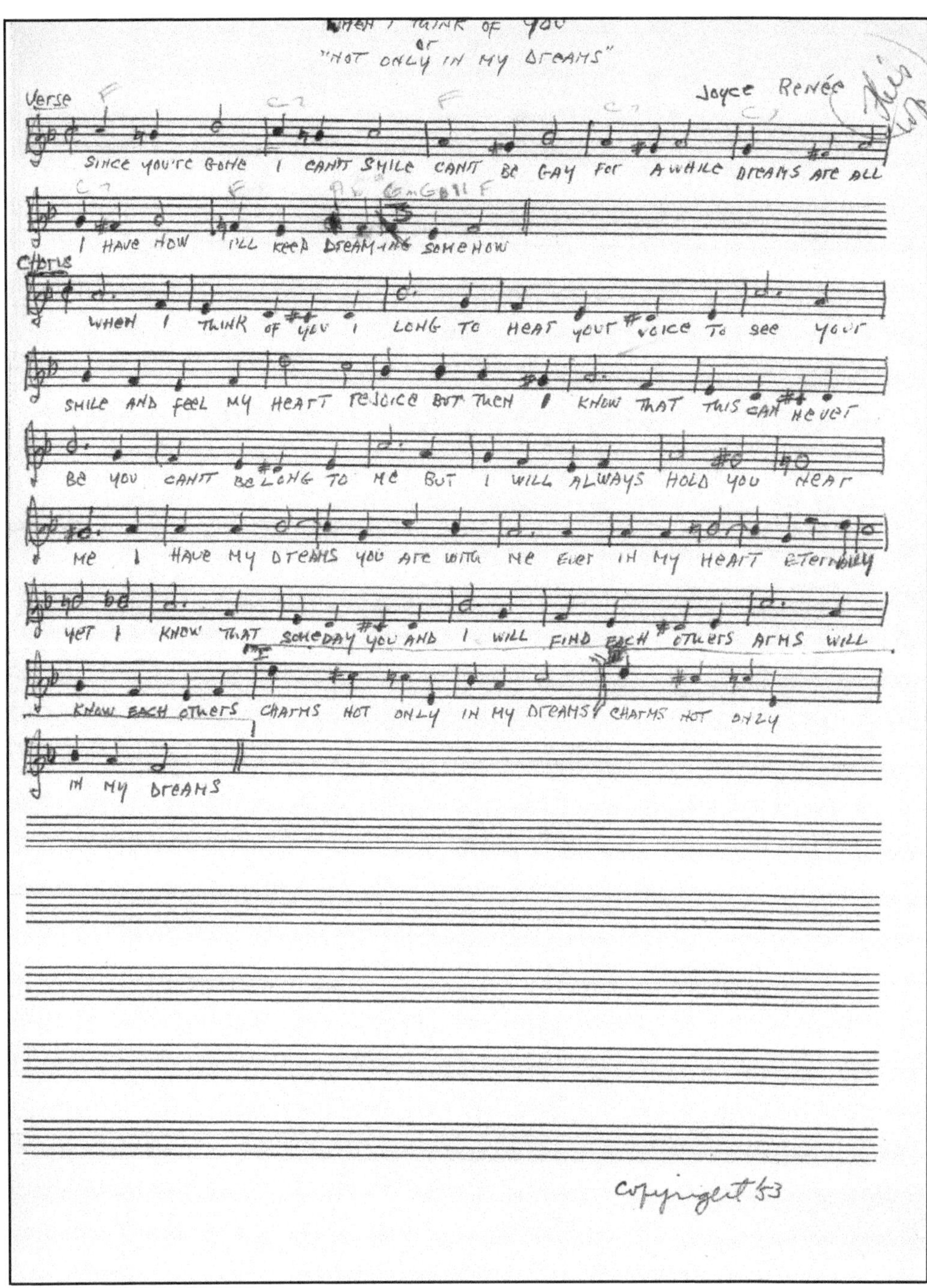
WHEN I THINK OF YOU
or
"NOT ONLY IN MY DREAMS"
Joyce Renée
Verse
SINCE YOU'RE GONE I CAN'T SMILE CAN'T BE GAY FOR AWHILE DREAMS ARE ALL
I HAVE NOW I'LL KEEP DREAMING SOMEHOW
Chorus
WHEN I THINK OF YOU I LONG TO HEAR YOUR VOICE TO SEE YOUR
SMILE AND FEEL MY HEART REJOICE BUT THEN I KNOW THAT THIS CAN NEVER
BE YOU CAN'T BELONG TO ME BUT I WILL ALWAYS HOLD YOU NEAR
ME I HAVE MY DREAMS YOU ARE WITH ME EVER IN MY HEART ETERNALLY
YET I KNOW THAT SOMEDAY YOU AND I WILL FIND EACH OTHERS ARMS WILL
KNOW EACH OTHERS CHARMS NOT ONLY IN MY DREAMS CHARMS NOT ONLY
IN MY DREAMS
copyright 53

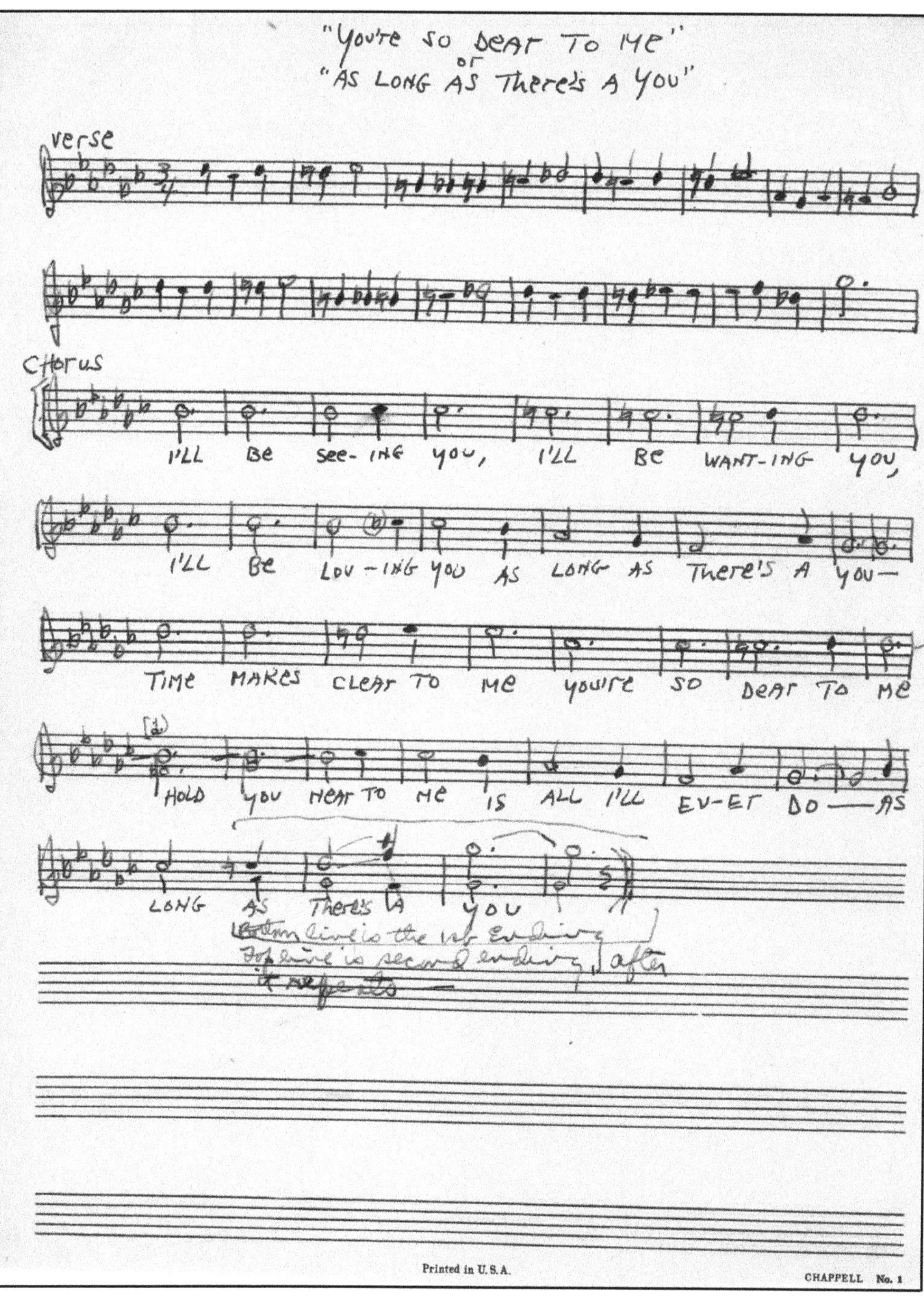
"You're So Dear To Me"
or
"As Long As There's A You"
verse
Chorus
I'll be see-ing you, I'll be want-ing you,
I'll be lov-ing you as long as there's a you—
Time makes clear to me you're so dear to me
Hold you near to me is all I'll ev-er do — as
long as there's a you
Printed in U.S.A.
CHAPPELL No. 1

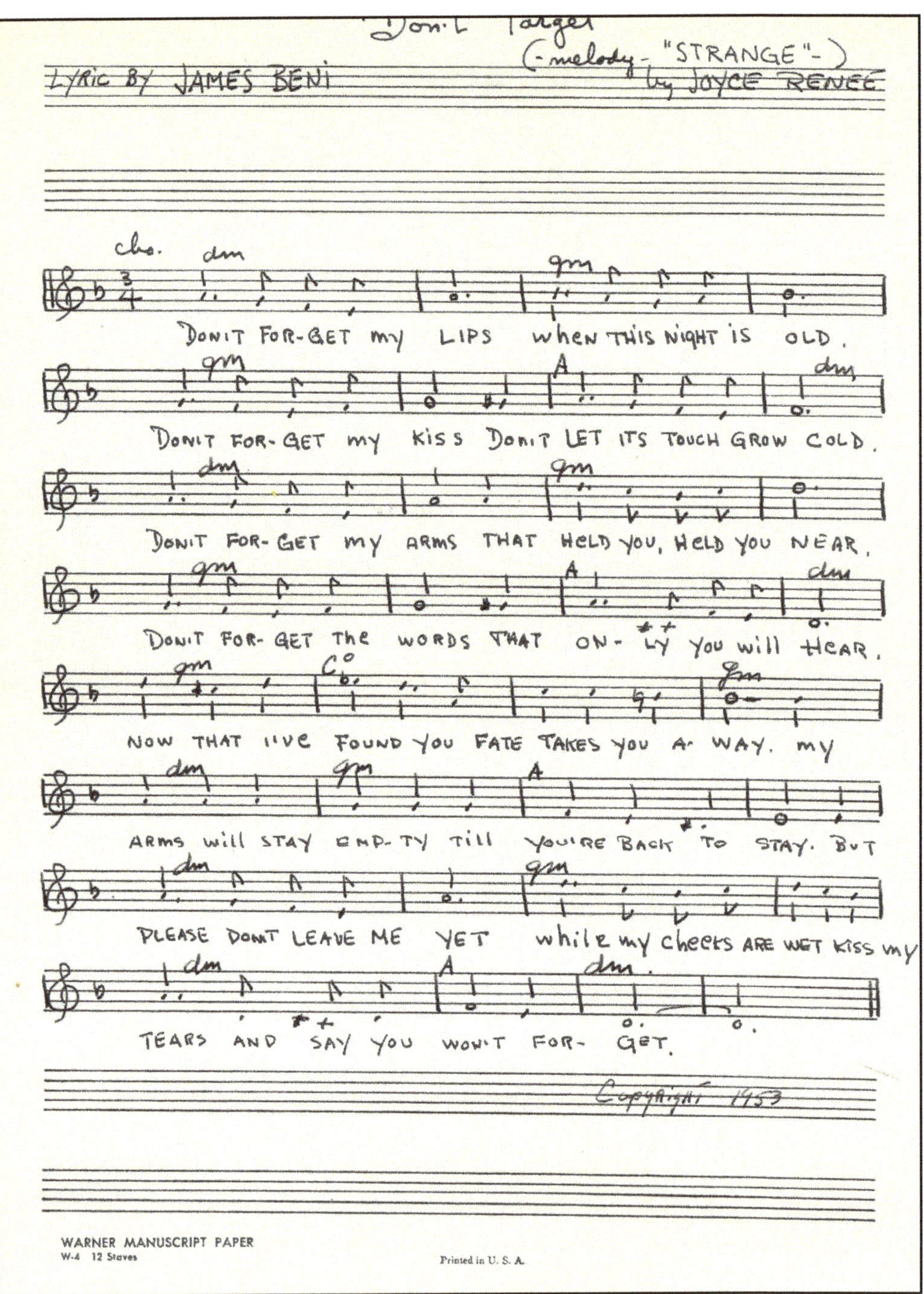
(-melody- "STRANGE"-)
LYRIC BY JAMES BENI
by JOYCE RENEE
cho.
DON'T FOR-GET my LIPS when THIS NIGHT IS OLD.
DON'T FOR-GET my KISS DON'T LET ITS TOUCH GROW COLD.
DON'T FOR-GET my ARMS THAT HELD YOU, HELD YOU NEAR.
DON'T FOR-GET THE WORDS THAT ON-LY YOU WILL HEAR.
NOW THAT I'VE FOUND YOU FATE TAKES YOU A-WAY. my
ARMS WILL STAY EMP-TY TILL YOU'RE BACK TO STAY. BUT
PLEASE DON'T LEAVE ME YET while my cheeks ARE WET KISS my
TEARS AND SAY YOU WON'T FOR-GET.
Copyright 1953
WARNER MANUSCRIPT PAPER
W-4 12 Staves
Printed in U. S. A.

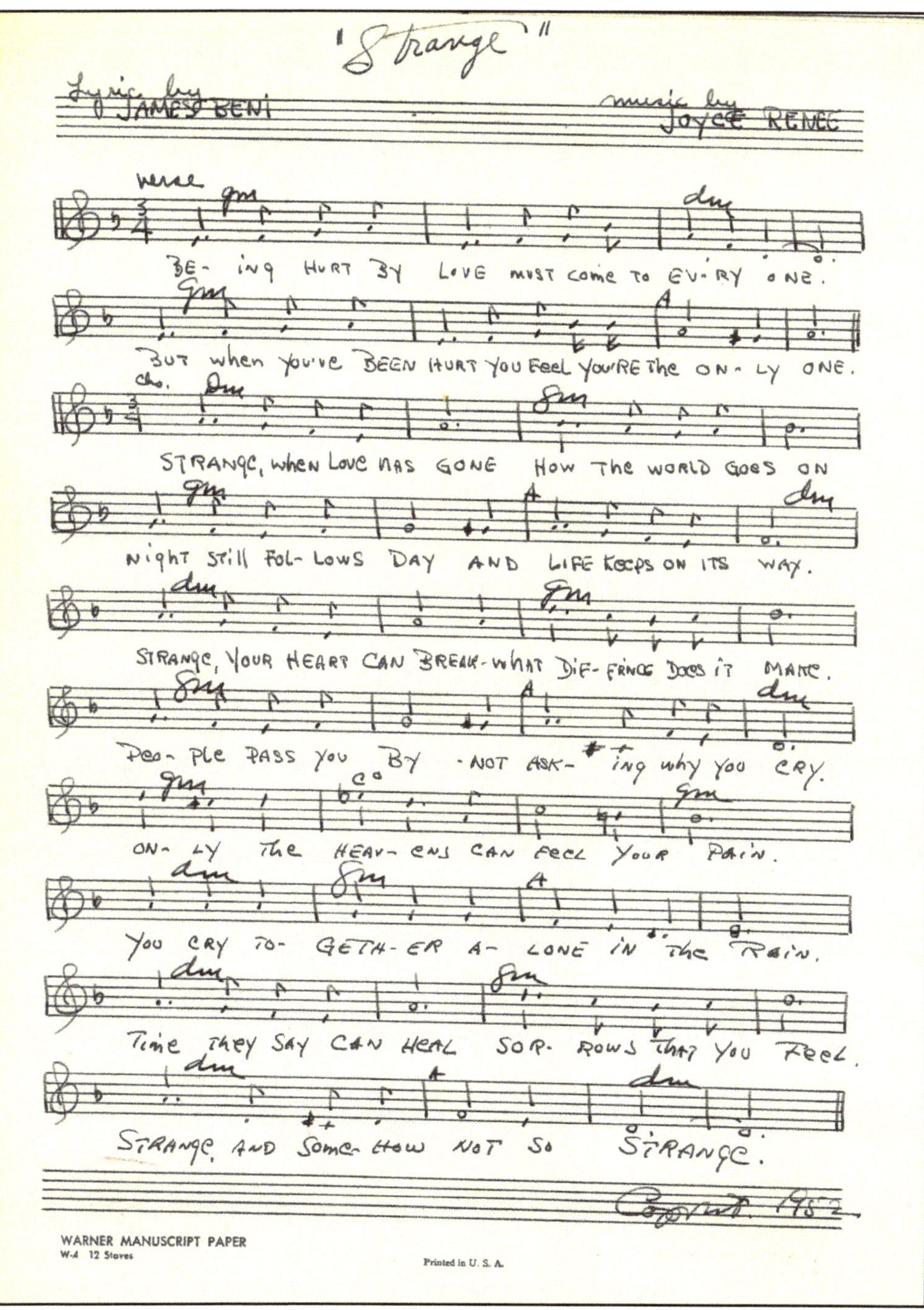
"Strange"
Lyric by JAMES BENI
music by JOYCE RENEE
verse
BE- ING HURT BY LOVE MUST COME TO EV-RY ONE.
BUT WHEN YOU'VE BEEN HURT YOU FEEL YOU'RE THE ON-LY ONE.
cho.
STRANGE, WHEN LOVE HAS GONE HOW THE WORLD GOES ON
NIGHT STILL FOL-LOWS DAY AND LIFE KEEPS ON ITS WAY.
STRANGE, YOUR HEART CAN BREAK-WHAT DIF-F'RNCE DOES IT MAKE.
PEO-PLE PASS YOU BY -NOT ASK-ING WHY YOU CRY.
ON-LY THE HEAV-ENS CAN FEEL YOUR PAIN.
YOU CRY TO-GETH-ER A-LONE IN THE RAIN.
TIME THEY SAY CAN HEAL SOR-ROWS THAT YOU FEEL.
STRANGE AND SOME-HOW NOT SO STRANGE.
Copyright 1952
WARNER MANUSCRIPT PAPER
W-4 12 Staves
Printed in U. S. A.

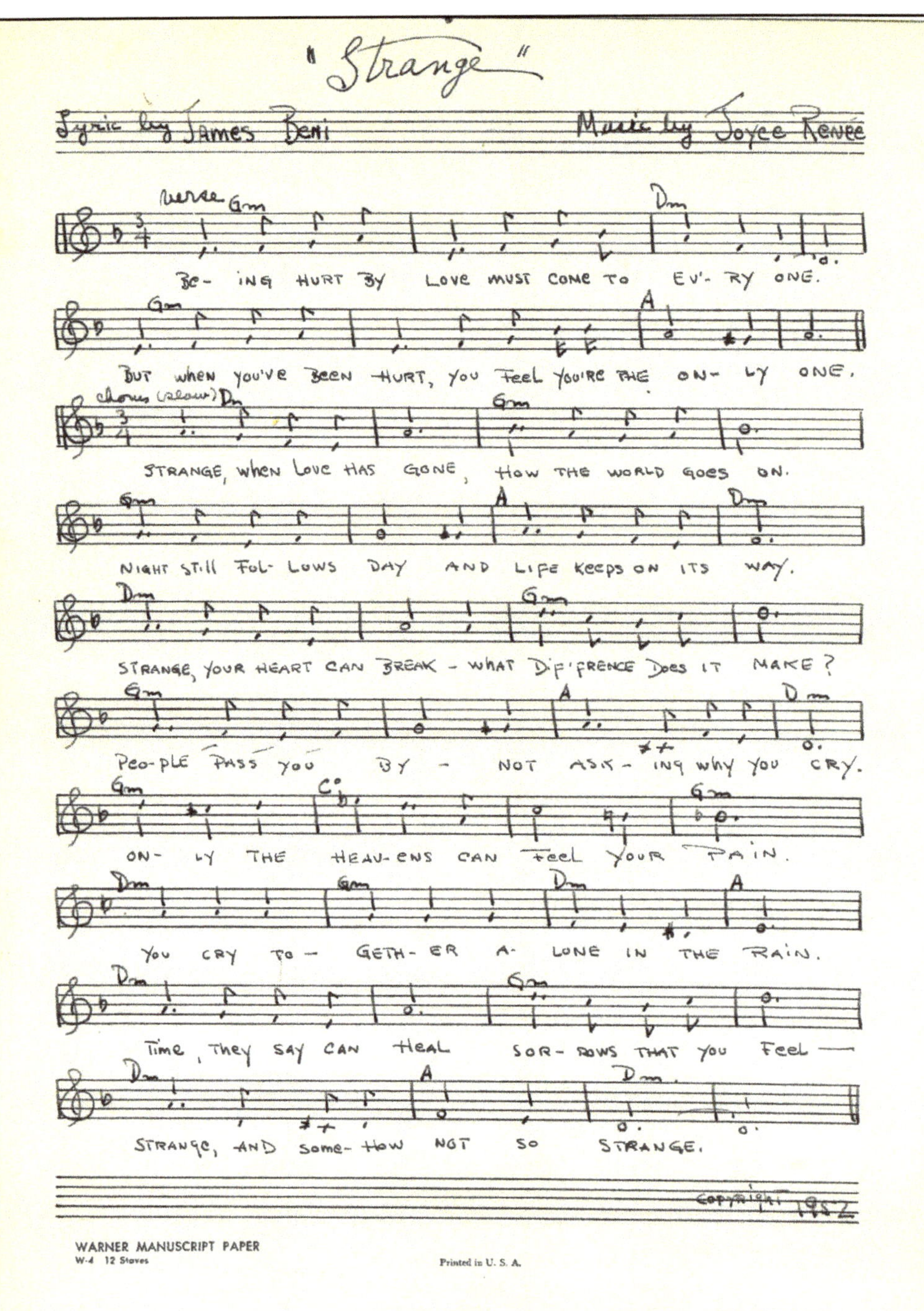
"Strange"
Lyric by James Beni
Music by Joyce Renee
verse
BE- ING HURT BY LOVE MUST COME TO EV'- RY ONE.
BUT WHEN YOU'VE BEEN HURT, YOU FEEL YOU'RE THE ON- LY ONE.
chorus (slow)
STRANGE, WHEN LOVE HAS GONE, HOW THE WORLD GOES ON.
NIGHT STILL FOL- LOWS DAY AND LIFE KEEPS ON ITS WAY.
STRANGE, YOUR HEART CAN BREAK - WHAT DIF'FRENCE DOES IT MAKE?
PEO-PLE PASS YOU BY - NOT ASK- ING WHY YOU CRY.
ON- LY THE HEAV-ENS CAN FEEL YOUR PAIN.
YOU CRY TO- GETH- ER A- LONE IN THE RAIN.
TIME, THEY SAY CAN HEAL SOR- ROWS THAT YOU FEEL —
STRANGE, AND SOME- HOW NOT SO STRANGE.
WARNER MANUSCRIPT PAPER
W-4 12 Staves
Printed in U. S. A.

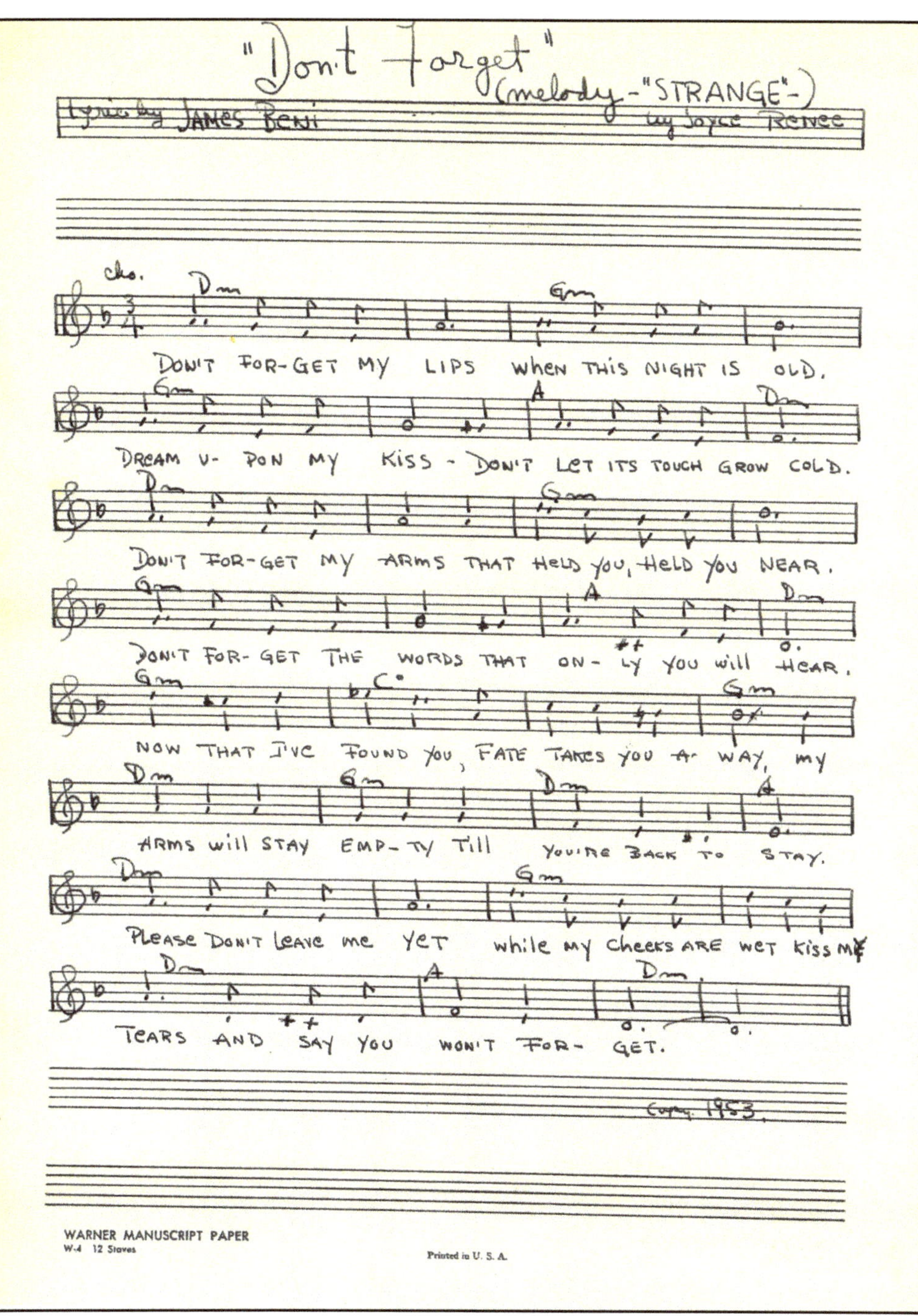
"Don't Forget"
(melody - "STRANGE" -)
lyric by JAMES BENI
by Joyce Renee
Cho.
Dm
Gm
DON'T FOR-GET MY LIPS WHEN THIS NIGHT IS OLD.
Gm
A
Dm
DREAM U-PON MY KISS - DON'T LET ITS TOUCH GROW COLD.
Dm
Gm
DON'T FOR-GET MY ARMS THAT HELD YOU, HELD YOU NEAR.
Gm
A
Dm
DON'T FOR-GET THE WORDS THAT ON-LY YOU WILL HEAR.
Gm
C°
Gm
NOW THAT I'VE FOUND YOU, FATE TAKES YOU A-WAY, MY
Dm
Gm
Dm
A
ARMS WILL STAY EMP-TY TILL YOU'RE BACK TO STAY.
Dm
Gm
PLEASE DON'T LEAVE ME YET WHILE MY CHEEKS ARE WET KISS MY
Dm
A
Dm
TEARS AND SAY YOU WON'T FOR- GET.
Copy. 1953.
WARNER MANUSCRIPT PAPER
W-4 12 Staves
Printed in U. S. A.

CLAPPING HANDS

by JOYCE RENEE

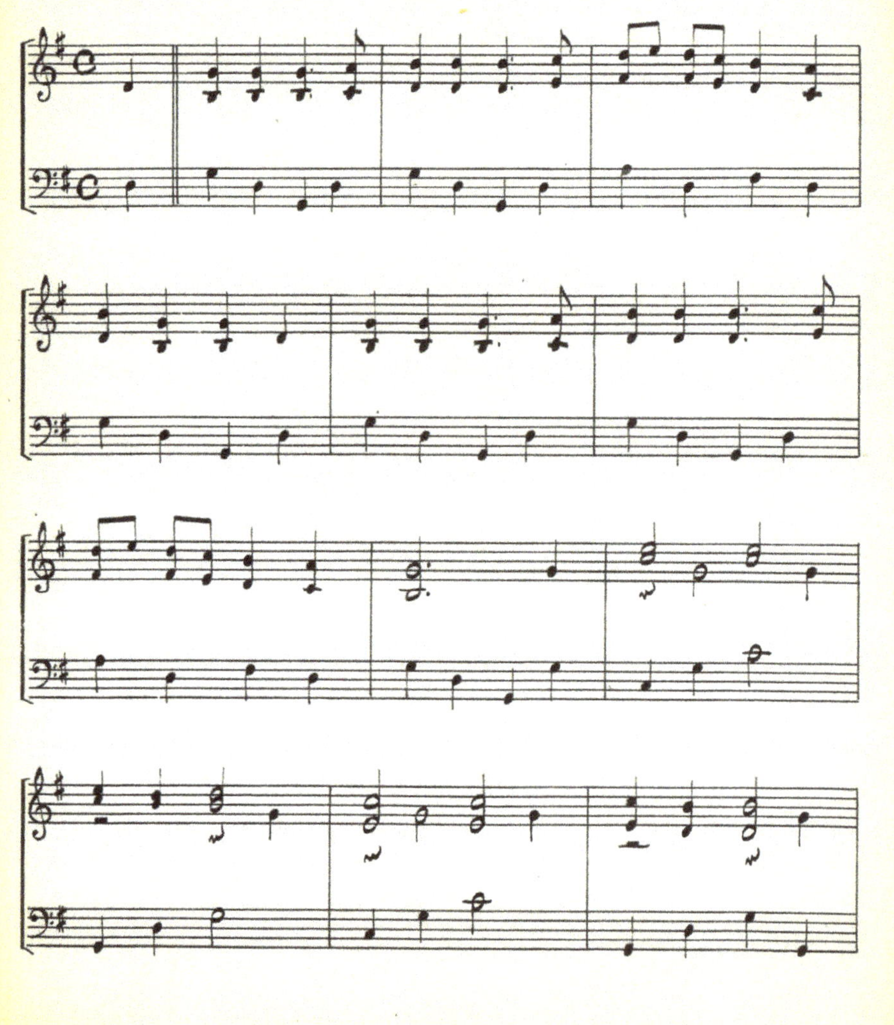

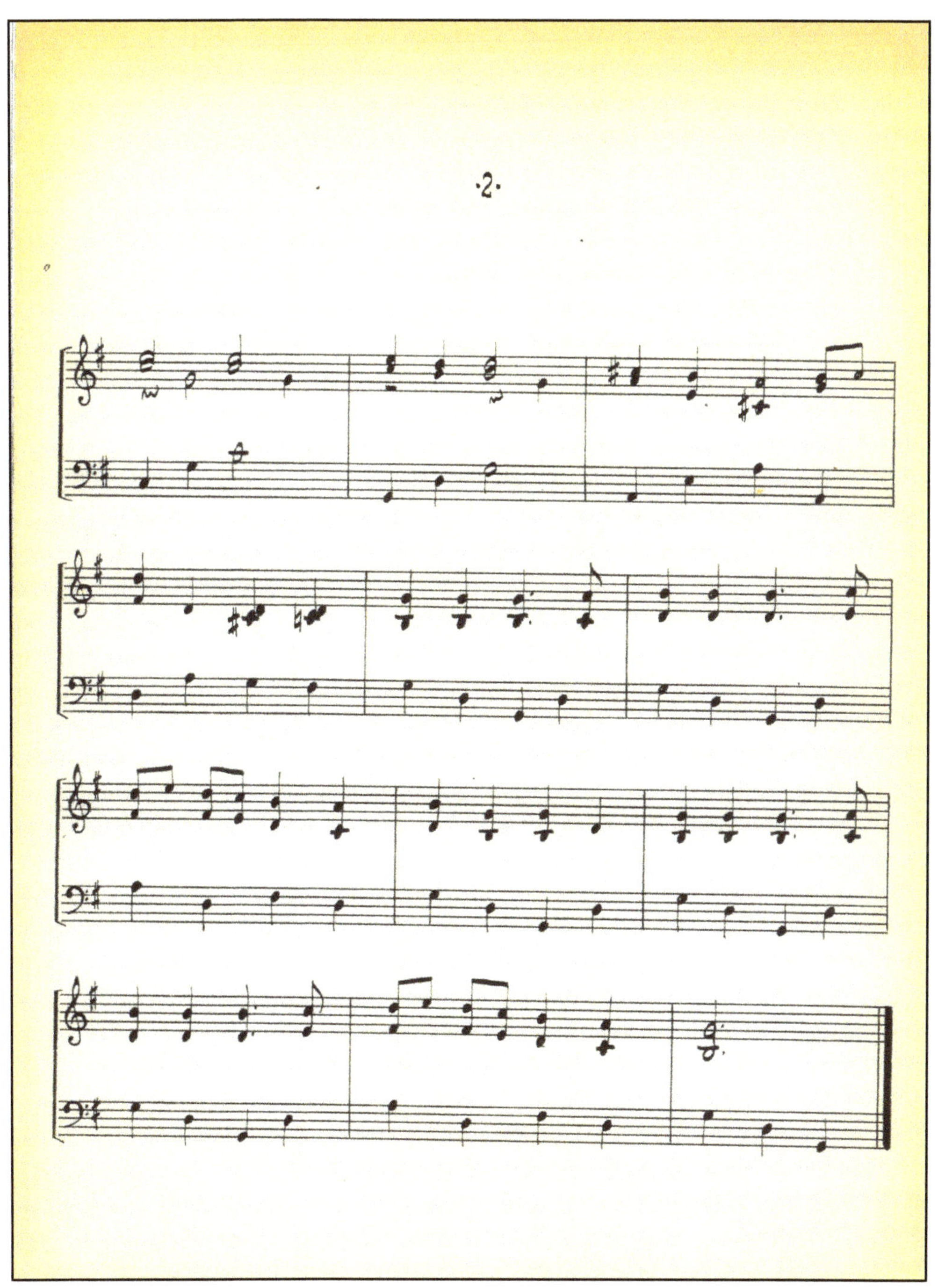

·2·

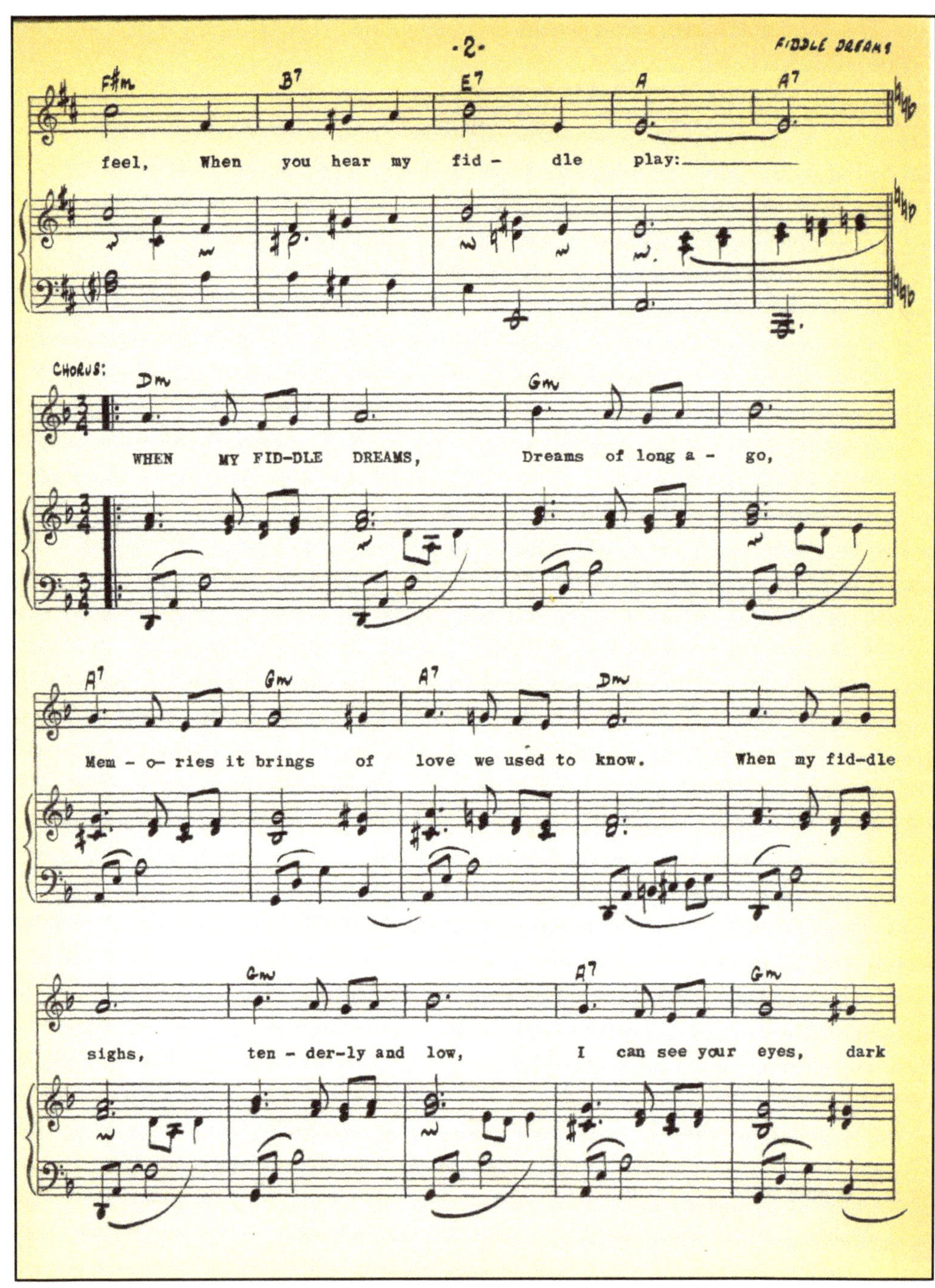
-2-
FIDDLE DREAMS
F#m B7 E7 A A7
feel, When you hear my fid - dle play:
CHORUS:
Dm Gm
WHEN MY FID-DLE DREAMS, Dreams of long a - go,
A7 Gm A7 Dm
Mem - o- ries it brings of love we used to know. When my fid-dle
Gm A7 Gm
sighs, ten - der-ly and low, I can see your eyes, dark

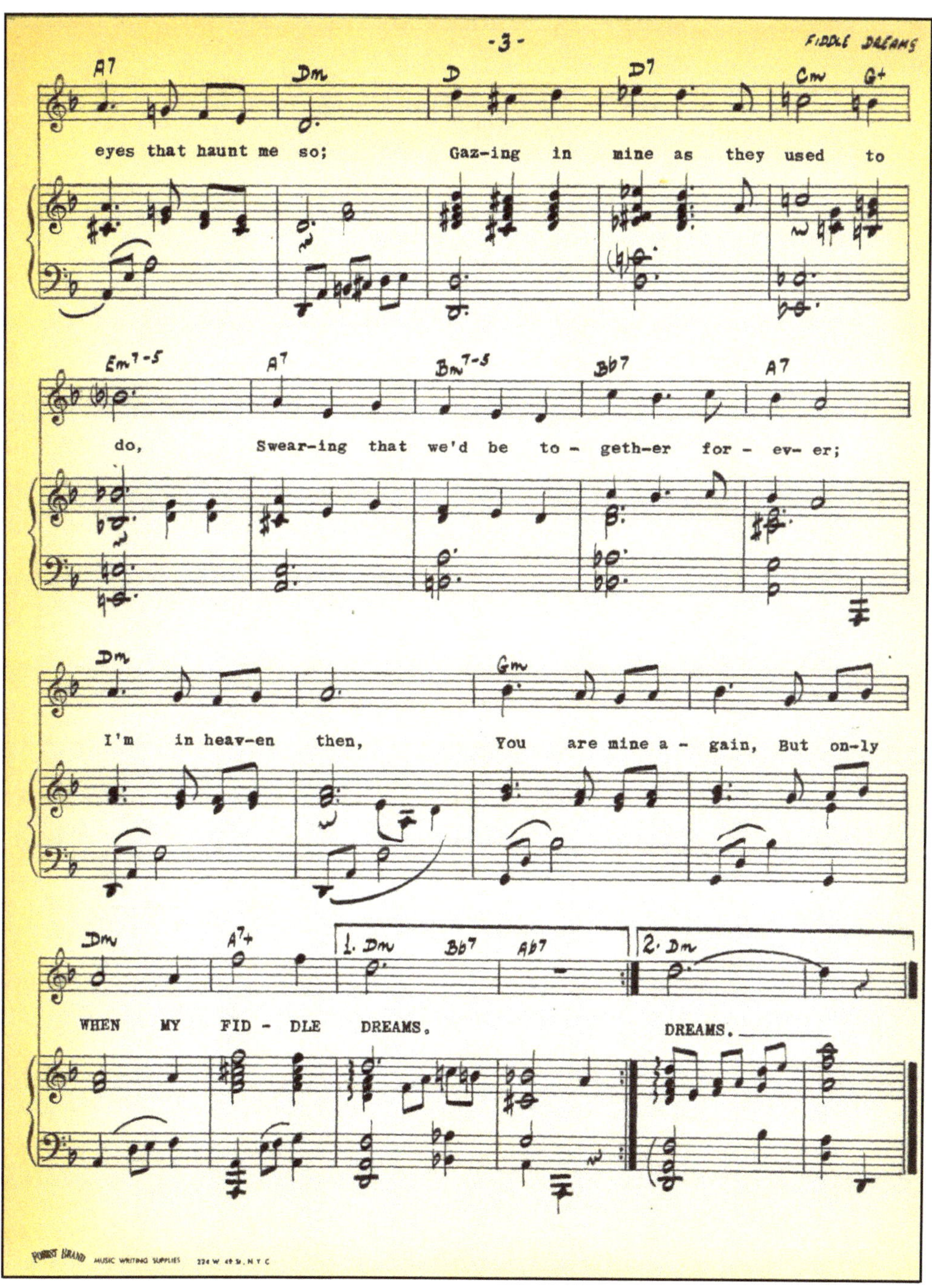

-3-
FIDDLE DREAMS
A7
Dm
D
D7
Cm
G+
eyes that haunt me so; Gaz-ing in mine as they used to
Em7-5
A7
Bm7-5
Bb7
A7
do, Swear-ing that we'd be to - geth-er for - ev- er;
Dm
Gm
I'm in heav-en then, You are mine a - gain, But on-ly
Dm
A7+
1. Dm
Bb7
Ab7
2. Dm
WHEN MY FID - DLE DREAMS.
DREAMS.
FOREST BRAND MUSIC WRITING SUPPLIES 224 W 49 St, N Y C

Works Cited

George Washington Carver: Textile Artist, Eulanda Sanders, Chanmi Hwang, DigitalCommons@University of Nebraska Lincoln, Textile Society of America Symposium Proceedings

Images of America, Jews of Cincinnati, 2007, John S. Fine and Fredric J. Krome, Arcadia Publishing

Julliard School Website

New York Journal-American, July 29, 1951

The *American Israelite*

The *Cincinnati Times Star*

The Jews of Cincinnati, by Jonathan D. Sarna and Nancy H. Klein, (1989), Center for the Study of the American Jewish Experience

The *New York Post*, column by Earl Wilson, June 23, 1951

The *New York Times, June 8, 1975*

Thesis by Christopher Chafee, Nov 20, 2003, University of Cincinnati

Town Hall website

United States Holocaust Museum website

Wikipedia, Édouard Lalo

www.jewishgen.org/Yizkor/Kamyanets_Podilskyi

www.jewua.org/kmanenets_podolski

www.zonta.org

ACKNOWLEDGMENTS

I want to thank my cousin Mike Aronoff for his help finding information, photographs, and news reports about my Aunt Joyce. The same goes for my cousin Missy Aronoff White who provided many of the photographs and ephemera I have relied upon. I want to thank my sister Margie Kessel for her recollections and assistance. Thanks also to my good friend Steve Rothstein for his assistance and comments. Steve was my historian regarding Cincinnati generally and specifically about the history of the Jewish community there. I also want to thank Adam Robinson of Good Book Developers for his assistance in the research, writing, formatting, and production of this book. Also, many thanks to my good friend Susan Lupica for serving as a "reader" of my draft—Susan is a great friend and expert literary critic.

A special thank you to Scott Fogelsong of the San Francisco Conservatory of Music for analyzing the works Joyce performed and composed, and for recording on piano several of her compositions.

Last, but proverbially not least, thank you to my wonderful wife Sharon for her comments and support as I worked my way through this project.

Steve Wasserman
February 2023

About the Author

Steven Wasserman is a retired attorney living with his wife in San Francisco. He is also the author of Grasping at Straws: Letters from the Holocaust, a memoir based on dozens of heart-rending letters written by members of five German-Jewish families from 1939 through 1941, in which the authors described their efforts to escape the Nazis. When he is not writing, Steve enjoys travel, running, gardening, and photography. Steve's photography can be followed on Instagram at WASSERMAN.STEVEN.

www.ingramcontent.com/pod-product-compliance
Ingram Content Group UK Ltd.
Pitfield, Milton Keynes, MK11 3LW, UK
UKHW062312290726
14090UKWH00018B/1027